TEACHING RELIGION

Fifty Years of Religious Education in England and Wales

TEACHING RELIGION

Fifty Years of Religious Education in England and Wales

Terence Copley

UNIVERSITY
of
EXETER
PRESS

First published in 1997 by
University of Exeter Press
Reed Hall, Streatham Drive
Exeter EX4 4QR
UK
www.exeterpress.co.uk

Reprinted 2003, 2007

British Library Cataloguing in Publication Data
A catalogue record for this book is available
from the British Library.

Paperback ISBN 978 0 85989 510 1
Hardback ISBN 978 0 85989 489 0

Typeset in 10/12pt Sabon
by Kestrel Data, Exeter

Printed and bound in Great Britain
by Edwards Brothers, Plymouth

Contents

Acknowledgements

To my friends and colleagues in the University of Exeter Department of Theology and especially Professor David Catchpole, my warmest thanks for the invitation to give the Boundy Memorial Lectures for the Lent Term 1996. This provided an opportunity to test some of the themes that were emerging in the research for this book. I am also very grateful to Simon Copley, a graduate in Politics, for assistance with research into the links that leading British politicians in the last fifty years have had with institutional religion, and to Gill and Claire Copley for help in preparing the index.

I was assisted by various key players in the events of this story. Kenneth Baker, Education Secretary at the time of the 1988 Education Reform Act, kindly spared time to discuss issues relating to the religious clauses in that Act. References to that interview appear at several points in the text, particularly in Chapter 5. Baronesses Caroline Cox and Nancy Seear also answered questions about the 1988 House of Lords debates about RE. Lord Rodney Elton wrote a reminiscence of the passage of the 1988 bill through the House of Lords in a letter dated 21 March 1996. Colin Alves (General Secretary to both the General Synod Board of Education and the National Society and responsible with others for briefing the Bishop of London in the Lords debates) helped me by telephone and by personal interview. He also documented the precise sequence of events in relation to the Anglican response to the original proposals in the bill. Liz Allen, Labour Education Policy Officer at John Smith House, answered questions about Labour and RE in the 1988 Act and provided information about comments by Derek Enright MP on the 1993 Act.

I met Sir John Acland several times to discuss the involvement of his late father, Sir Richard Acland, in religious education. Sir John generously allowed me access to various unpublished documents including his father's political diary for the war years and unpublished autobiographical writing which his father entitled 'A Political Record'.

Sallie Crispin and Kathryn Wright contributed Appendices 1 and 3, 'Starting Out in Religious Education, 1935' and '1995' respectively. These anecdotal accounts capture the mood of their respective times and together with Appendix 2, 'Starting Out in Religious Education, 1968', provide 'windows' into the period at three critical points.

Sir Geoffrey Holland, Vice-Chancellor of the University of Exeter and formerly Permanent Secretary of the DFE, generously, by interview, provided an insider view of DES/DfEE structures and operations and how RE was administered.

John Hull, Professor of RE at the University of Birmingham, generously supplied me with source lists in connection with the Birmingham Agreed Syllabus debate of 1975 and many cuttings from his personal collection. The *Bath Chronicle* supplied archive material relating to the controversy that took place over the City of Bath agreed syllabus in 1970.

Stephen Orchard, General Secretary of the Christian Education Movement, kindly allowed me access to the CEM archive in Derby, including Minutes of the Executive and the General Council. I spent several days there in December 1995 and also interviewed him about the past and present role of CEM. The record of that interview has fed into this text.

Gwen Palmer as Chairperson of the RE Council during the period of the 1988 Act generously described its work, in particular the lobby for RE before and after 1988. She supplied a list of key papers and dates in the lobbying process in addition to interview time.

Val Pearson, County Adviser for Religious Education in Devon, supplied me with press extracts relating to some national media appearances of RE in the 1990s.

Rheinallt Thomas of Canolfan Genedlaethol Addysg Grefyddol, the Welsh National Centre for Religious Education, was most helpful in identifying some of the key documents in relation specifically to RE in Wales.

To all these and other un-named helpers, thanks.

Preface

Every book is limited by its subject and its length, but more by the latter. We are concerned here with teaching religion over a half-century. School worship, the position and role of church schools and of religious education within them, are major subjects in their own right and space does not permit treatment here. Similarly moral education, later known as personal and social education, has been omitted, except where the debate about it directly impinges on RE. Space also excludes the different educational systems in Scotland and Northern Ireland in which RE has its place; this study is confined to England and Wales.

The period covered begins with the landmark Education Act of 1944 and ends with a controversial Circular from the Department for Education issued in 1994 to advise further on the provision for RE and collective worship after the equally momentous Education Reform Act of 1988. Each intervening decade had witnessed major change in religious education, so that, without forcing the subject matter to fit too strictly into artificial compartments, each chapter except the 1990s can be placed in the context of an approximate calendar decade.

Each chapter starts with a section on the wider political, social and religious change in British society during that decade. Selection of material for this has been inevitably subjective and has sometimes included the sensational, e.g. famous executions, which provided subject matter for ethical debate in some RE lessons, but the main aim of including this has been to provide a reminder for some or a flavour for others of the back-cloth against which religious educators were operating.

It is a characteristic that for much of the period under review language was more male-gender oriented than is now the case. Head-teachers were often presumed to be 'headmasters'. The child was usually 'he', etc. Quotations reflecting this are allowed to stand verbatim without further comment. The obsequious 'sic' has been kept to a minimum.

The half-century of this study was also a period of some significance for me. During it I experienced at first hand religious education as pupil and as teacher in half a dozen schools, then in many more classrooms in different parts of the UK as part of my work researching and teaching the subject within a higher-education context. Within a professional lifetime spent in RE I also taught theology in two universities and one college of higher education. The questions, creative tensions and opportunities that these very different experiences—of RE, of theology and of children—created in my mind, mirror those faced by religious education in the UK in the years ahead. What is its essential identity? Does religious education belong with the humanities, notably history and geography? Or with personal and social education? Or with the creative arts and subjects that seek to nurture the imagination? Or is RE a loner? Why do we talk about religious education, but not history education or mathematics education? Yet in the UK it is common to talk of 'teaching RE' or strictly, teaching Religious Education. A US commentator asks 'Does one teach the child education?'[1] Perhaps RE has suffered from the characteristically British neglect of the philosophy of education.

In the end, the system and practice of religious education we have is uniquely British, or to be more precise, Welsh and English. The story has its peaks and troughs. However 'bad', judged as education or theology, RE may sometimes have been, its removal from the curriculum altogether, a vague spectre that hovered around it from the late fifties until the early eighties, would have been far worse. For then implicit secular indoctrination in the curriculum might have reigned unchecked, pupil choice would have been further reduced and perceptions of religion among children would have been left to scandals misreported in the tabloid press and the more or less beguiling doorstep purveyors of religion. My decades of involvement in the process and profession we call religious education have convinced me that, above all, RE matters and that it can be both an entertaining and an intellectually absorbing quest—plenty to occupy a professional lifetime.

Terence Copley
School of Education
University of Exeter

x

Select Glossary

Education, including religious education, has produced a bewildering number of acronyms in the half-century treated in this text. For the benefit particularly of readers outside the UK education system a list of the main ones appears below.

Agreed Syllabus—The syllabus pertaining to RE and binding on all county and voluntary controlled schools, part of the 1944 and 1988 legislation affecting RE. It takes its curious name from the requirement that it be agreed locally at a conference consisting of different panels which each have one collective vote in the process. See pp. 31 and 146.

ATs (Attainment Targets)—National Curriculum targets post-1988 and as such not imposed on RE nationally. But agreed syllabuses can adopt locally binding ATs. The suggested national model syllabuses have two ATs for RE.

CAAW, See CCW

CCW (Curriculum Council for Wales)—Sharing NCC functions (q.v.) and extended to include assessment, later re-named CAAW, Curriculum and Assessment Authority for Wales.

CEM (Christian Education Movement)—Successor to the Institute of Christian Education (ICE), a liberal Christian movement concerned with education as a truth quest rather than evangelism. It is a charity, employing professional staff and producing published materials to support RE and school worship.

Church Schools—In the UK schools owned or part-maintained by churches, mainly Roman Catholic and Anglican, but with a sprinkling of Methodist, Quaker and other denomination schools. Some church schools are entirely independent (i.e. fee paying). Most are within the maintained sector as VA or VC schools (q.v.) where the LEA (or the DfEE after 1988 in the case of grant-maintained schools) meets most of the costs.

xi

DES, DFE, DfEE (Department of Education and Science, Department for Education, Department for Education and Employment)—Along with Board of Education these are the changing titles from 1944, with some reflection of changing role, of the government department responsible for implementing education policy. A description of the basic structure of this department appears on p. 130.

EKSS (End of Key Stage Statement)—These are more generalized than SoA (q.v.) and describe in broad terms what can be expected of pupils at the end of each KS. They apply to Art, Music, PE and some RE agreed syllabuses.

ERA (Education Reform Act (1988))—For the first time since 1944 this act legally re-defined RE and its position in the curriculum.

FARE (Forms of Assessment in Religious Education)—A field research project undertaken from the University of Exeter School of Education to try to develop forms of assessing religious education compatible with assessment processes in the national curriculum.

GCSE (General Certificate of Secondary Education)—This is the external examination system which merged and replaced the old Ordinary ('O') Levels and Certificate of Secondary Education (CSE). These had in turn replaced School Certificate. CSE had never been credible among many parents and employers, who viewed it as a second-best examination. Grade 1 CSE had been accepted as equivalent to an 'O' Level pass Grade C or higher. The GCSE pass grade range ran from A to G, with only U (Unclassified) below it. Coursework was introduced as part of the assessment, to an extent not seen before, and later cut back by government intervention. The idea was to record what children could do, rather than could not do, hence the wide grade range. Fairly rapidly employers and universities began to recognize only the 'higher grade' passes, A to C, which were held to be equivalent to the old 'O' Level.

Grant-Maintained Schools—Schools that after the 1988 Education Reform Act opted by majority parental ballot to leave LEA control and move towards central funding from the DfEE. Becoming grant maintained, also known as 'opting out', is a one-way move. There is no mechanism for a school to opt back into LEA control. LEA funding is reduced in relation to the number of schools 'opting out'. By 1994 some LEAs, e.g. Derbyshire, had lost a lot of schools whereas others, e.g. Cornwall, had lost none. See p. 133f and p. 146.

HMI (Her Majesty's Inspectorate of schools)—A part of the pre-privatized civil service operation based at the DES, which included a senior inspector for RE. After privatization HMI numbers were considerably reduced. By 1996 RE HMI were so few in number that the retirement of one had to be delayed by six months so that cover for his work could be organized.

KS (Key Stage(s) in the National Curriculum)—Age 5 children are designated Reception (R); KS1 is age 6 and 7 (Year 1 and Year 2); KS2 is ages 8 to 11 (Years 3, 4, 5, 6—formerly the junior school years); KS3 is ages 12 to 14 (Years 7, 8 and 9); KS4 is ages 15 and 16 (Years 10 and 11). Age 17 is Year 12 and age 18 is Year 13 (the former upper sixth form). Together Years 12 and 13 have been unofficially called key stage 5. 'Age' is taken to be the age of the majority of pupils in the year group at the end of the school year. Although the year naming system is optional it has become almost universal in schools. In secondary schools the following are equivalents:

1st Year Year 7
2nd Year Year 8
3rd Year Year 9
4th Year Year 10
5th Year Year 11
Lower Sixth Year 12
Upper Sixth Year 13

LEA (Local Education Authority)—The area body controlling education (except for independent schools, direct grant-schools, voluntary-aided schools and after 1988 grant-maintained schools, q.v.) and itself responsible to its county council or metropolitan borough council.

NCC (National Curriculum Council)—Based in York, the Council was formed to keep all aspects of the curriculum for maintained schools under review, advise Secretaries of State, carry out research and development work, and disseminate information relating to the curriculum. Replaced by SCAA.

OFSTED (Office for Standards in Education)—The privatized education inspectorate after 1988.

PCfRE (Professional Council for RE)—A wholly owned subsidiary of CEM (q.v.) but with a base clearly open to people of any religious commitment or none. Supports professional RE by conferences, courses and publications.

PoS (Programmes of Study)—The matters, skills and processes which must be taught to pupils in each key stage of the National Curriculum to meet the objectives set out in the ATs.

PM (Prime Minister)—There has been a surprising connection between British prime ministers in the period and institutional religion, which has also given them an interest in RE, referred to at various points in the text.

PSE (sometimes known as SPE, or PSME, Personal and Social Education, (the added M is Moral) known earlier as moral education) —Usually non-religious programmes in schools taken by form tutors or non-specialists, that deal with aspects of ethical and personal values. Part of the schooling of all British children. Also important by virtue of what it does not deal with, namely religion as a factor in human motivation and experience.

Public Schools—In the UK a term to describe privately owned, fee-paying schools and not as in the US state-funded schools.

RE (Religious Education)—In the 1944 Act RE was held to comprise teaching religion in the classroom (Religious Instruction) and school worship. In the 1988 Act RE was the name given to the classroom subject only.

RI (Religious Instruction)—The name confirmed for religion as a classroom subject in the 1944 Act.

RK (Religious Knowledge)—A name common for religion in the classroom in the 1950s and sometimes for GCE Ordinary and Advanced Level examinations.

RS (Religious Studies)—The name usually given to RE in external examination studies in secondary schools from the 1970s. See p. 123f.

SACRE (Standing Advisory Council on RE)—Set up in every LEA after the 1988 Act with three committees in Wales and four in England to be responsible for advice on RE and for producing and up-dating the agreed syllabus. An extra committee is added in LEAs where grant-maintained schools reach a specified level. See p. 32.

SCAA (School Curriculum and Assessment Authority)—Established in London in 1992 to ensure quality in the curriculum and to oversee assessment arrangements.

Scripture, Scripture Knowledge—The 1940s title which survived until the 1960s, also used in some external examination titles for the subject. Still surviving (along with Divinity) in a sprinkling of schools, usually independent, private ones.

Section 13 Inspectors/from 1996 Section 23 Inspectors—Inspectors appointed to examine RE, collective worship and spiritual development in voluntary-aided schools and collective worship and spiritual development in voluntary controlled schools

SHAP—Not an acronym but the name of a working party on world religions in education, which originally met at Shap (Lake District) in 1969. It produced curriculum materials and statements to affirm the importance of world religions in education from then on.

SoA (Statement of Attainment)—Each level of attainment in an AT can be defined by a more precise objective called a statement of attainment.

State Schools—Strictly an incorrect term but widely used in the UK to denote schools which are maintained by public funding rather than parental fees. In fact LEAs and dioceses maintain schools in the UK and the only 'state schools' are grant-maintained schools, which are centrally funded and accountable to the DfEE rather than locally.

VA (Voluntary Aided)—One type of church school, in which the church or foundation body appoints two-thirds of the governors and is allowed to require denominational worship and/or RE. Such RE is often in accordance with a diocesan syllabus. It must also be in general accordance with the Trust deed of the school. Such schools may legally advertise to appoint practising members of the foundation religion to serve on the staff. See p. 28.

VC (Voluntary Controlled)—Despite its name, the church or foundation body has only minority control in such a school. They appoint one-third of governors. RE must conform to the LEA agreed syllabus. Teaching is not permitted to be denominational. See p. 28.

Introduction

The Context

Each generation is taught by an earlier generation . . . The beliefs which boys . . . will hold in the Sixties will be largely those of the undergraduates of today [1948]. The moment we forget this we begin to talk nonsense about education . . . You may frame the syllabus as you please. But when you have planned and reported ad nauseam, if we are sceptical we shall teach only scepticism . . . if fools only folly, if vulgar only vulgarity, if saints sanctity, if heroes heroism. Education is only the most fully conscious of channels whereby each generation influences the next . . . A society which is predominantly Christian will propagate Christianity through its schools: one which is not, will not. All the ministries of education in the world cannot alter this law. We have, in the long run, little to hope or fear from government.

C.S. Lewis writing the preface to
B.G.Sandhurst, *How Heathen Is Britain?*, 1948 edition

Parliamentary debates about RE have rarely considered it in educational terms ; almost invariably it has been caught up in the unfinished debate on British national identity.

Geoff Robson, HMI, Staff Inspector for RE and
Ethnic Diversity, speaking in Birmingham in 1995

Religious Education is not, as might appear at first glance, one subject among others in the school curriculum of England and Wales. It has been influenced not only by its own history, for that would be true of any curriculum subject, but by the peculiar national identity of the UK, the position of the Church of England, the experiences and views of senior politicians, the attitudes of the public to religion and by the rapid social change of the last fifty years. What follows is an attempt to identify some of these factors.

Religious Education and National Identity

Religious education in any society exists in relation to the whole process of education and the life and traditions of the society in which it operates. A nation's religious heritage interrelates with its national consciousness to produce a feeling or mood in the public mind supportive of or indifferent towards religious education in its schools. One would not expect religious education in Britain and in Saudi Arabia to be alike. But national consciousness and religious heritage vary even within Britain. There are Scottish, Welsh, English and Northern Irish identities within the British. There are Cornish, Yorkshire, Liverpudlian and others within those. In England national identity is further clouded by the common assumption by many English people that English is synonymous with British. Jenkins (1975) held that the roots of religion and national identity are stronger, more tenacious and more intertwined than many people have believed. In Wales, for instance, it was through the life of dissenting chapels, financed and built by the Welsh people, that a road was found towards independence and identity which owed nothing to the English established church and arose despite its opposition. Northern Ireland, under its own Education Reform (Northern Ireland) Order of 1989 produced a core syllabus for RE in non-church schools including Attainment Targets that would not have suited the mainland (see p. 00) and a different curriculum position for RE to that in England and Wales. These complex interactions of living Christianity, religious heritage and local and national identity account in part for the broad if apathetic sympathy by parents for religious education in school, through most of the half century with which we are concerned.

> Our country is not Christian either in its faith or its actions. The majority of Englishmen do not believe . . . in the divinity of Christ nor do we truly love our neighbours as ourselves. On the other hand, England is not a nation of atheists. We have for the most part given up going to church. There is a great deal of ignorance about the Christian religion and much indifference . . . Nevertheless Christian values are woven into the fabric of English social life.

These words from a discussion group in 1947[1] reflect that British or perhaps uniquely English dalliance with Christianity that has simultaneously supported and undermined religious education in our period. It has supported a curriculum presence for Christianity, but tended to emasculate the power of Christianity to produce change in individuals and society.

The Church of England

One aspect of English identity is the unique position occupied by the Church of England. It has its role in English civic and national life as the established church. Residents in its parishes have entitlements, for example to marriages and funerals, by virtue of its status as national church. It is also the centre of that penumbra that Parsons (1993) calls diffusive Christianity. This is Christian adherence which sits lightly to institutional religion but which is insistent, under pressure, of its right to be identified as Christian. 'Diffusive Christians' attend midnight mass at Christmas and perhaps go to harvest festivals. The Church of England is a focal point for this group and its chaplaincy provision in hospitals, the armed services and prisons reflects aspects of this role. The Church of England is also part of the English landscape with its ancient churches and cathedrals, visited by many English people as part of an exploration of English history and identity rather than as a statement of distinctive Christian identity (pilgrimage) or commitment. Westminster Abbey is the key symbol of this aspect of the Church of England. This situation is not static ; the secular tide has advanced. 'No Smoking' notices are now found to be necessary in some cathedrals. Some church buildings are routinely locked, since they are in danger of robbery or simply attack from a small minority of the nation which is somehow excited against them.

The Church of England retains a major role as an educational provider and school owner both within the state provision and in independent education. In the English education system, but not in Wales, it is given as of right one committee in every Standing Advisory Council for Religious Education (SACRE). It is also a political reality that by virtue of two archbishops along with the Bishops of London, Durham, Winchester and the twenty-one most senior Anglican bishops with a seat in the House of Lords, the Church of England has more direct political influence over the nature of religious education in legislation than any group of professional religious educators. The religious provision within the 1988 Education Reform Act can be interpreted as a liberal Anglican settlement. Its final terms were framed by Kenneth Baker, Secretary of State for Education, himself a member of the Church of England, and Graham Leonard, then Bishop of London and education spokesperson for that Church. Leonard was briefed by senior members of the National Society, an Anglican charity based at Church House, Westminster, whose twentieth-century role is to promote religious education and to service and support the Church's work in education. They had consulted with diocesan directors of education, members of General Synod and also ecumenically. Not all teachers of RE had heard of the National Society or were even aware of the way in which the religious clauses in the 1988 Act came into being, but the major Anglican influence on it was no less real for that.

Attitudes to 'Other Religions'

Residual Protestantism within the English religious heritage has perhaps bred a suspicion and mistrust of teaching about religions other than Christianity and even until recent times of Roman Catholicism. This mistrust might be one strand in attacks on 'multifaith mishmash' and it may be reflected in the common remark that still distinguishes between 'Christians and Catholics'. If there is mistrust, there is also ignorance. BBC TV News reported at the opening of the new Hindu mandir at Neasden on 20 August 1995, the procession of 'idols' (sic) en route to their new home. No awareness of the concept behind a murti appeared at all. It was enough to assign the dismissive word 'idol'. Such ignorance about 'other religions' is not confined to England. In 1994 the UN dropped food supplies including pork to hungry Bosnian Muslims. It thereby unwittingly underlined a global argument for effective religious education.

Ignorance and mistrust are often partnered by prejudice. Clark (1982) also identified 'local cantankerousness' and produced evidence that suggested that some of the indigenous communities into which immigrant members of 'other faiths' moved could be complex mixtures of residual church and chapel loyalties, cyclic rhythms including spring/Easter and harvest, nostalgic religious emotions and inbuilt resistance to change. Those who differed in dress, diet and family customs could be stereotyped. Many immigrants themselves had moved from societies where religion was dominant and omnipresent to a culture in which they found religion being privatized as a personal or family matter and in which their ethnic religion was made to appear a small and deviant minority. For their British-born children the culture collision could be more acute. The furore over whether or not to require Sikh men to conform to motorcycle crash helmet regulations, or the realization in *The Satanic Verses* affair that the UK contained communities with different and sometimes conflicting values was a painful affair for all parties involved. Religious Education recognized the impact of the arrival of ethnic groups with different religions more quickly than wider society; wider society did not always respond with gratitude to the initiatives taken by Religious Education towards promoting tolerance, understanding and empathy.

Leading Politicians and Christianity

Religious education has a historic relationship with law and politicians as well as educational theorists and curriculum planning. Even in the increasingly secular times from 1944 to 1994 religion, or Christianity in particular, retained a tantalizing influence on those who held power in Britain. R.A. Butler's maternal grandfather was George Adam Smith, Old Testament scholar and one-time Moderator of the General Assembly of the United Free Church of Scotland. As a boy in India 'Rab' himself was riding at a gallop round a corner and was thrown by his horse. The fall broke his right arm badly. It never mended properly again. As he lay injured the first person on the scene, as it happened a Sikh, passed by and ignored him. In his autobiography Butler was to write that as Under-Secretary for India in later life he was 'quite unjustly cautious' of Sikhs.[2] It is unlikely that this experience delayed the arrival of multifaith RE in British schools, for in 1944 it would have been unthinkably reckless as a political move in a measure that needed church support to be carried through. In any case religion, for England and Wales, was then thought of as largely synonymous with Christianity. The connection between other leading politicians and institutional religion is impressive. Butler's Labour Deputy, James Chuter Ede, was a nonconformist who attended an Anglican school, later becoming one of its managers. Clement Atlee was brought up in a family which regarded scepticism as sinful and in which Sunday was strictly observed. High-mindedness was a family endowment and two sessions at Sunday school each week de rigueur. He rebelled against it but its stamp on his character remained. Churchill's first essay at Harrow School was about Palestine in the days of John the Baptist. His later less orthodox views on Christianity are referred to on p. 20. Harold Macmillan, who was dissuaded from converting to Roman Catholicism in his youth, went on to become a dedicated Anglo-Catholic. His official biographer recorded that he took more interest in church matters that any prime minister since Gladstone and enjoyed discussing them with the Queen. His view on the place of religion in society was quite clear:

> I don't think a nation can live without religion . . . If you don't pray every night and if you don't believe in God . . . eventually you can't solve all these problems and you can't even survive them . . . When you give up religion, you give up any kind of idealism.[3]

Alex Douglas-Home derived from his parents a strongly ethical Christianity. He took the view that Christianity is still the base of subconscious influence in the life of the British people and that they would respond if asked for service involving an element of sacrifice.[4] Harold Wilson attended the local Baptist Sunday school and grew up in its youth activities. He married the daughter of a Congregational minister. Later his occasional attendance at Methodist chapels became photo-call events. His religion was said to be more that of the social worker than the mystic.[5] Lord Longford described the Wilson Cabinet over- gloriously as one of the last 'Christian family Cabinets in modern times',[6] claiming eleven committed Christians among Wilson's colleagues. Even in 1996 Harries could claim that half the Labour Shadow Cabinet were Christian socialists.[7]

James Callaghan was the product of a Roman Catholic–Protestant 'mixed' marriage. His mother was a deeply religious fundamentalist who looked forward to the Second Coming and the certain joy of heaven. The young James went to the Band of Hope, the Christian Endeavour, the prayer meeting and the youth choir practice, all mid-week supplements to Sunday services. Sunday meant chapel service once, sometimes twice, and two Sunday school sessions. Even the journey to school was preceded by a short Bible reading. James created a stir by resigning his church membership when he found the Labour movement more real and true than fundamentalist Christianity. But he later wrote 'I never forget the immense debt I owe to a Christian upbringing nor have I ever escaped its influence'.[8] Norman St John Stevas, Conservative MP, one-time Under-Secretary at the DES and later as Lord St John of Fawsley, to play a part in the Lords' debate on RE (1988), was perhaps the leading Roman Catholic lay person of his day. He received an honorary Doctorate of Divinity in 1983.

Edward Heath had been an Anglican choirboy, growing up with Prayer Book mattins and evensong and reflecting his Christianity through his love of music. At one time he was a news editor at *The Church Times*, but his Christian commitment was largely unpublicized in his days of political fame.[9] David Steel, the Liberal leader, was the child of a Church of Scotland minister and grew up within a manse environment in of Scotland and Kenya. Margaret Thatcher's father was a teetotal Methodist with an unwavering sense of duty to his chapel and his neighbours. He was a lay preacher and trustee of some ten chapels in Lincolnshire. They often took tea or supper with chapel people. Thrift and hard work were in the air. She was later to write 'Our lives revolved around Methodism'. At one time she played the piano for the smaller children in Sunday school, followed by morning service in the church.[10] She described the religion she experienced in her youth as musical, sociable and intellectually stimulating. At Oxford her regular attendance at the Wesley Memorial Church included a vigorous Students' Fellowship. Thatcher was deeply influenced by C.S. Lewis's writings in her undergraduate days. The Methodist link was retained at her marriage at Wesley's Chapel, City Road, and even her economic philosophy was rooted in her 'Bloomsbury', Grantham with its 'Methodism, the grocer's shop, Rotary and all the serious, sober virtues cultivated and esteemed in that environment'.[11] In a letter to pupils in a Bristol comprehensive school (Green, 1984) she cited her favourite Bible passage as Psalm 46: God is our refuge and strength, a very present help in trouble. . . . Thatcher's arch-opponent Arthur Scargill, President of the National Union of Mineworkers, had a deeply religious mother to whom he was close. His own favourite Bible passage was Jesus turning the money-changers out of the Temple 'because he [Jesus] objected to their making profits out of other people's religious beliefs' (Scargill in Green, 1984). Neil Kinnock, Labour leader for many of the Thatcher years, was an exception in making no secret of his agnosticism, yet was still willing to sing in a Welsh congregation on BBC TV's *Songs of Praise*. His successor, John Smith, was an active member of the Church of Scotland. Next in the Labour succession, Tony Blair, had been top in Scripture at school on a number of occasions, was confirmed into the Church of England as an Oxford undergraduate, contemplated ordination for a time and remained a practising Christian, marrying a Roman Catholic.

Conservative Education Secretary Kenneth Baker went to an Anglican primary school in wartime Southport, later becoming a High Anglican. One of his successors, Kenneth Clarke, attended an Anglican primary school of Victorian foundation and discipline at Langley Mill. Clarke was later top in his form in RE at the independent Nottingham Boys' High School, having been bottom in the subject in his first term there. John Major, like Kinnock, was an exception to this history of connection between leading politicians and institutional religion. He was christened, however,[12] and in a written interview (McCloughry, 1996) claimed that he prayed 'in all circumstances'. Although 'essentially Christian' (Junor, 1993) the Majors were not a church-going family, but Sunday lunch with a roast joint of meat was a sacrosanct occasion. Perhaps this was the epitome of the English Sunday among 'diffusive Christians' at that time.

Britain's political leaders were not necessarily representative in their religious views and practices. But although the media in an increasingly secular society chose largely to ignore the religious commitment of national leaders where it existed, it is quite clear that many of them were greatly influenced by their faith or their childhood religious upbringing and wished that what was good in it could somehow undergird society. There was a tacit view that teaching Christianity to the young might provide an ethical base for them, even if they moved away from its doctrines or from church-going in adult life. Such views were not the highly publicized stuff of election campaigns, but they clearly influenced political attitudes towards religious education when legislation was framed in 1944 and 1988.

Indelible Influences of Schooling, Real and Fictitious

Schooling seems to be an ineradicable influence. Writing of Arnold of Rugby in 1844, only two years after his death, ex-pupil A.P. Stanley could note his influence in teaching religion: 'the union of reverence and reality in his whole manner of treating the Scriptures . . . the same searching questions, the same vividness, which marked his historical lessons . . . must often, when applied to the natural vagueness of boys' notions on religious subjects, have dispelled it forever'.[13] Generations of Arnold's pupils remembered the deep impression of his teaching. Generations of pupils everywhere remember their own teachers, for better or worse. In more recent time the premier political cartoonist of the post-war age, 'Carl' Giles, drew from his own childhood at Barnsbury Park School, Islington, his only character to be accurate in every detail including his name. This was the tyrannical, skull-headed schoolmaster, Mr Chalk. 'Chalkie' was recognizable to generations of elementary school pupils just as Henry Quelch was to independent school alumni. Quelch was the form master of the Remove at Grey-friars, in The Magnet comic.[14] Many adults who read of Chalkie and Quelch felt they had known them personally. They were archetypes. Bunter stories were written from 1908 to 1965, then reproduced in facsimile until the late eighties. The longevity of Bunter, Jennings and others is a testimony above all to the fascination that schooling seems to exercise over the public mind. This may have a significant bearing on a half-century of teaching religion in two ways. In the first place it may in part account for the surprising, direct, detailed and continuing interference by politicians in the eighties and nineties in the education curriculum. It is perhaps a British characteristic that many adults as ex-school pupils believe that they 'know' about education and can therefore pronounce on it. Second, their indelible adult memories of school-days include memories of RE. In the 1988 Act the perception by more than a few speakers in the parliamentary debates that RE was somehow a voluntary activity, different from other subjects, may owe more to their school memories of a generation previous than to informed commentary. But it helped to set the scene for post-1988.

Religious Education, the Wider Education Process and Social Change

Religious education is not, however, simply a matter for a national psyche or religious commitment by a nation's leaders, or of school-day memories by reminiscent parents. RE is sometimes, as in Britain, part of a formal curriculum process and as such has to be interpreted and understood in relation to the rest of the curriculum map. For example, by rewriting the whole of the rest of the curriculum the Education Reform Act (1988) inevitably changed the position of Religious Education as well. It was naive of the drafters of the bill to assume otherwise. Religious educators have long seen themselves working in relation to the wider education process and the peculiar position assigned to their subject within it in the UK. The changes in the name of their subject in school classrooms during the last half-century reflect a changing self-awareness about teaching religion: Religious Instruction, Divinity, Religious Knowledge and Scripture, give way to Religious Education or Religious Studies on the exercise-book covers and school reports of pupils and in the minds of teachers. Among parents this shift in how the subject is perceived is less certain.

But if religious education in any culture or society cannot exist independent of the whole educational scene, it cannot exist independent of social, aesthetic and moral trends and changes within that society either. It would be strange if religious education in the sixties, for example, had not been influenced by—or even itself have played some small part—in the ferment within UK society. Children who passed through school in the era when 'shotgun' weddings were the honourable or publicly expected way of dealing with pregnancies arising from extra-marital relationships, lived to see their children or grandchildren inhabit a society where living together with no expectation or desire to marry is regarded as normal by many and as an unremarkable matter for personal and private life by many more. The Victorians learned that doctrinal orthodoxy moves; what was doctrinally shocking in 1837 when the young Victoria ascended to the throne was orthodox, even passé, by 1901 when she died. The half-century since the Second World War has seen a similar discovery about moral orthodoxy, or a more radical shift away from orthodoxies towards a pursuit of individual hedonism within a climate of moral pluralism. The 'pic-'n'-mix' confectionery display in shops is a symbol of a deeper attitude to moral and religious values in society. What is certain is that children in schools in 1994 looked out on a world and unconsciously imbibed a mindset that had changed beyond recognition within the lifetime of their grandparents. Against this massive social change, religious educators have tried hard, not always successfully, to adapt their subject to make it relevant to contemporary society. On occasions they may unwittingly have adapted RE into something else entirely, like Social Studies or Personal and Social Education. In many primary schools RE may have disintegrated and disappeared within a notional context of integrated studies or Humanities. All these escape routes from teaching religion seem to be based on the premise that teaching religion itself is either intellectually suspect or socially unacceptable, a strange concession for religious educators themselves to make. Yet a loss of nerve on the part of religious educators would be understandable in a half-century which starts with them perceived as a state arm of the churches in schools and ends with society so secularized that the churches and their claims seem to have been eclipsed from the minds of many adults altogether. Distancing itself from the work of the churches may have been less of an option for Religious Education than the only route for its survival, especially as the religious presence in Britain became a plural as well as a minority activity. For if the growing awareness has been of secularization, it has been matched by an awareness that Christianity no longer stands alone within the religious scene in Britain. For example, by 1994 an estimated half a million Muslim children were pupils at British schools. But by then RE was confident enough and secure enough to stand independently without being seen as a version of the Christian Church in school.

Ecclesiastical Change and RE

If RE was changing, so were the churches. By emphasizing ethical Christianity after the Second World War some churches sought to make Christianity more accessible to the many and to stress its daily application, but in so doing they were perhaps promoting what Bonhoeffer and P.T. Forsyth would have called cheap grace, losing the challenge of the Gospel or losing what Otto called the mysterium. By emphasizing ethical issues in the same period, some religious educators sought to avoid the difficulties of doctrine and what they saw as the potential divisiveness of religion in the classroom—even to the extent of finding a less contentious name that omitted the reference to religion altogether. These efforts to customize RE may in the process have accepted and confirmed the very pupil prejudices about religions they sought to avoid, leaving religious belief and commitment to appear an incomprehensible minority hobby in the eyes of many pupils and as something even their teachers sought to avoid. In the 'retreat' from direct teaching about religion from the 1960s onwards (as we shall see, it was not strictly a retreat, because the tradition of direct teaching about religion was never really in evidence before then, only direct teaching of the Bible), God disappeared from many syllabuses. Even within the study of religious material itself, direct study of particular religions in themselves was replaced by 'themes' like sacred writings or places of worship or pilgrimage or festivals. The syllabus sliced or dismantled some religions in ways at which their members might have shuddered.

If RE was having problems about its nature and identity, so were the churches. This was not merely about denominational identity and relevance as the various ecumenical conversations (Anglican–Roman, Anglican–Methodist, Presbyterian–Congregational, United Reformed– Churches of Christ) bore witness, but also as to the very basis of belief. At the tabloid media level this lead to a fascination with various 'Atheist Vicar' stories. At a more educated level the debate continued via John Robinson's *Honest to God*, the various writings of David Jenkins and those of Don Cupitt. What these writings have in common is a desire to debate the nature of belief in a changed and changing world and a willingness to break away from what was perceived to be outmoded thought and into expression that is appropriate, comprehensible and acceptable to modern people. It was an exploration of what lay at the non-fundamentalist end of the rainbow of belief. It is significant that although all three men were once university teachers of theology, they were also ordained Anglicans, two of them bishops.

RE and Theology

While religious educators made attempts to engage with changing social trends they perhaps neglected to see themselves in dialogue with theologians, with the possible exception of the developments at Lancaster University in the 1970s. Even there the dialogue was strictly between Religious Education and the newly emerging subject Religious Studies, rather than theology. In the half-century of this study there have been times when what has been seen from the standpoint of education as trend-setting or even good RE must also be admitted to have been dubious theology. If the lament of theologians is that the churches failed to take account of decades of development in theology, one theologian (Hastings, 1991) can argue that failure of theologians to interest themselves in the world of the classroom accounts for much of the subsequent debit side of RE. Yet Religious Education went through a phase of disparaging theology as a biased and implicitly Christian activity compared to Religious Studies. It did not see that there are theologies in plural just as there are religions in plural—

Jewish, Islamic, Sikh, etc.—and that getting children to theologize could be a valuable educational exercise.

RE and the Fabric of National Life

Religious Education has also been caught into other debates because of its historic links with school worship. RE is an issue in voluntary (denominational or religious foundation) schools: should RE in such schools be governed by strictly educational or by religious nurture criteria? At the start of the period we are studying, religious education was also part of a debate about the fabric of national life itself.

> It has been noted in regard to the history of all Education Acts in England and Wales that the British only think seriously about their children and the future at such times as they are suddenly aware there may not be a future to which to look forward.[15]

Butler wrote that it was remarkable how in England educational planning and advance have coincided with wars.[16] It is certain that at the end of the period with which we are concerned there was no public debate about the fabric of national life and the place of religion or religious education within it. The contentious issue was the place of compulsory daily worship within the school system. But RE had gradually distanced itself from worship during this half-century and so was able to remain outside this particular controversy.

Butler and Baker

RE professionals around 1988 began to refer to 'the Butler's dream and the Baker's dream', after Genesis Chapter 40. They did not always remember that the butler was restored to a place of honour but the baker was hanged. It was Lord Graham of Edmonton in the Second Reading debate in the Lords (1988) who compared the Butler and the Baker with the Thatcher and the Hooper (Baroness Hooper led for the government in the Lords' debate). Reference to the Butler's dream was not original; it started with a Punch cartoon of December 1943 by E.P. Shepard. Butler is depicted seated at a table, wearing a suit, against a classical back-cloth, finger on his head like *Le Penseur*. Above him hovers Minerva, accompanied by an owl. Minerva is holding an unrolled scroll labelled Post-War New Curriculum. The bottom caption reads 'It all came out of my head'. Butler did not receive his commission from a Pharaoh, but he did receive his seals of office from a king, who wished him luck at the Board of Education and added 'I suppose you want to go there'. It was not then a high-status government position and contrasted with Butler's personal political dream at the time, to be Viceroy of India. Baker passed through Education on the way to the top, but Education was in many ways the zenith of his political career. The Home Office and the party chairmanship were to follow, but those were not halcyon days. The era that began with Butler's Act ended with another ERA, the Education Reform Act (1988). The first Act was introduced in the wartime coalition government by the President of the Board of Education, Conservative R.A.Butler. The second Act was introduced towards the end of the Thatcher premiership by Conservative Secretary of State for Education Kenneth Baker. Both men were Christians and Anglicans. But their dreams were quite different, as we shall see.

Chapter One

The Shadow of War: The 1940s

Nobody starting from scratch would ever have thought up the religious
clauses of the 1944 Act.

W.R. Niblett (1960)

The Background to the 1944 Education Act

It has become common, though mistaken, to view the 1944 Act as the
birth of religious education as a serious curriculum undertaking with
a philosophical base and a clearly defined framework. This view arose
because for nearly fifty years afterwards subsequent development
sought to relate itself back in some way to this landmark. It was not
until 1988 that further legislation affected the content and undertaking
of religious education in so major a way as to displace the earlier Act
almost completely from the horizon of religious educators. But the 1944
Act was not conceived in the abstract. It related to history and tradition
in British education, to a present wartime situation and to planning
and value judgements about the future of the nation. Debate and
planning of such a forward-looking, comprehensive and considered
nature has not occurred in British education since.

The year 1944 was not discontinuous with what had gone before. It
was the year in which Queen Victoria's last surviving child, Princess
Beatrice, died—her mother had come to the throne in 1837. Britain
was still under attack as V2 rockets fell on London. Only two years
previously the Battle of the Atlantic was going against Britain, with
victory over Germany still a remote, even unlikely, prospect. The
teachers who were to be called upon to implement the Act were the
ones who had survived the rigours of war, as combatants or civilians
under attack, trying to teach in the stressful circumstances of wartime
dislocation. The pupils in 1944 had lived and been taught through the
same upheaval. The plant—school buildings and resources—was what
remained after bombing had demolished parts of the cities, while in the

countryside school-building repair and refurbishment had taken a very low place in the priority of a nation on a war footing.

The War and Education

By 1939 the country already had a long-established tradition of parsimony in education, noted in the Norwood Report (1943) as a cause of poor pupil performance. After the Forster Act of 1870 spending on education only amounted to 1 per cent of the gross national product—from the then richest nation in the world. The school leaving age was raised to 14 in 1918, but stuck there. In 1939 most education for older pupils outside the senior elementary schools was private and fee-paying; the purchase of text-books and stationery was frequently a charge on the parent and, along with the cost of uniform, acted as an efficient barrier preventing children from working-class families attaining places unless they could achieve a much coveted scholarship.

The first effect of the war on education was dislocation brought about by mass evacuation. Board of Education Circular 1469 foresaw this and recommended improvisation—the use of drama, lantern-slide lectures, singing and dancing. But it did not anticipate that many small rural primary schools had no halls, or that they were already full of local children. Circular 1474 (23 August 1939) anticipated the double shift system for schooling: morning and afternoon shifts, or alternate days. By February 1940 9 per cent of elementary school children in evacuation areas were receiving no schooling at all. For secondary children the figure was 14.5 per cent—half a million children. Those in the cities fared little better. Blitz raids and the inadequacy of school shelters led to absenteeism. The teacher's daytime duties were often compounded by night-time fire watching, sometimes on the roof of the school they taught in by day. By July 1941, 1,000 of England's 23,000 schools were wholly or partially destroyed and 3,000 more were damaged. Fortunately for human casualty most schools were hit at night. Married women returned to teaching (marriage previously meant termination of employment for most female teachers) to replace conscripted men. Retired male teachers in shortage subjects returned to battle in the classroom in secondary schools, but much specialist teaching was lost. Unqualified young teachers also served.[1] If pupils were in schools with shared pencils (one between two or three pupils) no blackboards or chalk, where even bus or tram tickets were brought into use for rough paper, their lot was hard. Crises encourage resilience : cookery (Home Economics) developed pupil expertise in eggless cakes, boiled cakes, potato soup, carrot pudding etc. School meals at four pence ha'penny, later five pence (approximately 2p), were intended to relieve families with children billetted on them of feeding them mid-day. These meals, prepared under wartime rationing and limited food variety, gave birth to a new British mythology, jokes about school dinners.

Different forms of schooling arose. Nursery schools and facilities expanded to help working mothers. Several thousand city children were in house schools of eight to twelve children, a reversion to the dame schools of a previous age. More secondary children were in camping boarding schools, living under canvas for as long as three years. War brought curriculum change, not just in cookery. Gardening, including livestock keeping, was expanded. It was said to lead to improved mathematics, better animal drawing and elementary book-keeping. Local survey work was undertaken in geography or environmental studies. Autumn camps of older children helped to gather in the harvest. New youth training organizations supplemented guides, scouts, and the Christian-based Boys' and Girls' Life Brigades—the Air Training Corps (1941), Sea Cadets and Army Cadets (1942). A major advance in 'sex instruction' was applauded in 1942 when the Board of Education urged schools to keep rabbits.

Society and Church

War brought with it changes in patterns of social behaviour. 'Make do and mend' became as much a part of middle-class life—black market excepted—as it had always been of working class life. 'Black-out material was soon covering almost as many British women as windows'.[2] Slacks became common for women. In the early war years church-going increased. So did the sale of contraceptives and— despite that—the number of illegitimate births. Many families became de facto one-parent families with the father absent at war. Conventional religious belief was opened to discussion in the popular *Brains Trust*. Dorothy Sayers' radio play series *The Man Born to be King* (December 1941) provoked protest because in it an actor played the role of Christ. But it did not destroy her standing as a leading Anglican exponent of Christianity as author of *The Mind of the Maker*, alongside C.S. Lewis and T.S. Eliot. Calvocoressi (1978) argued that in the inter-war years the biggest boost to British culture came not from the education system but from the BBC ('wireless' only) and the creation of Penguin books. By the end of the war wirelesses were licensed in 9,700,000 homes, a growth of one million on the 1939 figure. Radio had become a potent wartime supplier of information and arbiter of tastes. Professor Cyril Joad's 'it depends what you mean by . . .' became as much a household phrase as T.T.F.N. and Mrs Mopp's 'Shall I do yer now, sir?'

The War and Religious Instruction

The April 1940 issue of *Religion in Education Quarterly*, in a smaller format owing to the shortage of paper, was devoted to issues arising from teaching religion in wartime. M.L. Jacks distinguished practical difficulties such as problems arising from evacuation, from intellectual and psychological difficulties: older children were questioning their attitude 'as Christians' to the war. Jacks' answer was to teach the Bible as religion rather than as ancient history, as it testifies to the indestructibility of spiritual forces and to the potential significance of the insignificant, however desperate the times may appear. Tatlow, writing on the results of evacuation, noted that girls were more anxious than boys and raised more questions about the meaning of the war, whereas boys tended to see the declaration and waging of war as inevitable and necessary. Some religious educators saw the war as a lapse.

> The Bible provides the foundations that 1939 has forgotten. It reveals the true relations of men to one another and to their Creator–Father.[3]

Planning for Post-War Education: Butler's Appointment

In 1926 the Hadow Report spoke of 'the gospel of individualism . . . being pursued',[4] suggesting that education should aim to promote social individuality, 'to offer the fullest scope to individuality while keeping steadily in view the aims of society'. 'Hitler's exploitation of youth only served to confirm our preference for this middle way'.[5] MP Richard Acland wrote enthusiastically about educational reconstruction (1942):

> We are not here concerned merely with the mastering of a few simple mental tricks called 'reading', 'writing' and 'arithmetic'. We are dealing with the introduction of a human being to the thrilling adventure of life.[6]

Acland proposed foreign travel and exchange for teachers, which was then rare; community service for a year for all school-leavers; married women teachers returning to the classroom. 'Even headmasters could well afford to take a six months course of lorry driving as a refresher.'

Richard Austen 'Rab' Butler, MP for Saffron Walden, arrived at the Board of Education on the day before Hitler invaded the Soviet Union. He was 39 years old, a product of a family that would in later times have been called Tory grandees. They had a long tradition in the public service and in the academic world. Butler himself later likened his life to the Cambridge tripos examination, divided into three parts between politics, Cambridge and India. His father, Sir Monty, had a distinguished career in imperial India, where 'Rab' had been born. At the onset of war 'Rab' was seen as a Chamberlain man and therefore suspect. Charmley (1993) suggests that as late as July 1939 Butler was still willing to support concessions to Hitler. Butler had been chafing to leave the Foreign Office where as Under-Secretary he was dealing with wartime red tape and trivia, such as arranging extra coupons for the Duke of Alba's socks.[7] Churchill took the view that running education was a low-status job and that Butler would 'do no harm' at the Board of Education. Cosgrave (1981) argued that Butler resented that Churchill thought it surprising that a young man like him should so tamely have accepted a post away from the centre of the War Cabinet and determined as a result to make his mark there. It is unclear whether Churchill moved 'Rab' there to rid himself of a potential enemy by placing him well away from the political centre or whether he had an admiration for him and wanted to give him a chance to prove himself in an unlikely situation. Whichever was the case, it fell to Butler as President of the Board of Education to try to translate into a plan of action a vision for post-war education on a national scale. It was the only major piece of domestic reform legislation undertaken during the war. There had been no major education Act since the Conservative Act of 1902. Butler wrote of his conversation with Churchill on his appointment:

> I said I would like to influence the content of education but this was always difficult. Here he [Churchill] looked very earnest and said, 'Of course, not by instruction or order, but by suggestion'.[8]

Exactly how much of the Act was Butler's own work is open to question. Gosden (1976) argues that most of the credit should go to civil servants at the Board of Education. Butler wrote afterwards:

> Towards the end of the war, the feeling was widespread among many sections of the community that in any future measure of educational reform religious instruction—and in the normal case Christian instruction—should play a larger part in the education of a child . . . My general aim and intention in framing the clauses dealing with religious education in what became the Education Act of 1944 was to recognise formally this special place of religion in education . . . I know that during the debates some doubts were expressed about the wisdom of making religious instruction and the corporate act of worship a specific requirement of the Act . . . But these doubts sprang, I think, mainly from the thought that it was unnecessary to make compulsory something in this field which was in practice universal,

and it is fair to say that they did not represent any hesitation in the minds of most members about the principle that there was in the general education of all children a vital role for religious education . . . Willie Temple and I were both schoolmasters . . .

Churchill had a less orthodox view of religion, writing as early as 1896 that 'one of these days . . . we shall go out into the fields to seek God for ourselves . . . We shall then be able to dispense with the religious toys that have agreeably fostered the development of mankind'.[9] Writing to his mother before the Battle of Omdurman (1898) he rejected institutional Christianity, yet he was to emphasize the importance of religion and the Christian ethic in later speeches. He presented the Battle of Britain (1940) apocalyptically:

Upon this battle depends the survival of Christian civilisation.[10]

He was also committed to religious instruction. In 1897 he had written that it should not be entrusted to the hands of any one sect, not even the Church of England, as 'all are partisan. I am in favour of secular instructors appointed by Government'.[11] Churchill saw religion as 'the fundamental element in school life'. In this he was being perhaps very English, certainly very Conservative. A report of the Central Committee of the Conservative and Unionist Party (1942) had included the following:

The State must do its best to ensure that every child is given every opportunity and help towards the awakening of its religious sense though it matters much less to the State what the particular dogmatic teaching given to the child may be . . . No permanent peace is possible in Europe unless the principles of the Christian religion are made the foundation of national policy and all social life.

This view was not universal. An article in the *Spectator*[12] attacked the new proposals as class-based, the product of MPs, peers, Board of Education officials and teachers who had all failed to consult working-class parents. It saw as suspect the principle of compulsion, on the grounds that the local school to which the working-class parent would be compelled to send their child might be appalling. Its author, Roger Clarke, also saw compulsion as carrying a deeper danger:

They [the education reformers] would no doubt like compulsory school feeding, compulsory school dressing, compulsory school dentistry and diphtheria immunisation. Already there is talk of compulsory religious *instruction* (quite undenominational, quite undogmatic, of course) and of compulsory inculcation of a 'sense of social purpose.' The totalitarian trend is . . . obvious.

Clarke was in a minority and he compared impending state reform of education in Britain with remarks made by Stang, the Nazi Youth Minister. The churches did not share his view. They were a forceful educational lobby, with their own concerns about pre-war decline as well as wartime damage. The number of Anglican schools had reduced from 12,000 to 9,000 in the first forty years of the century. Signs of the financial crisis in church education were reflected in the blacklist of school buildings compiled by the Board of Education just before the war. Church schools were blacklisted twice as often as council schools. Roman Catholic schools had increased, but only from 1,000 to 1,200 and they had the highest proportion of blacklisted school buildings (six per cent). The church lobby resented paying for county schools through the rates and also having to pay to maintain their own church schools. Their hope was that the Exchequer would pay seventy-five per cent of the costs of church schools. Butler argued successfully for a figure of fifty per cent instead. Wheldon, the Permanent Secretary for Wales, urged against this suggesting that pouring money into failing Anglican schools would be strenuously opposed by Welsh public opinion.

The Times concerned itself with religious teaching[13] when a leader attacked its neglect, blaming indifferent or ill-informed teachers. A letter appeared[14] from the Archbishop of Canterbury, the Cardinal Archbishop of Westminster, the Moderator of the Free Church Council and the Archbishop of York. The very fact of this letter was an ecumenical advance. It shocked those observers who were assuming that a post-war settlement in education would reflect the same inter-church feuding that had characterized earlier settlements. It urged that extreme inequalities of wealth and possessions should be abolished and that every child, regardless of race or class, should have equal opportunities of education, suited for development of their particular capacities and that the family unit should be safeguarded. It was followed[15] by a joint statement by the (Anglican) Archbishops of Canterbury, York and Wales. They asserted that Britain was fighting to preserve those elements in 'our human civilisation and in our national tradition' which owe their origin to the Christian faith. They regretted that many people were ignorant of what these were. They argued for the provision of 'Christian education' for all—with the existing withdrawal safeguards for teachers and for parents—in the hands of teachers qualified 'by personal interest, by knowledge and by training to give it'; support for enhanced training for teachers in RE, and upgrading Religious Knowledge to a full option subject not just an additional option, i.e. an enrichment or supplementary course within the Teacher's Certificate for students in training. Where suitable teachers for RI were in short supply in a particular school, they wanted the timetable to allow such teachers as were in place to teach different classes so that each class received its entitlement of the subject. They wanted religious teaching to be subject to inspection and each school day to begin with an act of worship.

They made a number of assumptions. One was that 'Christian education' and 'Religious Instruction' were identical. Another was that the school is the partner of the church, even where the school is a 'state school'. This reflected a pre-war climate. Implicit in the partnership idea is the principle that the nation was in some sense a Christian country, that Christianity was part of British identity. It would have been hard to challenge these assumptions when the war was being interpreted as a crusade between Christian civilization and its values such as democracy, versus a Nazi pagan empire. The archbishops called for a Christian lobby to support their proposals and declared their welcome for Free Church teachers to come into church (i.e. Anglican) schools to teach the Free Church children in them. This ecumenical surprise concealed another assumption, that in a post-war settlement denominational teaching was expected to continue, even beneath a welcoming Anglican umbrella, in the church school.

The Pre-Act Lobby and Circumventing Churchill

In July 1941 the Institute of Christian Education was founded. Its foundation pamphlet 'Why Christian Education matters' stated 'Neutrality is no longer possible. If God matters at all He matters more than any other fact in human experience'.[16] Meanwhile a formidable ecumenical coalition numbering thirty three, including the two Anglican archbishops and the most powerful nonconformist leaders, but no Roman Catholics, called upon the newly appointed President of the Board of Education less than two months after his appointment. They were there to assert the five points of the letter to *The Times*. Rab called upon the Archbishop of Canterbury, Cosmo Gordon Lang, to close the meeting with prayer. Chuter Ede recorded that it took everyone by surprise, including Lang himself, who mumbled his way through a collect.[17] He also claimed that on the morning of the deputation Butler was heard enquiring in the Board 'What is an elementary school?', a reminiscence that if accurate suggests that he still had a lot to learn before reforming the national education system. But Cosgrave (1981) argues that Butler was always completely briefed, patient, courteous and humorous, and that the request for prayer caused 'gratified surprise'. Butler's own account stated that he provided 'some innocent diversion and surprise' by requesting prayer.[18] 'Rab' clearly acknowledged the work of his team, including Chuter Ede and 'a quite outstanding group of civil servants'. Butler had had experience of negotiating with Muslims and Hindus in India in connection with the Communal Settlement which taught him that personal acquaintance with religious leaders and the building of trust were essential to progress in negotiation. Butler wrote to Churchill outlining his plans, including 'a settlement with the Churches about Church schools and religious instruction'.[19] Churchill, whose interest in education was later described by Butler as slight, intermittent and decidedly idiosyncratic, wrote a crushing rejoinder to tell him to get on with administering repairs to the disrupted school system and that a new bill was out of the question, adding: 'Meanwhile you have good scope as an administrator'.[20]

Butler's civil servants were not cast down by the reply; Holmes thought the demand for educational reform would become irresistible. But it took Butler the next year and a half and significant Labour Cabinet support (Atlee, Bevin, Greenwood) to circumvent Churchill's veto. It is possible that Butler himself would have delayed educational legislation on cost grounds, but was pushed by his Labour deputy in the coalition, James Chuter Ede, who warned that the Labour Party would create trouble in the House unless legislation was really moving. Chuter Ede (1882–1965), almost old enough to be Butler's father, was the son of a grocer. He had not been able to afford to finish his degree at Christ's College, Cambridge and became an elementary school teacher and an active member of the National Union of Teachers. At the Board he upheld the interests of the LEAs, the NUT and the Free Churches.[21] Butler wrote to Alec Dunglass (later Douglas-Home) that much of the drive towards a vaguely progressive future came from Labour.[22]

'Rab' eventually had to tell Churchill that he was working on an education bill. He decided to do it when he was summoned to the PM's bedroom for one of his late morning audiences. Churchill was in bed, smoking a cigar, deep in the papers on the counterpane. A possibly apocryphal detail adds that Churchill, looking at the large, sleeping cat on the foot of his bed, chided Butler that the cat had done more for the war effort than he, by keeping the Prime Minister's feet warm at no charge to the taxpayer. Butler is said to have replied that he doubted whether that were true, conceding that it was a very fine cat. Churchill told Butler that he must see the education plans when that they were ready and they were sure to be interesting. Butler fled from the room before he could change his mind.

The 1943 White Paper Discussion

The Paper noted

> a general wish, not confined to representatives of the churches, that religious education should be given a more defined place in the life and work of the schools, springing from the desire to revive the spiritual and personal values in our society and in our national tradition.

Meanwhile the church lobby had received a new member. William Temple, replaced Cosmo Lang who retired aged seventy-seven. Temple had been head-teacher of Repton School at twenty-eight and President of the Workers' Educational Association a year earlier. Temple and Butler found common ground, though Butler was negotiating not just with the churches about their schools, but exploring the possibility of bringing the independent schools into an entirely restructured secondary education system. Churchill himself wanted 60 to 70 per cent of their places to be filled by bursaries. Butler was forced to retract this radical intention, probably because the public school lobby, which overlapped the Anglican educational establishment, did not support him and he needed their support to reform the dual system.

Comments from Different Groups

The English ecclesiastical consensus which helped the Bill was also reflected in Wales. A joint conference of representatives of the Church in Wales (Anglican, but not established) and the Free Churches at the end of 1943 had amicably negotiated an agreed syllabus, although the Free Church ministers wanted it to be applied in controlled and aided schools. Speaking in the House of Commons in the debate about the bill, Professor W.J. Gruffydd, MP for the University of Wales, dismissed the religious controversies of the past, which 'to most of our generation are as comical as Dundreary whiskers and crinolines'. Viscountess Astor (MP for Plymouth Sutton) felt that there was a mood for a religious settlement: 'we do not want any more religious controversy.' T.M. Sexton (MP for Barnard Castle) took the view that there was never a religious problem inside a school: 'All the controversy came from the outside.'

The secondary school teachers' associations (GBA, HMC and the Joint Four) met Butler in May and June 1943 to voice their unease at the extension of agreed syllabuses from elementary schools to all secondary schools, arguing that in secondary schools the headmaster and staff were perfectly capable of their own approach to the subject, especially at sixth-form level. Butler stood firm, replying that the government had decided to make religious instruction a statutory obligation as an integral part of educational reform and could not change now. In Wales the teachers' union Undeb Cenedlaethol Athrawon Cymru placed constructive proposals, including the case for multilateral schools, instead of the tripartite system, in secondary school reorganization in rural Wales. Its president, Gwenan Jones, argued that reconstructed education should not be purely functional with the Welsh language a luxury, but education that would help children know, understand and feel. She continued that it should be 'ymbaratoi at wasanaethu'r gymdogaeth, sef cymdeithas y Cymry.'(To prepare for the service of the neighbourhood, namely Welsh society).

Churchill himself became fascinated by the idea of agreed syllabuses, referring to them as county council creeds and once as 'Zoroastrianism'. Churchill asked Butler whether he intended to start a new state religion.[23] Butler replied with characteristic gravitas and humour that the Roman legionaries in North Africa may have fallen for Zoroaster but that he was more orthodox. Neither of them could have imagined that one day (1995) Zoroastrianism would really appear on an agreed syllabus, for the London Borough of Brent, as an option for study in key stage 4.[24] Brent had a syllabus conference including representation of its Zoroastrian community.

The Roman Catholic Lobby

Butler found the Roman Catholic leadership more difficult to negotiate with than other church leaders. There was no special leader equivalent to the Anglican William Temple. Cardinal Hinsley's mental powers were in decline as a result of age. Downey was naturally combative and for some critical months in 1943 had to retreat to Ireland to reduce his weight by nine stones. Monsignor Godfrey, the apostolic delegate, told Butler uncompromisingly that Catholics had no intention of 'selling the true concept of religion' as the Anglicans had done. Archbishop Amigo of Southwark was frosty and demanding, concluding his first audience with Butler with the rather acid remark that if he [Butler] had belonged to his community he would have suggested that they pray. Butler maintained with dignity that he was very ready to do so, since he was also a churchman. He had to visit Roman Catholic bishops on their territory and they sometimes received him rather formally in full vestments.

'We were all filled with a certain awe,' he wrote of one of these occasions, at Ushaw College, 'which was no doubt intentionally administered'.[25] Butler had to go as far as asking the papal envoy to stress to His Holiness himself that the proposed religious settlement would pose no threat to the religious liberty of Catholics. The reply came[26] that His Holiness was pleased to hear that, but it was clear to him that British Catholics were being placed in a very difficult position financially by the proposed terms, which would threaten their exercise of freedom of conscience. Kenneth Baker would later face a frosty response from Cardinal Basil Hume about his bill, on the grounds that grant-maintained schools were fundamentally unacceptable to the Roman Catholic Church on moral and ethical grounds (see p. 147).

Wider Public Debate

But against these difficulties there was also a growing public desire to do a good job in education. This was fuelled by the shocking behaviour, as it seemed, of children described by Iremonger as half-fed, half-clothed, less than half- taught, the products of the education system of which the British claimed to be proud.[27] 'The educational problem must never be separated from the social problem. It is all part of the great enterprise of civilization—the provision of a truly civilized society'.[28] In *Education For a New Society*, Ernest Green wrote: 'The educational provision of the nineteenth century was short- measured. That of the twentieth century has been short-sighted'.[29] Dent (1944a) echoed this, writing that a new order in society necessarily involves a new order in education and that such an order would be better shaped deliberately than by circumstance. *The Times Educational Supplement* discussed more equality of educational opportunity, what it meant and whether it was desirable.

Mass Observation surveyed 1900 teachers about RE. Ninety per cent were in favour of it in state schools, 71 per cent opposing denominational instruction in such schools. Church people, politicians, industrialists, professionals, public opinion, were all seeking for the right settlement for post-war education. People seemed to value religion as a heritage and saw that its effect nationally could be to unite rather than to divide. If people did not always want to practise religion, they seemed to want it to be available: children were sent to Sunday School in numbers that far exceeded those parents who went to church. The Christian ethic, or what was widely believed to be the Christian ethic, was accepted as a base for living even by many who felt unable to accept Christian doctrine. English country church bells at evensong, the hymn-singing of the Welsh chapel, the Whitsuntide processions in the north of England, were seen as part of the fabric of the nation that 'we' were fighting for. In contrast, the Nazis had taken deliberate steps to weaken the place of religion in school life by excluding questions about religion from school-leaving examinations and making school worship optional (1935). Ironically, views about RE were linked with views of education for citizenship and even political education both in the UK and Germany. In his speech at the bill's Second Reading Butler alluded to this :

> Let us hope that our children—to use words found in one agreed syllabus 'may gain knowledge of the common Christian faith held by their fathers for nearly 2,000 years; may seek for themselves in Christianity principles which give a purpose to life and a guide to all its problems'. But remember that in so vital, personal and individual a subject as the teaching of religion, the State cannot claim to possess absolute authority, or to speak the final and decisive word. The churches should never forget their own responsibility.

Perhaps educated public opinion was impressed by the involvement of the churches in social questions : church, community and state (Oxford, 1937), faith and order (Edinburgh, 1937), industry and daily living (Malvern, 1941), the British Council of Churches (founded 1942). Temple's credentials as a former head-teacher, supporter of the Workers' Educational Association, involvement in the Student Christian Movement and his writings—*Christianity and the Social Order* was a best-selling Penguin Special (1942)—were impressive by any standard. He died in October 1944, not before having made a contribution to the new Education Act with Fisher, then Bishop of London, J.S. Whale, and Scott Lidgett. There was even input from Cardinal Heenan and later from RC Archbishop Griffin. Cardinal Hinsley's earlier criticism of agreed syllabuses as 'disembodied Christianity' was tempered by the Roman Catholic retention of separate schools with their own syllabuses. Niblett commented that the expectation undoubtedly was that religion as a school activity would be upgraded and that RI would go beyond Bible teaching. Butler's initial preference was for a select committee to examine the religious provision with much of the debate on the rest of the bill to be left to the floor of the House. He thought that controversy about religion on the floor might 'come undignified.' But the chief whip argued for the whole bill to be taken on the floor, requiring major business time from the end of the Christmas recess to Easter 1944. His view prevailed.

1944 Act Overview

The Act of 1944 addressed almost every aspect of education: abolishing 169 of the 315 local education authorities; promoting common salaries nationally for teachers; laying down machinery for creating articles for school government; dealing with 'state', i.e. LEA, boarding schools; nursery education; 'special educational treatment' for pupils with 'any disability of mind or body'; provision of school meals, milk and clothing including shoes; rights of women teachers to retain their jobs after marriage; children infested by vermin; school transport; responsibility of the Minister for ensuring that proper facilities for teacher training and supply exist; employment of children out of school hours; abolition of fees in all LEA secondary schools, but not direct-grant schools; setting up of a register for independent schools and arrangements for their inspection; intention to raise the school-leaving age to 16 (not achieved until 1970); establishing a school health service to include dental checks; provision of facilities for physical recreation; part-time and continuing education after leaving school. Within this comprehensive legislation appeared the mission statement (Section 7):

> It shall be the duty of the local education authority for every area
> . . . to contribute towards *the spiritual, moral, mental and physical development of the community* [Italics mine] by securing that efficient education throughout those stages shall be available to meet the needs of the population of their area.

With regard to church schools the categories of aided school (voluntary aided), controlled school (voluntary controlled) and special agreement schools were defined. In controlled schools the LEA took over the plant and appointed two-thirds of the managers/governors. No capital obligation was left with the school—and very little independence. Cash shortage edged many church schools towards state control via VC status. Aided schools, in which the church appointed two-thirds of the managers/governors, had to raise half the money required for the plant and exterior repairs, excluding playing fields. The salary bill and other (interior) charges were taken on by the LEA. Only 2,000 out of 9,000 Anglican church schools survived as voluntary aided, roughly equal to the total of Roman Catholic schools. Special agreement schools were a product of the 1936 Education Act retained in 1946 for schools whose governors had entered a special agreement with the LEA on an individual basis entitling them to similar funding and status as VA schools. Most RC schools came into this category.

In the secondary sector the Act required LEAs to submit development plans to show how they were going to provide schools suited to the age, aptitudes and abilities of their pupils. It did not spell out organizational detail, but the famous or infamous tripartite system of secondary grammar, secondary modern and secondary technical was introduced via the Green Book and the Board, though other alternatives such as bilateral, multilateral and even a handful of comprehensive schools (ten by 1951), appeared soon afterwards for LEAs unwilling to impose the tripartite model on their schools. Although the 1943 White Paper had explicitly stated that the different types of school might be combined in one building or on one site, variance on other than geographical grounds, such as population spread in rural Wales, was discouraged. Only Penlan and Mynydd-bach schools were allowed in an authority (Swansea) which wanted multilateral schools. The 1944 Act left education under LEA control but strengthened central and professional elements in policy-making. Butler was applauded in the House when he spoke of leading boldly and not following timidly. The President of the Board of Education, later to be ranked as Minister and in 1964 upgraded as Secretary of State for Education, had powers of intervention in school admissions, amenities, repairs and teacher qualifications. He, for such it then was, also had the power of the purse. Chief Education Officer appointments in LEAs were subject to ministerial confirmation. Teacher training was a separate branch of education within the dual system; some training institutions were LEA controlled and some church controlled. These were the training colleges, soon to be involved in emergency short-course training (one year) for teachers after the war, although for graduates no training course was compulsory prior to entry into teaching.

The passage of the bill through the House witnessed the first defeat of the National Government in the war: an amendment calling for equal salaries for men and women teachers was carried against the government by one vote (117 to 116). Butler was furious, not because he opposed equal pay but because he felt the defeat endangered the bill. Churchill, who was exhausted at the time from conduct of the war, was not amused, especially since the amendment came from the Tory Reform Committee. But at least by now the religious clauses had ceased to be contentious. Churchill made the defeat a matter of a vote of confidence to bring various rebel MPs into line and won it, thus making it easier for the rest of the bill to be passed, including the more contentious legislation abolishing 'Part III' LEAs. Equal pay was not introduced until 1955 and only then phased in over some years.

Religious Education in the 1944 Act

Butler said in his opening speech:

> There is religious teaching over the length and breadth of this country, accompanied by forms of religious worship in schools, but, like many

debates in this house, the standard is uneven, and it is the government's intention that this shall be put on a better basis . . .[30]

He was aiming to conserve and improve. The Education Act of 1870 had introduced board schools (named after the local school boards set up to run them) to fill the gaps in the provision of voluntary, i.e. church, schools. It had provided a withdrawal clause from religious instruction, not so much to protect atheists as those Christians who found their children in a school belonging to a denomination they did not support. The background to this clause is outlined in Appendix 4. In order to facilitate any such withdrawals, the period of religious instruction had been restricted to a fixed time at the beginning or end of a session, i.e. a half-day as marked on the register. A picture of religious education in this era appears as Appendix 1. Francis Cowper-Temple (1811–88), the Liberal MP for South Hampshire, had also introduced a clause stating that no religious catechism or formulary distinctive of any particular denomination should be taught in a board school. But the 1870 Act had not made RI universally compulsory. When school boards were abolished by the 1902 Act to be replaced by education committees of the local authorities, the provision for RI and for withdrawal were left unchanged.

Contrary to what was assumed later by many religious educators, the 1944 Act did have a concept of religious education as well as religious instruction, even if it was ill-defined. The phrase 'religious education' was not a later invention but is present by name in the 1944 Act. RE in the Act is held to embrace Religious Instruction, i.e. the classroom subject, and also the whole-school act of worship at the start of the day. Although these two had previously been 'virtually universal in the schools' (Dent, 1944b) they had never been made statutory obligations, and there was some protest about the new obligatory nature, partly by teachers' organizations trying to protect the right of their members not to take part. Chuter Ede, Parliamentary Secretary to the Board of Education, addressed these objections in the House of Commons :

> There is, I think, a general recognition that even if parents themselves have in the course of life encountered difficulties that have led them into doubts and hesitations, they do desire that their children shall have a grounding in the principles of the Christian faith as it ought to be practised in this country.[31]

Religious instruction was to take place every week in every county school and every voluntary school. The Act did not lay down a set number of occasions on which this should happen. Once a week was clearly the absolute legal minimum required to conform to the statute. Another change was that religious instruction was no longer confined to the beginning or end of a day. This opened up the possibility of specialist teaching more widely. Otherwise a start- or end-of-day arrangement requires more specialists than can be fielded when RI is running, but leaves them to be deployed into other subjects for the rest of the day, a majority of their teaching time. RI was also to be open to inspection. The 1870 conscience clause was retained. A parent could withdraw their child from the subject, including the receiving of religious instruction elsewhere during the school day. Religious teaching was to be based on an agreed syllabus—agreed at a conference between various defined panels: the LEA, the Church of England except in Wales, other denominations and the teachers. Butler referred to agreed syllabuses as 'extremely successful' because of their undenominational nature and avoidance of credal formularies. The 1870 Cowper Temple clause was retained. RI in county schools 'shall not include any catechism or formulary which is distinctive of any particular religious denomination' (1944 Act, Section 26) A VC school was included in this, so the originating denomination lost even its hold over religious teaching, except that where the parents requested that their children receive RI in accordance with the trust deed that set up the school or previous practice (i.e. before its controlled status), then such instruction could be given for not more than two periods in every week.

VA and special agreement schools retained the right to provide denominational instruction for their children under the control of the managers or governors, in accordance with the trust deed or previous practice in the school and without obligation to adopt the agreed syllabus. In some cases a diocesan syllabus was substituted. In schools where the teaching staff exceeded two in number, up to one-fifth of the staff were to be 'selected for their fitness and competence to give religious instruction'. These were known as 'reserved teachers'. Headteachers were ineligible to act in this capacity. Section 30 offered the protection to teachers that those who had doubts about compulsion feared. Not merely could a teacher decline to participate in RI or worship or both, but 'no person shall be disqualified by reason of his religious opinions, or of his attending or omitting to attend religious worship, from being a teacher in a county or voluntary school . . . and no teacher shall be required to give religious instruction or receive any less emolument, or be deprived of, or disqualified for, any promotion or other advantage by reason of [this]'.

A further provision in the Act was that each LEA was empowered if it chose to establish a Standing Advisory Council on Religious Education (SACRE). This was 'to advise them upon matters connected with the religious instruction to be given in accordance with an agreed syllabus and, in particular, as to methods of teaching, the choice of books, and the provision of lectures for teachers.' The method of appointing members and their terms and condition of office were left to the LEA to dispose. LEAs were to have regard to a unanimous recommendation that their agreed syllabus conference might make in respect of establishing a SACRE. By 1952 only 31 out of 163 LEAs had established SACREs, though ten stated that they were in process of setting them up. The role of a SACRE was strictly advisory.

The Act did not specifically require RI to be Christian, but it has to be noted that this was a tacit and unchallenged assumption all the way through the consultations inside and outside Parliament. At the time the words Christian and religious were nearly synonymous in an way which is no longer the case.

The Immediate Aftermath of the 1944 Act

The Act intended to reflect vision and purpose for the whole of education and the religious clauses were central to it. Writing an introduction to the new London agreed syllabus three years later, F.A. Cockin, Bishop of Bristol, commented:

> It is for those who are convinced that a religious understanding of man's life as the essential basis, not only of true education but of the moral health of society and of individual character, to see to it that such teaching is wisely planned and given with conviction.

He continued

> What is religious instruction ? What is it that teachers are meant to be doing when they give it? . . . Immediately we find ourselves in a situation in which the issues are confused in a tangle of ignorance, misunderstanding, conscientious scruple and the relics of past controversy . . .

Durham County produced a new syllabus in 1946. The introduction states:

> It will be generally agreed that the Christian people of this country desire to secure in all schools sound instruction in Christian faith and morals as an integral part of education. The fulfilment of this desire

has for long been hindered by ecclesiastical divisions; and this hindrance is the more obviously deplorable in view of the menace of anti-Christian forces in the modern world . . . Religion is not merely a matter of Biblical knowledge, but primarily a way of living, and of looking at life, and of meeting the various situations in life, inspired by a conscious relationship with God . . .[32]

Middlesex County, replacing in 1948 a syllabus used since 1929, stated the principles on which their syllabus was based: that 'the primary function of Christian religious teaching is to show the way in which Christianity offers the right relationship between God and man', that teaching should be based on the Bible, that the chief task of the school itself is 'to train for Christian citizenship', and that the child should be given an opportunity to gain 'Christian religious knowledge appropriate to his or her age'.[33] One of the clearest insights into critical thinking immediately post-war comes from Cambridgeshire, revising (1949) a syllabus devised in 1939. The introduction said of the war:

It is clearly impossible to pretend that it was fought on the issue of Christianity versus Paganism. In this twentieth century there is only one cause that can enlist, for the waging of 'total war', the whole energies of peoples, and that is a threat, real or imagined, to their freedom. The history of these last four centuries in the West is the history of a struggle for freedom— individual, social and national . . . The unquestioned assumption of medieval Christendom, that men are *too sinful to be free* [Italics theirs] . . . was consciously or unconsciously abandoned . . . In every sphere this pursuit has determined the characteristic features of modern civilisation in the West . . .

It went on to review the rise of science, its assumption of authoritative status in the minds of people, the rise of 'Machines' and the power of 'Money'. Communism and Democracy are then reviewed, neither uncritically.

The Christian can be a democrat because he believes that all men for all their weaknesses are meant to be free and responsible beings. But he can never identify Christianity with Democracy. It is the death of true religion to be accepted merely as the bulwark of social order. If instruction in the Christian religion is rightfully included in our educational system, that cannot be because we want the support of religion for the principles of Democracy: it can only be because we believe that those principles are vanity unless they are rooted and grounded in the faith and service of God . . . To teach Christianity to our children is to inspire them with the vision of the glory of God in

the face of Jesus Christ, and to send them into the world willing to
follow Him who was among us as one that serveth, because they know
that in that service alone is *perfect freedom* [my Italics].

It might now be argued that this is a charter for confessional RE, i.e.
religious education that assumes or works to promote a religious, in
this case Christian, base in its teaching and as such indoctrinatory. This
would be simplistic and anachronistic comment. What the Cambridgeshire syllabus and others are commending was intended as a
statement of the base values for the whole of education, not just the
teaching of one subject. If religious education is deemed to have 'failed'
in those early post-war years, it must be partly because the wider vision
out of which it was born quickly evaporated in a rapidly changing
post-war Britain. Few syllabuses in any subject have ever, like the
Cambridgeshire one, sought to justify and set themselves within
the context of the cultural history of the Western world; the 1988
Education Reform Act was deficient of all such reasoning. Moreover
the notion in more secular times that education can somehow be
value-neutral has only recently come under proper scrutiny. The values
of our times may seem as transparent to those who come after as the
values in these 1940s documents, but our values will have been less
publicly discussed in their contemporary setting. Cambridgeshire again
is clear on this:

> The form and content of education must always be conditioned by the
> view taken by the educators concerning the proper end of man. And
> it is neither the arts nor the sciences but religion which is able to say
> what this end should be. The most important element in any educa-
> tional system is its religious element, for whether the system expressly
> includes or excludes the teaching of religion, whether it is based on a
> positive or negative effect towards any particular set of religious ideas,
> its effect will be determined by whatever answer to the religious
> question is implied . . .[34]

To translate this principle into practice not only is subject content
detailed but the syllabus provided a checklist for head-teachers about
their own school including:

> Is the school so organised as to encourage co-operation as well as
> proper forms of competition?
> Are opportunities given whereby the stronger and cleverer may help
> the weaker?
> Is the love of animals and birds encouraged?
> What does the child do for his school?

What does the school do for the village or town . . . .
Is the school emphasising 'Thou shalt' as the rule of conduct rather
than 'Thou shalt not'?[35]

To Reid (1951) RE is important because religion is important for
national survival. Without sound religion a state may become corrupt
and decay. But he accepts that religion has its proper autonomy and
does not exist simply to serve states. The current danger as foreseen by
Reid is that scientific humanism may be absorbed by people un-
thinkingly and in the end threaten Christianity itself.

The Effects of the Act

The development work that went into agreed syllabuses in the years
immediately after the Act were one of its great contemporary successes
for education and for the developing ecumenical movement within the
churches. These were days when the reunion of most of British
Methodism was still within recent memory (1932) and co-operation on
agreed syllabus conferences was a surprise and pleasure to some
denominational participants, even if the desire for agreement meant
that heavier emphasis was given to the Bible than might otherwise have
been the case. Other development work, production of materials for
the classroom, better training for RE teachers and a higher profile for
the subject in training colleges and university departments of education
also followed. But as the vision of a religiously inspired education
system, in terms of its basic values faded away, to be replaced by no
particular vision at all, RI became a classroom subject among other
classroom subjects.

The seeds of later problems arising from its difference from other
subjects and its latent Cinderella status were sown. The joke quickly
was that RI was simultaneously the only compulsory subject (the law
said it must be provided weekly) and the only optional subject (parents
could withdraw their children). The other joke that RI teachers soon
tired of was that compared to English Literature, for example, RI had
only one set book, the Bible. This was often literally true. But the
Bible could be said to be out of date in language at least until a
clergyman, J.B. Phillips, produced Letters to Young Churches (1947)
for children he was working with. A whole New Testament followed.
The theological debate instituted by Rudolph Bultmann and others that
suggested that the New Testament might be out of date in its thought
mode and framework did not percolate to agreed syllabuses and
classroom RI at all, although the Durham syllabus was one of a number
to recognize different ways of interpreting scripture[36] perhaps under

35

the influence of Canon, later Archbishop, Michael Ramsey, who served on the Anglican committee of the agreed syllabus conference.

W.O. Lester Smith, one-time Director of Education for Manchester and professor of education in London, reviewed the workings of the 1944 Act (Smith,1949). He concluded that its debit side was the failure to communicate to children leaving school even the minimum knowledge of and interest in religion envisaged in the Act, the evidence coming from inspection of 'tepid teaching', the rapid dating of those religious clauses in the Act designed to prevent church squabbles and their subsequent 'provincial' appearance. 'The world is so much smaller than in 1944 . . . and the number of non-Englishmen so much more apparent to us.' Hull[37] noted that although syllabuses were concerned to nurture the religious lives of pupils in the present, they were concerned to study only the past as a means of doing this. Lawton (1992) argued that as the 1945 Labour manifesto Let us face the future contained nothing on education except a statement of support for the Butler Act, Labour lacked an education policy and therefore initiatives were lost in the immediate post-war years which affected RI along with other curriculum areas.

It is easy to be harsh on the failures. But there was a shortage of specialist teachers in RE that has had a limiting effect on the development and delivery of the subject at classroom level over the whole half-century. Nor can the provisions of the Act be blamed for failing to predict not only the rapid disappearance of its value-base in education and society, but the massive demise of the church presence within British society in the next half-century. Set against those two trends, RE can be said to be both durable and resilient for even in 1946 Sandhurst, using interviews with army cadets and a questionnaire survey of 4000 former pupils at independent schools, was judging RI a failure in more than half the nation's schools. He made the questionable assumption that RI in state schools would be worse than his sample from the independent sector.[38] He blamed parental indifference to Christianity as the root cause of the failure of RI. When Avery wrote her book for teachers she identified the climate of the time as insecure, frustrated, unsettled, noisy to an extent not known, and 'in the grip of the machine and the machine-made outlook', lacking a coherent philosophy of life and therefore ready prey for communism.[39] The immediate post-1944 years were not a golden age for RI. But it did not sink as Sandhurst feared; it adapted and survived.

The 1944 Act had been steered through Parliament mainly by devout Anglicans who hoped to see church influence in the whole of education rather than merely in the ghetto of church schools. Temple won here, with his vision of the national church. But Hastings argues that 'the

36

quickly advancing secular consensus of middle England in the sixties owed a great deal to the educational choices made in the 1940s'. Certainly from then on the churches, Roman Catholicism excepted, seem to have tried to appease the state in their efforts to retain what was left of their role in education, rather than challenge post-war and 'post-Christian' values. The Free Churches, having already given up nearly all their schools, were already marginalized in terms of influence except in the 'Other Denominations' panel of the agreed syllabus conference. But some of their ministers had influence as individuals among a growing number of RE advisers being appointed by LEAs. Anglicans and Roman Catholics could offer their clergy opportunities for non-parochial work within their own church school system. A Free Church minister had few options of this sort within the employment of the church, so some opted into county school RE jobs. There was still a perception that these schools were where the Free Church children were and that working in them was service to the church in this wider sense.

Most immediate post-war agreed syllabuses were intensely biblical. It would later be assumed on the basis of psychological study of child development (Goldman,1964) or pupil interview (Loukes,1961) that this biblical study was largely ineffective. But as early as 1939 Heawood argued that sensitivity was required. In an imaginary staffroom discussion one of his teachers says:

> No-one should thrust his views on immature children . . . The difficulty is to prevent oneself from foisting one's own half-baked views on young things who should be trained to grow their own.[41]

Before the war it had been seen that religious instruction might need to develop away from its 'instructional' base. The war delayed this, adding a tendency to return to the traditional in the 1944 settlement. In the later mythology of RE it was presented as if only in the sixties was it perceived that things were going wrong. It would be more accurate to state that it was only in the sixties that people were willing to listen to evidence that things were going wrong. Evidence had been in existence for more than thirty years.

The Holocaust and Immediate Post-War RI

The question must be raised, in the light of post-war knowledge about the Holocaust, whether RE syllabuses and the Act can be criticized for failing to grasp an opportunity to examine two religions at least, Christianity and Judaism, rather than to reduce Judaism to an almost extinct prologue to Christianity in the form of the Old Testament. Was this a chance to present Judaism as a religion of the present, to undertake some examination of the roots of anti-semitism, and to learn something of contemporary Jewish values and practice as well as a Jewish view of their scriptures ? Acland wrote[42] 'My Twenty-First Century Christianity is something which will recognise how much of the truth it missed when it broke from Judaism.' But he was atypical.

Persecution of Jews under the Reich had been openly reported in the UK in the 1930s. A White Paper (October 1939) appeared on German atrocities but by 1941 the British Ministry of Information had banned horror-based material about the treatment of Jews. Despite the best efforts of publisher Victor Gollancz and Eleanor Rathbone, MP for the Combined Universities, and campaigning by the *Manchester Guardian*, government response was mute. *The Times* of the 4 December 1942 spoke of a deliberate plan to exterminate the Jews. Temple made an impassioned speech in the Lords on 23 March 1943, but was almost a lone voice. Koestler's 'The Transport' (end of 1943) was rejected by some readers as atrocity propaganda. By then three-quarters of the killings had already occurred. Kushner (1994) argues that public knowledge of the Holocaust in Britain actually declined from 1943 until the end of the war. In cinema terms, *The Great Dictator* (Chaplin, 1940) presents camps as ridiculous rather than evil. Mass Observation (1946) revealed some anti-semitism among British opinion: the Nazis went too far but the Jews brought it on themselves, etc. Morgan[43] refers to anti-semitism in post-war Britain in small but real ways such as the membership rules of some Home Counties golf clubs.

Perhaps the legislators and syllabus framers wanted to forget the horrors of war and bury the past. Or perhaps there was an uneasy guilt that many more Jews could have come to Britain and survived, if the government had been willing to admit them and if public opinion could have stomached refugee influx in large numbers. Another part of the answer to the omission of Judaism and the Holocaust from RI lies in the equating of religion with Christianity by those involved with the Act. If Christianity is seen, even implicitly, as the culmination and end of religious revelation, then study of the other religions becomes akin to studying phlogiston in chemistry. It has potential historical or antiquarian interest but is of no use for daily living.

Equally important was the situation in Palestine under British mandate. The government was caught between the Arabs, who wanted no Jewish immigration, and the Zionists, who wanted unlimited immigration. Police stations and offices were attacked by the Zionist groups. In 1946 explosives planted by Irgun in milk cans at Jerusalem's King David Hotel killed ninety-one people and led to immediate clamour for British withdrawal back in ̶B̶r̶i̶t̶a̶i̶n̶ ̶i̶t̶s̶e̶l̶f̶ The Irgun massacre of the Arab villagers of Dir Yasin in April 1948 left 200 dead and on May 15 the British evacuated Jerusalem. It must have seemed to many people in the UK, hearing on the radio of British police being shot in Palestine, that Jew, Zionist and terrorist had become synonymous. The bomb that blew up that hotel blew up with it any faint possibilities of an early development of multifaith RE or of Holocaust education within the British educational system.

Varying Attitudes to RI in 1943/44 Despite Apparent Consensus

It would be a mistake to look back on the 1944 provision as monochrome, reflecting a coherent and static national consensus about Christianity and education. The Commons debate illustrated a wide variance of view, both about the religious provision and the effect that state-supported teaching of religion might have both on the state and the public perception of religion, as the following quotations from *Hansard*[44] illustrate:

> We sometimes say that this is an irreligious age. I believe that this is entirely wrong. Religious topics which a few years ago were regarded as almost improper, are now freely discussed in trains, in buses, at the fireside, in clubs, everywhere . . . and I believe that the people of this country have never been more ready for spiritual leadership and guidance than they are today . . . It is only on the basis of a true religion that men can have the courage to adventure and strength to achieve . . . Therefore the awakening of this religious consciousness is a fundamental necessity for the production of [a] . . . more closely knit society.
>
> Sir Harold Webbe (MP for Westminster Abbey)

> If religion is to mean anything different from mere Scripture and ethics, it seems to me that the proposals are impossible. The relation between the religious teacher and his pupil must be a spiritual one . . . I am certain that no teacher, however well-trained, in any day school, would ever have given us the understanding of the faith of our fathers which those teachers who were not trained did in the churches. I can think of no more certain way of raising atheists in this country than to place religious instruction . . . in the hands of secular teachers . . .
>
> Professor W.J. Gruffydd (MP for University of Wales)

> It is a commonplace today that education is not a matter of mere mental instruction . . . We need to provide for the whole man, physically, mentally and spiritually . . . The state is now to have control up to

the age of 18, and it must not develop lop-sided men . . . Education which fails to stir up and strengthen the religious instincts of man is incomplete . . .

R.D. Denman (MP for Leeds Central)

We in the Labour movement, particularly in the trade union movement, have no wish to see the expansion and development of a particular kind of religion [denominational teaching]. We see its adverse effects in other countries . . . [citing Spain, Italy and Ireland as examples] . . . Usually the denominational schools are deplorable places.

A. Walkden (MP for Bristol South)

C.W. Key (MP for Bow and Bromley) had been for fifty-three years a pupil and then a teacher in elementary schools. He recalled that a reputedly religious teacher had caught a boy commit a minor mis-demeanour during morning prayers and caned him with the words, 'My God, I will teach you reverence'. Key added : It cannot be done. Reverence is not a subject of direct instruction, even at the end of a stick . . .'

Defending denominational teaching Major Sir E. Cadogan (MP for Bolton) said:

I take the view that undenominational religious instruction has been an egregious failure in this country. Disraeli said that religion without formularies is a new kind of religion. I suggest that it is no religion at all. Undenominational religious instruction has failed because it is so dull and uninspired. There is nothing in it to kindle the zeal of youth, or fire the imagination of the boy. Thanks to the undenominational instruction in schools we now have a generation of parents who know nothing and care nothing about religion . . . However ingenious your syllabus may be, the general indifference to religion is an appalling indictment of the system of religious instruction that has obtained over the last 30 years. Can we be surprised . . . when we have relegated religion in the training colleges as an unconsidered extra not to be calculated in the certificate examination?

Major Cadogan was not alone in this view. The Economist[45] had already argued that the reason for the weakness of religious teaching in county schools was the Cowper-Temple clause of the 1870 Act, as it 'forbade the teaching of those religious formularies and doctrines which alone could interpret and inspire'. Mrs Cazalet Keir (MP for Islington East) saw teaching the Bible as a gateway of opportunity:

I hope that the Bible . . . will be used widely. It is the only book which can, through study and understanding, give us real equality of opportunity.

Sir George Schuster (MP for Walsall) saw RE as an antidote to over-vocational education:

> Many people in the course of this debate have warned us against regarding education as a process by which boys and girls are trained to earn their living. That is very wise, but we must also remember that it is a process which should be training them for life—how to stand up to life—how to know and maintain true standards or values in life. It is in that spirit that I look to religious teaching . . .

Viscountess Astor (MP for Plymouth Sutton), herself a convert to Christian Science, unwittingly reminded Members of the ambivalence of the English towards religion:

> I believe that though the people of this country do not talk so much about religion and do not attend churches as much as the people of other countries, deep down in their hearts they live it probably more than any other country in the world. So we do not want any religious controversy . . .

The seeds of many of the later issues about the relationship between religious education and education and society as a whole were present in this debate about the Act. If consensus emerged, it cannot be equated with uniformity and it was a consensus that glossed over difference. An issue of the *Religion in Education Quarterly* in 1953 could look back eulogistically on the Act as having brought firmer standing ground, more assured freedom and clearer purpose for RE.[46] But the legally-enacted provision was by no means the only factor affecting how RE was to develop in the early post-war years.

The 1945 General Election

In the July 1945 election Labour polled 47.8 per cent of the vote against the Conservatives' 39.8 per cent, producing a majority of 146 seats, including some in the 'unwinnable' south east. Even the Independent candidate who stood alone against Churchill polled 10,000 votes to Churchill's 27,000. There was a new prime minister, Atlee, and a new priority under Labour, social reform. Before the general election Richard Acland's idealistic Common Wealth Party had 15,000 members in 300 branches and four seats. Of these they retained only Chelmsford: their campaign for 'Beveridge now' was lost in Labour's ability to deliver it. The National Insurance and Health Service Acts of 1946 brought into being the National Health Service. A programme of state ownership was beginning: rail, roads and electricity (1946), coal, cables and wireless (1947), gas (1949). The Empire was breaking up: India became independent in 1947, Ceylon and Burma in 1948. There was war damage to put right, estimated at three billion pounds, excluding one billion pounds of lost overseas assets. External debts had increased by 3.3 billion pounds. Exports were only paying for a fifth of the cost of imports. British costs of feeding Germany rose from $60 million in 1946 to $240 million in 1947. Inflation was rising and the pound had to be devalued from $4.03 to $2.80 in 1949.

Education was dropping down the list for priority attention and investment, taking religious education with it. The British wartime tradition of make do and mend applied to the education system in peace: no-one could have known in 1945 that the outdoor toilets in existence at Sheffield's prestigious Firth Park Grammar School since 1920 would still be in existence in 1994. The complex forces that swept Atlee to power turned attention to the immediate present. Education was displaced by the urgent needs of the broken economy and by programmes of social reform. The Act was being implemented, within cash constraints and without further debate, but the vision was fading.

Chapter Two

Post-War Reconstruction: The 1950s

Four related words acquire special significance [in the fifties] . . .
Austerity and Affluence, Status and Image.

Peter Lewis (1978)

Society

Images of the early 1950s are those of austerity, of prefabs, of weeds growing on bomb sites, high income tax and shortage of houses, steel and coal. A third of all houses lacked bathrooms, their inhabitants either using 'tin' baths in front of the fire, or making a weekly visit to the local wash and bath house. National Service was compulsory throughout the decade. The new Conservative Prime Minister, after the 1951 election had ousted Labour was the old Churchill on a salary of £10,000, then equivalent to $28,000. In the USA the President of General Motors at the time had an income of $581,000. Britons looked at American affluence with envy. US supermarkets and their product packaging made the British grocery and its plain brown bags for hand-weighed products drab.

Gradually the British economy seemed to recover. A growth rate of 40 per cent became the basis for large pay rises, almost doubling wages during the decade. Labour recruitment encouraged people from the New Commonwealth, notably the Caribbean, to come to Britain for work. Thrift was discarded in favour of acquisition—refrigerators, washing machines, televisions (4.5 million licences in 1955 from 2 million in 1952) and cars, which doubled in number during the decade. For the aspiring younger motorist there was the motor-scooter. Macmillan made his famous 'You've never had it so good' speech at Bradford (1957), returning as Conservative Prime Minister with 100 majority in the election two years later. But the pound fell by a third while the economies of Germany and Italy were growing at 150 per cent. A 150 per cent rise in German and Italian exports was matched

43

by one of 28 per cent in Britain. Britain was disappearing as a world trading power. In 1950 it had 25 per cent of the share of world trade, but by 1962 only 15 per cent. Suez (1956) highlighted Britain's reduced world status and led to further rapid decolonialization in Africa.

There seemed to be a quest for easy money. Premium Bonds were established (1956) with a minimum one pound bond. There was some Christian opposition to this gambling, since the real non-refundable 'stake' was the interest on the capital investment in the bond. Covetous eyes watched TV quiz shows from the USA, like *The $64,000 Question*, which made Lancashire home-spun radio star Wilfred Pickles with his prize of 'five bob' (five shillings or 25p) meagre by contrast. *What's My Line ?*, a BBC quiz show, featured panelist Gilbert Harding, one of the first celebrities created by television, a rude, intimidating, former schoolteacher. ITV (1955 onwards) exploited the quiz show medium further.

It was not all money seeking and affluence. Kinsey's second report, *Sexual Behaviour in the Human Female* (1953) revealed that half the 6,000 women interviewees claimed to have had intercourse before marriage, about a quarter claiming an extra-marital sexual liaison. It did not correspond to the stereotypical fifties family picture. If the fifties convention remained that a woman's place was in the home and in the bed—and a third of married women were confuting this by returning to employment—Kinsey suggested that it was less clear whose home and whose bed. London police estimated (1950) that there were about 3,000 prostitutes there and Billy Graham is said to have remarked on a crusade visit that the London parks were turning into bedrooms. This caused a question in the House to 'Rab' Butler, who as Home Secretary reported that half a dozen prosecutions a day were arising from illicit activities in Hyde Park. The contraceptive pill was invented in 1952, although its use did not spread extensively until the sixties. Divorce quadrupled on pre-war figures—and this in the decade before the so-called permissive society. The quest for hedonism was chasing the quest for affluence. In 1953, the year of the coronation of Elizabeth II, the conquest of Everest, of Billy Graham addressing two million people in Britain, *Playboy* magazine for men was launched. James Bond in *Casino Royale,* was screened in a Britain finding espionage fascinating in the context of the Cold War.

The fifties saw the debate on capital punishment intensify, especially with the execution of Derek Bentley, a retarded accomplice to the murder of a policeman in a case in which the murderer himself was too young to be hanged (1952). The execution of Ruth Ellis caused such furore (1955), that years afterwards the hangman felt obliged to deal with continuing controversy over what she said on the way to the scaffold.[1] This case and the retirement, not entirely willingly, of the eighty-year-old Churchill in the same year were symbolic turning points mid-decade from the old era to the new. Butler did not succeed him, although he had been in charge of government in 1953 during the illness of Churchill and Eden. Macmillan ensured that Butler did not succeed again in 1963. Perhaps Butler's anti-Suez stand had not expunged what was seen as his pro- appeasement stance in the thirties. It looked as if education would be his apogee.

The Campaign for Nuclear Disarmament was founded (1958), following the production of a British H-bomb (1957) after extensive nuclear tests in the atmosphere. On Good Friday a protest march, a mixture of pilgrimage and pop festival, went to the atomic research establishment at Aldermaston. Other marches followed. From the mid-fifties a different form of protest—by clothing—emerged in the form of Teddy boys and girls. It was a blend of gang instinct and new youth culture with money to spend. Rock, skiffle and jazz each had their young devotees. Youth culture soon gained martyrs—actor and rebel James Dean, killed in a car crash aged twenty-four (1955) and Buddy Holly, killed in an aeroplane crash (1959). Youth non-conformist behaviour became a media-inspired and media-manipulated phenomenon and gave rise to values for youngsters only, from which 'oldsters' were excluded. They did not wish to listen to the juke-box or to spend the evening in the milk-bar. Television was novelty enough for parents. Growing manipulation in advertising was exposed by Vance Packard in *The Hidden Persuaders* (1957). It shocked its readers and quickly went through reprints, but the growing advertising industry continued unabated. It was followed by *The Status Seekers* and *The Waste Makers*, symbolic titles for the late fifties.

Within the revolution in entertainment the Bible was not eliminated: *The Robe*, *The Ten Commandments*, *Ben Hur*, and *Quo Vadis* brought it to the cinema, the gospel according to the director and the size of the budget. Cinerama with its bigger screen and bigger effects boosted epics, including *The Greatest Story Ever Told*. The first Sputnik (1957) travelled round the earth in the time it took to watch the film. On radio, later TV, Anthony Aloysius St John Hancock, of Railway Cuttings, East Cheam, a brilliant mixture of real life character and fiction, became a national figure. Holiday camps were another form of entertainment, but throughout the fifties camps declined in popularity as people forsook communal holidays with a thousand or more sitting down to eat at the same time in favour of individual or small group holidays. Growing numbers used the 'freedom' of their cars to crawl and swelter on the Exeter by-pass, the slow way to exotic, distant Torquay or nearly foreign Newquay. Some were sampling the rapidly expanding coastal villages in southern Spain. Transatlantic jet flight was making big liners redundant.

Church

The religious scene was also changing. Stafford Cripps, the gaunt Labour Chancellor, said by Macmillan to be a monastic man who lived by eating watercress grown on the blotting paper on his desk, was one of the nation's prominent lay Christians, but Labour left office in 1951. Cripps's Christian Socialist tradition continued through Methodist Donald Soper, Labour supporter, pacifist, and minister at Kingsway Hall, London. He appeared weekly at Tower Hill and in Hyde Park to argue Christianity with the crowd. Soper was not, until his elevation to the peerage, a politician in either House. Nor was he a typical clergyman or even a typical Methodist. Clericalism generally was becoming conservative. Archbishop Fisher of Canterbury was no radical, though he did understand one sector of education, as an ex-head-teacher of an independent school (Repton School). Two of his six sons became head-teachers. His successor, Michael Ramsey, was a distinguished theologian, a man of deep spirituality, but not a politician or media persona. His television appearances conveyed an air of a displaced but benevolent Father Christmas.

With the arrival of the welfare state it seemed that clerical radicals had run out of steam. The churches seemed to turn inwards. Cathedrals were rebuilt. Tindal Hart (1959) noted that even in the countryside the status, role and educational background of the parson was changing, with clergy collectively fewer in number, older in years and reduced in influence. In terms of religious experiment there was some interest in house churches, based on the French worker priest movement, an attempt to get a church presence into new big housing estates, but worker-priests seemed too political and smacked of communism. E.R. Wickham was pioneering industrial mission in Sheffield and there were experiments in inner-city ministry, such as those by Alan Ecclestone at Darnall, Sheffield, or Ernest Southcott at Halton, Leeds. But these were exceptions, and it is notable that immigrant Christians (92 per cent of Jamaican immigrants were Christian) felt on the whole unwelcome in the indigenous churches and set up their own.

Many Free Church families still would not do washing on Sundays or watch television or let their children play outdoors, but as more and more women returned to work or remained at work after marriage and their husbands washed the car on Sunday morning prior to a 'spin' in the country after lunch, the sabbatarian Sunday was eroded just as surely as the starch-requiring separate collar shirt was displaced by drip-dry human-made fabrics. Traditional Free Church strongholds—afternoon Sunday school and Sunday evening worship—had to move to Sunday morning or accept steep decline or eclipse. If the churches turned inwards, there were some benefits. There was some ecumenical thawing including the exchange of pulpits, but nothing as radical as inter-communion. As Hastings has noted:

> Faced with the rather dreary reality of post-war England, the Church of England as an institution sat tight, tied on every side by its venerable customs, pastoral amateurishness, and immensely complex separation of powers.[2]

Post-War Public Image of Religion

The Reverend Wilbert Vere Awdry wrote his Tank Engine books from 1949 onwards. The train-spotting or model-railway clergyman was one element in a media image of the clergy that was growing. It is best described by the crime novelist H.R.F. Keating, who noted that if a novelist wrote ' "The vicar came into the room" . . . almost all of us will at once see a vague, benificent figure, blinking owlishly'.[3] In Awdry's case this was less than fair. Just as it was forgotten that he appeared in his own books as the Thin Controller, it was also forgotten that he had been controversial enough to be sacked from his second curacy in 1940—for pacifism. But fiction in the media image of religion was to become more powerful than fact. The benign clergyman was to come to full fruition in the late 1960s TV series *Dad's Army* with the wartime vicar portrayed by Frank Williams. Millions of adults and children with no links with institutional Christianity imbibed these portraits of bumbling, well-intentioned, rather harmless prigs. It was miles distant from the 'Red Dean', John Collins, and from Trevor Huddleston, whose *Naught for Your Comfort* appeared (1956) after he had been forced to leave South Africa. Christianity could still be a crowd draw—Billy Graham's missions and Jehovah's Witnesses conventions were fielding 40,000 to 50,000 people, but there was among many Christians and non-Christians alike a feeling that these groups were 'them' and not 'us'. The media image of religion also became associated with decline: chapel closures were unabated, not simply caused by falling congregations but also by rationalization, delayed by the war, from the Methodist union of 1932. Some chapel communities were tribal, inter-related, extended families dating back to Victorian times or earlier. Closure often meant that substantial elements in the congregation did not transfer elsewhere. Their roots had gone in rationalization, though statistics suggest that moving house was just as likely to dislocate and displace the habit of church-going. Sunday-school anniversaries might still fill the small or medium size rural chapel to standing, but in most there was a growing shortage of children to go on the platform. Performances of *Messiah* or *Creation* had to advertise augmented chapel choirs ; there were no longer enough in one chapel to manage without help.

Roman Catholicism during the fifties was not very influential outside its ghetto; that must not obscure its quiet growth and consolidation at a time when other churches were in decline. Its schools seemed integral to its sense of purpose, especially with the adage 'Every Catholic child to be taught by Catholic teachers in a Catholic school'. Merton's *Elected Silence* (1949) had an influence well beyond its church of origin, presenting in the pages of an autobiography all the appeal of old-fashioned supernaturalism and uncompromising claims for Mother Church. In that sense it was a backward-looking book.

Christian culture was represented by Benjamin Britten, C.S. Lewis, Basil Spencer, Graham Sutherland and delayed recognition for Stanley Spence. But it is hard to avoid the view that in general, the churches were heading one way and society another and that the gap was increasing rather than diminishing. Almost unnoticed on the religious scene in the same period was the arrival of immigrants from different cultures and countries, some of them different Christianities such as Caribbean, others from different religions altogether, notably Indians (80 per cent of Indian immigrants in this period were Sikhs) and Muslims from Pakistan and Eastern Bengal (later Bangladesh). By 1960 they numbered half a million.

Religious Education in a Changing World

The task faced by religious educators in the 1950s was fully to implement the 1944 settlement. This had been arrived at on the basis of consensus between the churches, the politicians, those responsible for RE and the educational community. Even by the early fifties it is clear that this consensus was disappearing, if it had existed at all. Yet the will to re-write the 1944 settlement for RE was not there either. This might be because of the hegemony of 'Christian Educationists' in RE, from the mid-1930s to the early 1960s. They were perhaps never so self-conscious as a 'school', but they did share largely unquestioned assumptions about the nature and purpose of RE. Added to the lack of specialist teachers and (at this time) lack of identity for religious educators as a professional group, it looked as if religious education was being called upon to address an unworkable situation. Granted this context, some of the stinging criticism that developed in writings of religious educators in the early 1960s was misplaced. After Loukes (1961), Acland (1963) and Goldman (1964, 1965), it seemed hard to believe that anything of value had gone before. If 'bad' RE developed, it must have been at least in part due to the unpredictably changed situation in which the 1944 settlement now found itself. But did 'bad' RE develop at all?

The whole of education was not yet as unsettled as society appeared to be. This was still an era when a single person could dominate a subject market in school text books for many years. In French, for example, W.F.H.Whitmarsh was producing books for several decades from 1940. So was Ronald Ridout in English. The equivalent in Religious Knowledge was Bernard Youngman, a one-time secondary modern head-teacher who wrote a series of text-books, *Background to the Bible*, including black-and-white photographs of scenery and buildings. These were used for many years and constituted a complete secondary course in RK. There were four volumes: (1) Patriarchs, Judges and Kings; (2) Prophets and Rulers; (3) The Palestine of Jesus; and (4) The Spreading of the Gospel. There was a supporting book for teachers and students in training, *Teaching Religious Knowledge* (1953). In the preface to the third edition (1958) Youngman commended closer relationships between day and Sunday-school teachers and urged the need for a specifically secondary modern school syllabus, distinct from the grammar/technical school one. He perceived that there were serious problems in RK teaching even in imparting the most basic knowledge.[4] He referred to a radio *Top of the Form* quiz programme in which the round of questions on Scripture was a dismal failure. The 'top forms' could get only two out of eight answers correct. The questions were:

Who fed on locusts and wild honey?
What was Paul's name before he was converted?
Who refused to leave her mother-in-law?
What occupation did Peter follow?
Who was the oldest man mentioned in the Bible?
Under whom were the people of Israel exiled?
What is the name given to the Latin form of the Bible?
Name any one modern version of the Bible.

The second and sixth were answered correctly.[5] They were tests of knowledge, not religious understanding. Like many quiz questions since, some might be deemed trivial. But it is significant that the problem of knowledge retention was again being identified and discussed almost a decade before the 'shock' of public awareness of the issue was produced by Loukes (1961) et al. Youngman's answer was to appeal to teacher commitment to the subject and call for more interesting and effective teaching methods. He appealed not to the Butler Act but to the Spens Report (1938) as a basis for teaching:

> The traditional form which that [religious] way of interpretation [of life] has taken in this country is Christian, and the principal justification for giving a place in the curriculum to the study of the Scriptures is that the Bible is the classic book of Christianity and forms the basis of the structure of Christian faith and worship.[6]

He was equally clear:

> After every war we plan to make the world a better place, a Christian brotherhood. England is always to be the new Jerusalem . . . The cynics say 'What a hope!' The teachers say 'Here I am. Send me.' Like the prophets of old, they seek *to inspire their children to be good citizens* [my Italics] . . . Let us make no bones about it. The teacher of Religious Knowledge must be a Christian teacher . . . His work is equal to that of the minister of the gospel.[7]

He lists qualities required by RK teachers: knowledge and study, personal conviction, sense of vocation, sincerity, tolerance, infinite patience, great determination, 'a tremendous sense of humour and a hide like a rhinoceros'.[8] It was too much to ask. But Youngman pointed to other reasons for the failure of Scripture lessons: they might be at the start of the day and be eroded by collection of national savings or school meals monies or hymn practices or medicals; they might be ruined by rote Bible reading round the class, or by rote learning of long, unsuitable Bible passages; thousands of children had experienced wartime disruption of all timetable subjects, not just RK; some schools were merging classes for Scripture. One such class had 103 boys aged eight plus.[9] Youngman provides a window into some of the practical difficulties of immediate post-war Religious Knowledge teaching and awareness of the problems in pupil learning.

He also offers alternatives: more timetable time; basic English Bibles instead of 1611 Authorized Versions; making links with current news ('the escape of a Borstal boy may introduce the Prodigal Son'[10]); curriculum links with other subjects and activities; choosing material that presents Christianity as a way of life. He commends as a syllabus for seniors:

1st Year
Term 1: New Testament. Life of Christ, based on Mark

Term 2: Christian Church. Acts 1 to 8
Term 3: Old Testament. History up to the exile

2nd Year
Term 1: Old Testament. From the exile to the world Christ knew
Term 2: New Testament. Teachings of Christ (Synoptic gospels)
Term 3: Christian Church. Acts 9 to end.

3rd Year
Term 1: Christian Church. Spread of Christianity to Middle Ages
Term 2: Old Testament. Covenant. Religion developing into worship of the one God
Term 3: New Testament. The New Covenant. Personal and corporate religion

4th Year
Term 1: The Bible. The Testaments and the Apocrypha. The making of the Bible
Term 2: Christian Church. Reformation to the present day.
Term 3: Old and New Testaments. Jesus the Messiah. Jesus for the Jews. Jesus for all men

5th Year
Selected themes. Bible literature; letters of Paul; great religions; personal and social problems; creeds; questions.[11]

It is easy to see this as educationally effete, not child-related, too content-driven, inept theologically and naive in its expectation of success among a young generation already caught up in the changes described above. But the year of writing—1953—is significant, for many of the upheavals in British society in the fifties still lay ahead. Youngman did recognize a major problem in pupil learning and attempted a solution which needed further evaluation, which was to come with a vengeance in the early 1960s. What he proposed for RK was not so dissimilar an approach from other content-heavy subjects of the time, such as History. Moreover, Youngman also perceived that the C and D stream children would need a special scheme and not just a watered down A stream syllabus.[12] He viewed teaching method as of crucial importance, not just content. If it seems amazing now to present Christianity entirely through a book, the Bible, when it was alive in Christian communities all around the schools, to have presented it via a study of churches might have appeared to introduce the element of denominational controversy which was feared. The boast was in some county schools that even the Roman Catholic children attended RK lessons, if they were not in separate schools, because they were

Bible-based lessons and the Bible was seen as a lowest common denominator between Christians where doctrine was not. A Bible was presented by some LEAs to each child on their arrival at secondary school as a sign of its civic and national importance. It was still an uncontentious part of heritage.

Youngman's recommended teaching methods were story-telling, rote learning of key passages, painting, use of a classroom question box, drama including mime, puppetry, mock radio scripts, newspaper-type accounts, question and answer, listening to children's questions, discussions, debates, brains trusts,[13] lecturettes by pupils, topic work (projects), choral speaking, visits and visiting speakers, maps, murals, films and epidiascopes, flannelgraphs, modelling, newsboard (newspaper cuttings from archaeology, etc.), quizzes and games, even a revival of lantern slides, which he thought might appeal to a now sophisticated TV generation. He did not intend Religious Knowledge to be dull.

The window offered by Youngman into 1950s RK is that of one person, albeit a major contributor, to the developing theory and especially the classroom practice and presentation of the subject. Victor Murray (1953 and 1955) takes a similar view. He recognizes the limits of RE. Knowledge of religious history and doctrine does not bring a person into the presence of God. Something is required in the person 'which no teacher can ever supply'. But religion is never simply an uninformed emotion. Wherever it is found it possesses content, tradition, externality, sacrament, something that is personally communicable. Murray urges the reader to beware lest religious education become a substitute for religion itself. 'Knowledge can so easily stand proxy for faith.' He was aware that RE 'has been a wonderful playground for amateurs' and attacked the view that biblical knowledge has itself some magical quality which affects character. Equally he attacks the view that religion can be taught by 'atmosphere', without any form of education. Murray was conscious of an issue of control: 'the Church wishes to control the teachers and safeguard the position of religion in the schools. The teachers feel they should be the judges of professional competence in this as in all other such matters. The Education Authorities wish to have all education in their hands and they look upon Church control as a nuisance and an anachronism.'

Murray recommended similar teaching methods to Youngman. He also includes specimen lessons, all biblically based. But the Bible should not be read around the class; children should hear it well read and they should learn key parts of it by heart. A lesson on Naaman starts with recapitulatory questions about Elijah from a previous lesson, moves to a map to locate Syria, Carmel, border country and leads into question and answer about the God of Israel and information (from the teacher) about a god of Syria, Rimmon. The teacher then reads II Kings 5.1 to 19 without note or comment and children follow the sequence of events in their own Bibles. Two pages of expository comment follow for the teacher to work through with the class, using question and answer. The lesson ends with Naaman attending the worship of Rimmon as a duty, which is compared with the Roman Catholic Duke of Norfolk or Hindu and Muslim princes from India attending the coronation.[14] The didactic style characterizes all the lesson samples.

Mid-Fifties Survey Evidence

Religious Education in Schools, (SPCK, 1954) for the Institute of Christian Education resulted from an inquiry into the working of the 1944 Act. This offers a different perspective to that of practitioner evidence like Youngman. It was based on varied research methods: questionnaires to teachers in Birmingham and Norfolk, including those in voluntary and special agreement schools (except for RC schools in Birmingham), selected as contrasting LEAs. There were other in-gredients: 1500 questionnaires to independent, direct grant and county grammar schools across the country; in-depth visits to 94 London secondary modern schools and to sixteen further ones in Hull; an inquiry into agreed syllabuses in use in the LEAs of England and Wales and 1,500 questionnaires designed to test the amount of religious knowledge retained in pupils in the Leeds area aged 16 to 19.

The survey revealed that in some secondary schools, Religious Knowledge was receiving three or four periods per week. In others it was being omitted altogether in the examination years, apart from pupils entering school certificate in the subject. Lack of clarity in the 1944 Act about how much time should be allocated to RK meant that in many schools it was minimal. The Birmingham school survey revealed that on the whole primary schools were putting more hours in per week than secondary; the percentage figures for grammar and secondary moderns allocating more than two hours per week to the subject were 14.4 and 14.3 respectively. Grammar schools made the worst individual score, with 43.3 per cent out of a sample of 90 schools allocating less than one hour per week. The highest score came from the 135 remaining all-age schools in the sample, 97.8 per cent of which were providing more than two hours per week. Norfolk all-age schools were similar. The Birmingham grammar schools had the highest proportion of specialist teachers. Norfolk data revealed that only 19.2 per cent of their schools surveyed had moved away from start-of-day religious teaching using the new freedom of the Act. This is a significant return, because start-of-day teaching severely limits the use of specialist teachers; they cannot be in all lessons then and deployed elsewhere for the rest of the day. It was still a real impediment to the development of the subject.

The Joint Four Committee (of teacher associations) national survey of grammar, direct grant and independent schools found that out of 674 respondent schools, 303 allotted only one period per week at 11+ to RK. A great many set no homework. Girls' schools were sometimes more generous in their time allocation than boys' schools. In some mixed schools RK was taught separately to girls and boys as it was timetabled against PE. Schools reporting this stated there were some advantages to this segregation owing to the different rate of maturation between girls and boys.

Syllabuses, Equipment and Examinations

Agreed syllabuses were not always being accurately used, or even used at all. Some 291 independent or direct-grant schools were using their own syllabus, either as thematic syllabuses based on the Bible or as 'an orderly development . . . based upon the evolution of religious ideas in the Old and New Testaments'.[15] One school reported an emphasis on the Bible, 'a neglected study today'.[16] The ICE report itself urged distinctive syllabuses for secondary modern schools[17] to take into account their pupils' characteristics and needs and the unsuitability of heavily academic syllabuses for them. Among agreed syllabuses in use, there was most homogeneity in Wales where apart from Breconshire, which was using the 1949 Cambridgeshire syllabus, the other LEAs were using a syllabus devised for the Welsh Society of the Institute of Christian Education (1949). England was predictably more varied, with Cambridgeshire's syllabus the most popular among LEAs using the syllabus of a different LEA. The oldest syllabus in use in 1954 was Cornwall (1936), itself an adaptation of an earlier York City syllabus. Several LEAs were using the syllabuses of others with local supplements, e.g. Southampton, which was using the Durham syllabus with a supplement on the history of Christianity in Wessex. Only one syllabus, Salford, had within its title awareness of multifaith presence. It was using 'Cambridgeshire (supplemented with Old Testament material [sic] for Jewish children)'. Equipment in use for RK was surveyed. The Bible was the leader, mainly in Authorized Version or Revised Version, but with a wide range of children's Bibles in minority use. Library provision at school and county level was discussed and then a whole range of non-book aids was examined. In grammar schools the most common in order of use were pictures and charts as joint first, followed by maps then radio. Secondary moderns used pictures and charts as joint first, followed by maps then drama. Primaries made the heaviest use of pictures and charts, with models next and drama third in order. The report recommended that the BBC consider selling records of its religious broadcasts to schools.

The question of entering pupils for external examinations—and internal ones too—was still unresolved. There was still a feeling in some schools that it might 'spoil the spiritual atmosphere in which teaching is given' or reduce RK to rote learning of facts or theological formulae. The report sided with the benefits of thorough, systematic study offered by examination work. Biblical 'gobbet' or context questions in the emerging GCE were already a dreaded feature. Heavily factual rather than interpretative Ordinary Level questions were criticized—this did not prevent the same criticism applying right up to the time of GCSE, whose first examinations were held in 1988. Work on the effectiveness of retention of religious knowledge among children suggested un-surprisingly in view of the syllabuses that the highest rates of retention were among children with a church background, though there were some hints in the sample that children from practising religious families did better in some other subjects as well, e.g. History.

Teacher Shortage

As far as the shortage of specialist teachers was concerned the report drew a distinction between specialists, semi-specialists and non-specialists. The specialist was defined as a main subject two-year college-trained teacher or university graduate in theology. The non-specialist was not trained in RK but was teaching it as a minority part of an overall timetable. The semi-specialist was someone with either some initial training in the subject, or one who had undertaken later part-time courses or private study such as would give them 'no difficulty in passing an examination at Intermediate B.D. level'. In 1952–53 final-year students in colleges taking Religious Knowledge as an advanced course numbered 234 men and 697 women. There were 83 colleges offering such courses as against 101 (History) and 102 (Geography). 'One of the chief problems confronting Divinity lecturers is the ignorance of the student . . . concerning elementary biblical facts'.[18] Another problem was that many college students had not found studies in the Bible in their school-days to be relevant. One wrote:

> Had the effect of making me indifferent to religion: am finding difficulty now in having any definite ideas on the subject.

Another said of school-days:

> We did not understand the Bible and it was considered rather boring.[19]

The report later comments:

> It is evident that a generation has grown up which has no appetite for reading the Bible.[20]

This pre-dates by ten years the much publicized 'discovery' of the same evidence. The report went on to recognize the problem of specialist knowledge required to teach the birth stories, the feeding of the five thousand and the resurrection even at infant level.[21] It was recognized that the RK teacher needed skills as well as knowledge. Murray (1955) noted a similar problem, that in Scripture (sic), 'it is still very unusual for a teacher even in a grammar school to have so much as a diploma in the subject, to say nothing of a degree'.[22] The great difficulties imposed by tokenistic teaching of RK in one period per week were also noted. Despite the evident difficulties in teaching the Bible and in the attitudes of alienation towards it among many children, the emphasis for RK in the report remained unshakeably biblical.

> It was not, however, for its cultural worth and importance that the Bible was unquestionably given a place of primary importance in the schools . . . It was because the Christian faith and morals . . . were regarded as the foundations of national life and of individual character and happiness. The Butler Act regularized what had long been part of the normal tradition in all types of school.[23]

The existence and work of Standing Advisory Councils on RE was reported as enormously varied. Some were arranging residential week-end or day courses for their teachers. One had issued a bibliography for teachers. Several had liaised with the county library service to provide books. Another arranged for missionary visitors to schools. Many LEAs did not have a SACRE, as these were not mandatory under the Act. Some SACREs were inactive. Their role as potential stimulators for educational advance is stressed in the report.

Interpreting the Report

Interpreting this differently assembled and varied data is not easy. A picture is appearing of RK as a disadvantaged subject, under pressure for curriculum space in its early years as a legally compulsory subject.

Religious educators seem aware of the learning needs of children but unaware of the unsuitability of much syllabus content and of how fast society was moving away from what remained of its Christian consensus. At the same time there were glimmers of hope. Some schools were providing a generous time allocation for the subject. The beginnings of a professional rather than a merely confessional approach to the subject are in evidence. It was beginning to be possible to think of RK teaching as a career, even if such thinking was still rather too worldly for some observers. If RK in schools was still seen by many as a secular arm of the churches, foundations were being laid that would provide it with the independence from ecclesiastical connection that would enable it to survive the decline of the churches and the Sunday school movement.

End of Decade: the Bristol Agreed Syllabus (1960)

The Syllabus of Christian Education was produced by the City and County of Bristol Education Committee in 1960, revising a 1946 syllabus. The first page shows an awareness of the less than idyllic scene besetting the 1944 vision. The language is itself revealing.

> A small boy was getting ready for Sunday School one Sunday morning: his father was sitting in his shirt sleeves, slippers on his feet, reading the Sunday paper in front of the fire. 'Dad', said the boy . . . 'when shall I be old enough to read the paper on Sunday morning like you?' How is the father to answer? Is he to be honest and say, 'Look, my boy, I am just a rotten slacker; you stick to your religion ; it's the most important thing in life'? Or is he to say, 'It's all a lot of kid's stuff and when you are older you can throw it up and read the Sunday papers instead.'? This story raises the question of the importance of religion in life and highlights the influence of the home in religious education . . . It is the completely negative attitude of a great number of our homes today which makes the religious teaching of church and school so difficult . . .

The syllabus goes on to distinguish vocational training and training for living a full life, locating RE within the latter. No true education, it argues, can be merely secular, utilitarian or materialistic. It must be religious, which for this country means Christian.[24] The child is 'more than a growing, communicating, thinking, potentially earning individual. He is a spiritual being with an eternal destiny. The awakening of this spiritual apprehension is the aim of the Scripture lesson . . . We cannot create our own spiritual life. It needs to be called

forth, stirred, kindled either by our surroundings or by contact with
someone who knows the impact of the Spirit in himself.'[25]

There never would be enough Christian teachers to perform the task.
But implicit in the syllabus is the notion of entitlement, that if pupils
go on to reject Christianity as an option for their life, they are at least
entitled to be told about it. Another sign that this syllabus was
awakening to a different situation to the 1944 settlement is that it
includes a section entitled 'Is the Bible true?' At least its teacher readers
are allowed legitimate doubts and questions.

Notes on places of interest in church history in and around Bristol
are included along with a history of Christianity in Bristol. Then the
primary syllabus is introduced by a section on the spiritual needs of
children. The infant material revolves around the seasons and the
church year. First year juniors spend a year on New Testament
background and stories of Abraham, Joseph, Moses, Samuel and
David, then stories of men and women who have 'tried to follow Jesus':
St Christopher, Dr Grenfell, St Hugh, Florence Nightingale, St Patrick
and Mary Slessor. The scheme develops in the same way until the
fourth-year syllabus, the Kingdom of God (Term 1), the Apostles'
Creed, the Lord's Prayer and the Ten Commandments (Term 2), what
worship is, including its background in synagogue and early church
(Term 3) and then the Gospel of John. Memory work, sixty-nine
passages in all, is included for secondary, eg the Beatitudes (Matthew
5.3 to 12), Judge Not (Matthew 7.1 to 5) and the New Jerusalem
(Revelation 21.1. to 4). Fifth-year work was intended to pursue options
not used in the fourth. The syllabus includes sixth-form work on the
faith of the creeds, ethics, the transmission of the Bible, the church in
the twentieth century, science and religion and world religions:

> The ultimate question that must be raised is this: is Christianity wholly
> true and the other religions wholly false, or can we say that while there
> is truth in all the great religions Christianity supplants what is false
> and completes what is true in all of them.[26]

Religious Education is here starting to address the issue of truth
questions rather than operating simply as instruction. That the question is raised at all constitutes a move towards the changed situation in society. The next two sections are even more surprising:
scientific humanism and Marxism. The aim for teaching the former is
stated:

> Those with religious convictions need to realise the impact and
> challenge of scientific and humanistic thought, and the more agnostic

need to be taught to appreciate the Christian response to the work of scientists and humanists.[27]

This illustrates another emerging idea in RE—balance. Marxism 'raises many fundamental problems: the existence of God . . . free will and determinism . . . right and wrong, the rights of the individual and the meaning of the historical process. It is in the light of the Christian approach to these problems that the affirmations of Marxism can be profitably discussed'.[28] These sections are options on a syllabus devised for the small minority of pupils then staying on at school into the sixth form. The unit on Marxism is worthy of note, ten years before public debate flared up about its inclusion in the proposed Bath and Birmingham syllabuses. The Bristol document is one agreed syllabus in one LEA. It can provide no evidence about how much of its own content was being used in Bristol classrooms or how effectively. But it contains the seeds of some later development in RE and as such is evidence that such ideas were beginning to gain ground.

Corroboration for the potential of sixth-form RI was provided by Wright (1962). In his survey pupils were asked to fill in a rating scale on RI lessons. There was a slight tendency for favourable comments to outweigh unfavourable, although favourable constituted lukewarm favour rather than enthusiasm, but 21 per cent drew a comparison between the failure of RI lower down the school and a more positive effect in the sixth form. 'A constant theme was appreciation of opportunity for frank discussion . . . contrasted with dull Bible study lower down the school. Only 3 per cent thought there should be more Bible study.' There was a message here which religious educators were not quite ready to hear.

We may briefly contrast the Bristol syllabus with the revised Syllabus of Religious Instruction for the Schools of Wales (1963). Although it falls outside the decade, its content and outlook place it in the 1950s. The most important Welsh syllabus changes were the introduction of a common course for the first two years of secondary education, whichever type of school the child was attending, a new course on the Christian faith designed for the school-leaving year, with new course options for sixth forms. The syllabus aims were:

> to ensure that when pupils leave school they know the main content of the Christian faith . . . to make pupils aware of the claim the Christian revelation makes upon its hearers, of the consequent call for decision in response to this claim, and of the inevitable challenge to identify themselves with a worshipping community.

It was further evidence for a shift away from aims which were expressly to convert. Although the syllabus remained biblically Christian in its content and framework, even eight of the twelve sixth-form pages remaining solidly biblical, pupils were explicitly being allowed and acknowledged to possess the freedom to decide for themselves. Instead of inducting children into a received Christian tradition, it sought to challenge them by it. RI had moved on a little from 1944, and British society had moved on a lot. The chief gains for RI in a decade of uneven progress were consolidation within the curriculum map and an emerging professionalism, spearheaded by an increasing amount of specialist teaching. But RI was about to see its assumptions about syllabus and lesson content and its implicit view of the pupil learning process castigated in a rapid series of devastating revelations.

Chapter Three

Iconoclasm in RE: The 1960s

Theologically the present time is an age of demolition, not of reconstruction. We have 'a site but no house'. The symbols and modes of
thought in which religion has been expressed since the Reformation
have been shown to be either misleading or meaningless to a generation
whose thought is regulated by the scientific temper.

Edwin Cox (1966)

Society and Church

Stories of the Swinging Sixties can be overdone in a decade that
witnessed progress in more mundane matters like preventing the
nation's sewers from choking up with foam from detergents. But by
the mid-sixties certain social themes or values seemed to be in the
ascendancy. Niblett noted (1960):

Teddy-boyism and existentialism at their different levels are both
protests against being simply 'carried along'. People need to feel they
are alive as well as to be so . . .[1]

The dominant values seemed to be materialism, hedonism and almost
total personal freedom. The only limitations acceptable on this freedom
were the law and the moral acceptance that one should not 'hurt'
anyone else, though hurt was usually construed in a physical rather
than an emotional sense. Drug-taking became more common: cannabis
and amphetamines were more easily available along with LSD. Pop
lyrics and the much publicized behaviour of some pop stars promoted
the new ways. 'Lucy in the sky with diamonds' (Beatles, 1967) was a
thinly disguised advertisement for the LSD experience. By then the
Beatles' MBE was two years old. They were, in a sense, part of the
establishment. In this climate Sunday closure of cinemas (England) and
public houses (Wales) was as easily swept away as freezing and drying

overtook canning in food preservation. Sexual indulgence became more public. Living together started to be acceptable, rather than something to be concealed under pretence of marriage and false names. As skirts got shorter, so men's hair became fashionably longer. Short back'n'sides became the outmoded badge of national service and the fifties, except in certain cult groups. The mods and rockers' seasons ran from 1962 to 1964. The Penguin paperback of *Lady Chatterley's Lover*, sold at three shillings and sixpence (17½p), emerged with the court case against it dismissed, not least after the prosecuting counsel's question to the jury 'Is it a book you would wish your wife or servants to read?' That the remark was funny then showed how society had changed, though it still shocked many that the book was defended in court by an Anglican suffragan bishop, John Robinson.

Robinson reached fame, or in his opponents' view, notoriety, when SCM Press published his paperback *Honest to God* (1963). It was a badly written book which called for British Christianity to face the issues raised for honest faith by the writings of Tillich, Bonhoeffer, Bultmann and others about making theology relevant to contemporary thought. The reaction was unexpected. It sold a million copies. Its author received 4,000 letters, ranging from the scholarly to the abusive. It opened up a debate among thinking Christians and effectively ended the ecclesiastical, though not the academic, career of its writer.

Other questions were being openly discussed. Homosexuality became legal in 1967, five years after *Gay News* began. Despite Roman Catholic and other opposition, David Steel moved a successful abortion bill in 1967. Even Roman Catholicism, fresh from Vatican II, seemed to relax in the later sixties. An unlikely alliance was discussed in 1963 when the Macmillan Cabinet debated a joint propaganda offensive with the unreformed Roman Catholic Church against the USSR. It did not happen. But changes within Rome did. The vernacular mass was introduced in 1967 and quickly became the norm. Mass was celebrated by priests who now faced the people. Greater lay participation in the liturgy was introduced. More traditional practices—Rosary, Devotions to the Sacred Heart, Stations of the Cross, Friday as a meat-free day, declined in favour of parish prayer groups, Bible studies, discussion groups and ecumenical co-operation to a degree not seen previously. Even the backward-looking encyclical on birth control, Humanae Vitae (1968), did not stem this tide.

As a result of government encouragement to fill gaps in the labour market there had been a steady influx of immigrants since the war. In the fifties these had been mainly from the Caribbean and Ireland. Immigration from India and Pakistan peaked in the sixties. Some immigrants were refugees, e.g. from Kenya or Uganda, who held

British passports. But the consequence for the religious scene was that pluralism became much more evident, especially since employment took the immigrants into conurbations. The Irish and the Poles were one factor in the growth of Roman Catholicism. Hindus, Sikhs and Muslims arrived from the Indian subcontinent. The Chinese and Greek Cypriot population of the UK also grew in the sixties, as did smaller groups of Iranians, Iraqis, Egyptians, Palestinians and Sudanese. The UK, not often conscious of its mixed ethnic past of Celtic, Angle, Saxon, Jute, Roman, Dane, Norman, etc was growing into a new multi-ethnicity that was not unopposed. A political backlash was to lead to Immigration Acts (1962 and 1968) designed to restrict entry. In Walsall, Enoch Powell made his first attack on immigration, referring to the Kenyan Asians. As a former professor of Greek he recalled the ancient Roman who saw the River Tiber 'foaming with much blood'[2]. Politicians nearly foamed at the mouth to disown him but dockers' marches in the East End of London and the popularity of Alf Garnett, a fictitious but credible working-class, Queen and Country, Tory in TV's *Till Death Us Do Part*, showed that Powell was not without support outside Parliament. The 1968 Race Relations Act followed as an attempt to restore liberal harmony. The Roman analogy cropped up again[3] when Keith Joseph spoke about the inner-city crime rate and the danger that some areas were becoming ungovernable, comparing ancient Rome being destroyed from the inside.

Ethnic minority musicians were to exercise a strong influence on popular music, but there were other shifts in the entertainment world. The role of the Lord Chamberlain in censorship was phased out (1968). Even the BBC lost its Reith image with a satirical current affairs show *That Was The Week That Was* (1963). Mrs Mary Whitehouse's 'Clean-Up TV' campaign (1964) seemed a tiny force against the tide, though in 1994 it would still exist as the National Viewers' and Listeners' Association. The sixties were not all liberal. 'Rab' Butler, now Home Secretary, sanctioned the execution of James Hanratty for the 'A6 murder' (1962) even though shortly afterwards (1966), capital punishment was abolished. The last two executions were held in Liverpool and Manchester at exactly 8 a.m. on 13 August 1964, for the curious Home Office reason that no-one could claim that their relative was the last person to be hanged. Despite reports to the contrary two sets of gallows were retained, dismantled, in case the decision was ever reversed. At 3.03 a.m. on the 8 August 1963 a mail train stopped at a red signal. Criminals robbed it of two and a half million pounds. The Great Train Robbers acquired celebrity status despite virtually killing the train driver. But even trains were changing. *Evening Star*, the last steam locomotive, commenced service in 1960. More sleazy than the Train Robbers' image was the Rachman property and vice ring in London, exploiting women and tenants. Media preoccupation with salacious stories was reinforced by the Profumo affair. John Profumo had been Secretary of State for War, resigning (1963) when it became public that a prostitute whose services he had used, Christine Keeler, had also liaised with a Russian diplomat. In Wales Gwynfor Evans, President of Plaid Cymru, won a by-election against the Wilson government in Carmarthen (1966), a Labour seat held by Lady Megan Lloyd George until her death. Harold Wilson installed George Thomas as Secretary of State for Wales to try to curb the rising tide of Welsh nationalism. More extreme direct action—attacks on government offices, on second homes in Wales owned by English visitors and the defacing of road signs were part of a campaign by Cymdeithas yr Iaith Gymraeg, the Welsh Language Society, which had been formed in 1962. The Welsh Language Act (1967) under Cledwyn Hughes at the Welsh Office was also intended to placate Welsh feeling over increasing pit closures and the troubles of the farmers. The fortress Labour strongholds of Rhondda West and Caerphilly nearly fell to Plaid Cymru in 1967 and 1968 respectively. The Welsh tradition of nonconformist radicalism which had moved from Liberalism to Labour in Wales seemed now to be moving to Plaid Cymru. Cynics identified the investiture of Charles as Prince of Wales at Caernafon in 1969 as the government's response to Welsh agitation. Welsh Christianity was involved in this Welsh resurgence, or parts of it were. The Bishop of St David's sanctioned the use of church bells as a warning to villagers at Llangynderyn who were obstructing the surveying of a new dam. Archbishop Simon visited nationalist leader Dafydd Iwan in prison. Welsh Independent R. Tudur Jones saw a degree of political emancipation as a prerequisite for the spiritual revival of Wales. A new Welsh translation of the New Testament was to appear in 1975.

Violence seemed to be increasing. Kennedy was assassinated in 1963, an event that seemed so cataclysmic at the time that for decades afterwards people could remember what they were doing when the news came through. In Northern Ireland from late 1968 onwards disturbances about the role of the Royal Ulster Constabulary and its part-time special constabulary led to the abolition of the latter and the arrival of more troops from the mainland. 'Bloody Sunday', 30 January 1972, in the Catholic Bogside area of Londonderry and its aftermath made Ulster look ungovernable and led to direct rule. Even England's football World Cup win over Germany[4] was marred by soccer hooliganism, a sign of things to come. Football, once a family spectator sport, was being turned into a contest for young men, some of whom were lured by the excitement of the battle off the pitch, rather than the ritualized battle on it.

If there were social troubles, the troubles of the economy were dire: growing industrial action and a continuing balance of payments deficit. The pound was devalued. Labour Chancellor Denis Healey cut defence costs. But wages continued to rise, as did the number of people holidaying abroad, often in Franco's Spain. Foreign holidays rose from seven million per year to ten during the decade. Money in the form of credit cards had become more easily available with the arrival of Barclaycard (1966). Payment could come later.

Education

A fairer deal in education seemed ahead. The consequence of the tripartite system had been that almost as soon as it was implemented, the secondary grammar schools reverted to their simpler pre-war name of grammar schools and the secondary modern schools, sometimes abbreviated to modern, at others to secondary, acquired secondary status. Not to be selected for grammar school was to be deemed to have 'failed' the eleven-plus examination by many parents, employers and pupils themselves. There were serious problems with selection at eleven. Some were ideological, such as whether the system was making for two nations at the tender age of eleven and whether it was desirable to separate children in this way. Some problems were technical, such as whether the tests used were reliable indicators and how to cope with borderline cases. Some problems were local, like the lottery element caused by one LEA having a higher percentage of grammar school places than its neighbour, which meant if you resided in one LEA you 'passed' and if you lived in the neighbouring one you 'failed'.

Department of Education and Science Circular 10.65 required all LEAs to produce programmes for a switch to comprehensive schooling. The intention was to provide better opportunities for all. 'Green field' site schools or schools which became comprehensive without merger, by taking a non-selective entry, fared better than schools that were forcibly married, often with split sites at some distance (in at least one case ten miles) and resentment by non-graduate and often former secondary modern teachers that they were passed over in newly created and contested head of department posts. Suspicion that the ex-grammar school teachers would never cope with difficult low-ability children were countered by sneers that the ex-modern school staff would not be academically competent to teach to 'A' Level. Ex-grammar comprehensive schools continued to attract parental esteem for years after their changed status. But the whole move to comprehensive schooling was done without adequate staff training (or in many cases, without staff training at all), without adequate funding and without proper consideration of curriculum provision. Circular 10.65 requiring change led in the event to some excellent comprehensive schools and some extremely poor ones. En passant it destroyed some fine grammar schools and—less publicized at the time—some excellent secondary moderns. Major school re-organization without major school funding was a hazardous business. By the time a new Conservative government under Edward Heath, himself an ex-grammar school boy, rescinded the Circular under Education Secretary Margaret Thatcher in new Circular 10.70, leaving the organization of schools a matter for each LEA, 32 per cent of secondary pupils were in comprehensive schools. Under Thatcher's Secretaryship more LEAs submitted comprehensive plans than did under Labour, including Conservative LEAs. But some had their proposals turned down.

It was not just the eleven-plus examination that was under fire. Debate about whether eleven was the best age at which to move pupils from primary to secondary school led to another major departure from the 1944 Act. The 1964 Education Act allowed LEAs to set up 'middle' schools, usually for nine- to thirteen-year-olds, where they deemed it a more appropriate age to move children. In such authorities there were then 'first schools' (4 to 7 years), middle schools (9 to 13) and upper or high schools (13 to 18). Another alternative model of movement at 11 and 16, the latter to a sixth-form or tertiary college, was yet to be established.

Religious Education

Hilliard
F.H. Hilliard (1963) did not attempt to defend RK on the basis of the nation being Christian. But he did assert that the nation had not moved to atheism, rather to a reluctant agnosticism which still regarded it as desirable that children should learn about religion in school or even attend Sunday school. He did not defend this as an intellectual base for RK but as a social reality which could not be ignored. Hilliard's intellectual defence of religion in the curriculum was that without it education would be incomplete. Children would lack the cultural key to Western history, music, art, architecture, law etc. Moreover, it offered children an option, a religious interpretation of life, which they might otherwise lack. He did not use the later fashionable word entitlement to describe this, but he did use the word 'right'. He did not feel that schools could fill a gap of religious influence left by parents

or church but he did think they could arouse interest in the subject of religion. Hilliard noted that it was no longer possible to equate religion with Christianity but argued that Christianity should properly continue to dominate RK because it was to be seen as the key to understanding Western culture. It forms part of school life, not because of a historical legacy from pre-Reformation and pre- Renaissance times, perpetuated in the dual system, but because education itself would be incomplete without a religious (in England and Wales, Christian) dimension. But he did countenance children 'learning about the other great religions which attract millions in other parts of the world'. Hilliard maintained that this teaching should take place after the child had received a thorough grounding in their own culture and tradition.

> It is in its Christian form that religious faith and experience will most obviously make any appeal that it is to have . . . It is hardly to be expected that many of them would be likely to become practising Muslims, Buddhists or Hindus, however much sympathy with and interest in other men's faiths they may later come to have. 'Indoctrination' of a sort this may perhaps be, but then all education is inevitably a form of indoctrination, not least in this second half of the 20th century.[5]

He cites as examples of positive indoctrination, teaching the freedom of the individual, or teaching acceptable standards of social behaviour. Repulsive indoctrination aims at 'foisting upon the individual a point of view without giving him as full a picture of the salient facts as possible and the freedom to come to his own conclusions'. Religious education is a crucial phrase, for it is the component of education that can prevent indoctrination in the bad sense. Hilliard quoted from a *Daily Telegraph* article:[6] 'Religious education is not slavery, but compulsory freedom.' He conceded it could resemble punishment in the classroom, if it became like a protracted visit to a museum, a catalogue of facts or a matter open to such various interpretation that it becomes obscure. As Bible teaching comes alive, so teaching about religion is properly turned into teaching religion. The analogy is with music or art or literature: through teaching the techniques, the teacher hopes to lead children into the experience that lies behind these spheres of human activity.

Hilliard noted that much RE in secondary schools in particular was failing to make an impact. Lack of esteem by pupils, lack of support by some head-teachers, the failure of many agreed syllabuses to relate Christian principles to the reality of daily life; a continuing serious shortage of specialist teachers especially in grammar schools and a climate in which a superficial demands for 'facts' and 'proof' is dominating the thinking of children are cited as examples. He did detect inconsistency in noting this lack of specialist teachers alongside his own strong recommendation that RE specialists should teach in another field to prevent the setting apart of religion from the rest of school life and work. But a steady increase in examination entries at Ordinary and Advanced Levels was noted with pleasure.[7] Girls outnumbered boys in all RE entries by between two and three to one. Hilliard feared that the comparative low Advanced Level entries stemmed from 'Divinity' being thought of as an abtruse, speculative subject. Advanced Level syllabuses were beginning to include sections on science and religion, world religions and ethics. He argued for entering pupils for one biblical and one non-biblical paper.

The RE teacher's qualifications should include: personal concern about religion; broad sympathy with its different manifestations; academic study of theology and an understanding of life. 'Those who would lead others towards spiritual understanding and insight must themselves know the life that the others really live'.[8] The RE teacher should blend the human concern of the subject with the mysterium. What Hilliard did not say is as noteworthy as what he said: the claim that the teacher must be a committed, practising Christian, has gone. This was perhaps a mixture of a philosophical shift of perception of the role of the RE teacher alongside a practical sense that if only the committed Christian were available to teach the subject many good teachers would be excluded and the subject would collapse through lack of staffing. Niblett supported this (1960) arguing that the crucial point was that in RK the teacher should understand what religion is really about. Although Hilliard's recommended teaching methods were no different from those of Youngman a decade earlier, curriculum development in all subjects moved more slowly then.

Hilliard marks one of the last conservative attempts to refine the tradition of teaching in RK that had gone on before and after the 1944 settlement. The Surrey Agreed Syllabus was another. Alongside a biblical syllabus with the addition of study of selected famous Christians[9] was an awareness that 'one of the aims of education is the training [sic] of imagination, wonder, reverence and awe'. RE was seen as having a very important part in that training. Jones (1963) writing for teachers takes a similar view. His chapter headings were all based on aspects of the Bible: biblical history, biblical theology, biblical religion, biblical geography and biblical archaeology. The final chapter, significantly, was called Problems of Communication. The front cover of the book showed a photograph of a gowned male teacher facing a blackboard next to a relief map of 'The Holy Land' while a pupil with a wooden pointer indicates Nazareth on the map. On the board are written the words: 'St Peter preached that Jesus was the Son of God. He proved this by three things . . .' It was the end of an era. Five books appeared shortly afterwards that cast doubt on the effectiveness, though not always the principle, of the whole enterprise of RK as it was being conceived and delivered in school. These were written by Harold Loukes, Richard Acland, Ronald Goldman and Violet Madge.

Loukes

Perry (1956) had already written about the problems being caused by unrealistic agreed syllabuses for the secondary modern school.[10] Garforth (1961) wrote about 'Doubts about Secondary School Scripture'.[11] He cited the meagre time allowance, the absence of teaching comparable to external examination standards in many schools, the lack of specialist teachers, the non-provision of text-books, the low status of the subject in the eyes of parents and the failure of RI in county schools where there was no adequate link to the church. He used the term Cinderella to describe the position of RI. The phrase caught on.

When Loukes published *Teenage Religion* (1961) he was Reader in Education at Oxford. His book grew out of the results of an inquiry, sponsored by the Study and Research Committee of the Institute of Christian Education in 1958, intended to investigate the state of RE in the secondary modern school. It was not concerned with statistics or even with the factual knowledge of and about the Bible which teenagers retained but with how far Christianity made sense as an instrument to help school-leavers make sense of their own condition. Niblett had hinted (1960) that limiting RK to biblical history, church history and Christian doctrine was like 'confining sexual education to biological descriptions'. The Institute inquiry tested this idea further. The enquiry method was tape-recorded class discussion in the normal classroom setting. A selection of comments from the tapes was then put to 500 children for their further comment, to try to estimate what those who remained silent in a class discussion might be thinking. The book presented one complete class recording and extracts from the others. Topics included: belief in the Bible; the nature of God; Jesus Christ; heaven and hell; suffering; is Christianity worth dying for?; prayer and worship and the Scripture lesson itself. The answers showed an honest and at the time shocking vocal mixture of ignorance and negation within a wide spectrum of viewpoints. They also reflected an assumption that the teenagers' questions and challenges to belief were not welcome as an integral part of the lesson. They assumed that the teacher was there to promote belief. Scripture lessons, for instance:

Well, when we have Scripture it's like the teacher dictating to the class
. . . I think it should be more of a discussion.

We used to keep going back over the same things and they'd flog the
same old things to death . . .

Yes, it's a very controversial subject [religion], but Scripture lessons
are totally boring.

Interviewer: You wouldn't do away with RI ?
Answer: No
Interviewer: So you just want to change it ?
Answer: Yes, it needs some radical changes.[12]

The cumulative evidence of the interviews was that the pupils were
more sympathetic to Christianity than one might expect, although they
demanded the right to personalize it in statements of belief that were
quite unorthodox by standards of the creeds and other definitive
statements from institutional Christianity. There was a suspicion of the
Bible as an unquestionable authority for belief:

The Bible is just a collection of tales and song and poetry made up by
some people to explain the world in my opinion.

ther is a lot of rubis in it techers admit ther is so that I do not think
that it is true.

It could be [true] but was it? I was not there so I do not know. Are
any stories true? As we grow up we realise that Father Christmas and
fairies were unreal, so why not the Bible?[13]

Loukes saw some of the difficulties as being caused by the attitudes of
the churches towards children, and perhaps as a result of his own views
as a Quaker took the view that the churches should not press for
conversions as these were emotional rather than intellectual or truly
volitional. More importantly for RE he saw that its future must be to
advance a theory which corresponds to its actual role, rather than the
role which Christians might hope it would fill. It must accept the
integrity and freedom and questions and complex personal life of
peer-group pressure as well as the emerging sexuality and search for
an identity of the adolescent. Loukes had made clear in his first editorial
in *Learning for Living*[14] that he believed the situation in schools had
radically changed: Parliament had raised the school-leaving age at the
same time as nature had reduced the age of puberty. The result was

that young adults were now spending two years of their adult lives in
school. He saw, but did not develop, Piagetian analysis of child
development as a helpful tool in this process. So Loukes' syllabus was
'problem-centred', on the grounds that adolescents would see the issues
as relevant and interesting. His spheres were:

> problems of personal relations: authority, friendship, sex and marriage
> and snobbery; problems of personal responsibility: money, work,
> leisure and prayer; problems of meaning: suffering, death and learning.

His recommended teaching approach was to raise the problem in an
opening discussion, to analyse it by moving from the general to the
particular, to introduce Christian teaching on the issue, and to refer
the problem back more widely to society as a whole in the light of the
earlier phases. Discussion is to be the central method and no longer
peripheral, although Loukes registers awareness of the danger of
uncontrolled or uninformed discussions. He made a big move away
from a generation of agreed syllabuses and Bible-centred learning but
his effect on agreed syllabuses was by no means immediate. In 1965
Darlington produced an entirely biblical new syllabus. Even so, it
contained questions for discussion as part of each section for older
children, e.g.

> Is there room for God in this world of space and atoms? If astronauts
> can find no trace of him, where is he? Can we get in touch with God?
> What do Christians mean by saying Jesus is the Son of God? And what
> do they mean by saying that He is still alive? How do we know whether
> what they say is true?[15]

It was a small but significant step for so cautious a committee document
to be accepted as an agreed syllabus. Within a biblical and church
history syllabus, Cornwall (1964) was recommending small group
work and structured use of discussion, within a staple diet of class
teaching in which often 'the best visual aid is the blackboard dia-
gram'.[16] Goldman's work was to move syllabuses further and faster.

Acland

Richard Acland had a long history of involvement in religion and
education. He had made a dramatic intervention in the 1943 education
debate as Liberal MP for Barnstaple.[17] He strode across the floor from
the National Government benches and spoke passionately from the
opposition front bench about society needing to live up to the principles
it teaches children rather than teaching them implicitly that 'You shall

be personally responsible for carving out as big an income as you can for yourself'. Acland viewed Big Business and Materialism as enemies. He was a crusader, a visionary, the only MP to have served in the ranks of the armed forces (as Lance Bombardier, writing books after lights out, typewriter on his knees). He was likened by some including himself to an Old Testament prophet. His belief in God was a derivative from his political ideas and experience rather than the reverse. His book *Unser Kampf* (*Our Struggle*, 1940) was written to rebut *Mein Kampf.*

> We have used the Bible as if it were the special constable's hand book—an opium dose for keeping beasts of burden patient while they were being overloaded.[18]

Acland acknowledged his quotation from Conrad Noel, Christian Socialist vicar of Thaxted from 1910 to 1942. Noel in turn was quoting Charles Kingsley, one of the founders of Victorian Christian socialism. Acland was conscious of himself within that tradition and his involvement in RE is to be interpreted in that context.

In a book specifically about RE, *We Teach Them Wrong*, he described how with no more qualification than that of being an Anglican lay reader, he was persuaded into teaching RE when he was on the staff of a secondary school in Wandsworth. He did not, however, describe his own background, which was very different from that of most schoolteachers. Born in 1906 he was the fifteenth baronet of a family dating back to the twelfth century. In 1944 he gave his house and estate at Killerton, Devon, to the National Trust because of his belief in common ownership. He abandoned the Liberalism of his upbringing to found a new political party, Common Wealth, which had received some support from William Temple. Losing as Common Wealth Party candidate for Putney in the 1945 general election, a seat he fought as a result of 'a stupid muddle'[19] and witnessing the virtual obliteration of his party, he eventually became Labour MP for Gravesend, resigning on principle when Labour accepted nuclear weapons. The need for employment took him to the Wandsworth school. Yet Acland was perpetuating a family interest and commitment towards religion, education and religious instruction, including efforts by his forebears Sir Thomas Dyke Acland to reorganize arrangements for religious instruction (1887) and by Sir Francis D. Acland, whose wife Eleanor had written an essay in 1914 on RI in a changing society. There was a dynastic interest in teaching religion. With disarming honesty Acland wrote about his RI teaching that he could not hold the boys' attention for five minutes. He could not even keep them quiet. In the end he had to ask the head-teacher to relieve him of his duties. He described what was going on as 'the religious fiasco' and felt that, in part, his lack of specialist training in the subject was to blame for the pupil riots. Licking his wounds from the safer vantage point of a lectureship in History at St Luke's College, Exeter, he reached the conclusion that something was going radically wrong in the delivery of RE that no minor tinkering would put right.

He saw in the sixties some symptoms that others had seen a decade earlier: the retention of religious knowledge by pupils who had passed through the process was abysmally bad. But the effect of some Bible teaching on children was far more negative. In a survey of some 200 pupils in the Taunton area, asking the open-ended question 'What do you think of the story of Jonah and the Whale?' he analysed their replies as follows: 21 knew nothing of the story; 27 could retell it as a story but expressed no opinion about it; 23 believed that with God all things are possible; 8 thought it might be based on an exaggerated historical event; 14 saw it as possibly some sort of myth or parable, 14 dealt with it as clearly unhistorical parable but, most disturbingly of all, 125 (62.5%) dismissed the whole thing out of hand as quite impossible. Acland concluded that the Bible was being taught without interpretation, hence quite literally, even by teachers who were not themselves literalists. Faced with the simple proposition, 'believe this as literal truth or reject it', he was convinced that most children would choose the latter. He felt that the longer the teacher plodded on with the implicitly literal approach, the more alienated the child would become from the Bible and from the lesson. Partly on anecdotal evidence, partly on personal experience and partly on survey evidence (Sheffield and Nottingham Institute of Education surveys) he came to believe that pupils despised RK. 'It is the period in which, by long-established tradition, we muck about, and see how much we can get away with'.[20] Part of the reason for this was that they had imbued the view that the church was opposed to science, but that Science was 'true' and its progress irreversible. He related the failure of RK teaching to a wider Christian failure to present truth in a non-literal way and to a growing feeling outside the classroom that RK did not matter:

> Teacher stands there saying it matters; the whole outside world says it does not.[21]

What Acland said was not new. Sandhurst had said it in 1946 but his sample had been ex-independent school pupils who were sometimes more polite than Acland's:

I found the clearer explanations were from laymen. The parsons were hopeless.

It [the Bible] was discussed slightly, but I think it should be discussed more fully, as it broadens the mind.

The don was a padre who . . . only pointed out the Christian point of view.

RE was limited at my school to numerous visits to the chapel and to incompetently run divinity classes.

Let them quit this [the Bible] and teach the present problems and the way to overcome them.[22]

Disaffection with RK had a demonstrable problem that stretched much further back than the sixties. Acland's solutions to this were to rename the subject Religion and Life Discussion Period, to provide it with two periods per week instead of a token one, to adopt Loukes' lesson themes, to explain to children that a new direction was being taken, to provide teaching that questions common assumptions about what constitutes proof, and to present Christianity in a non-literal and non-anthropomorphic way. Noting that George Adam Smith had seen Jonah as an inspired parable as early as 1896, Acland pondered why that had not percolated to the classroom of 1963. Presenting Christian belief as a spectrum of views and not a monolithic view was a task of the church which he believed the religious educator should build on. He hinted that what was going on in classrooms had its roots deep in the developing history of the Western world: Luther had challenged the divine right of popes, Cromwell the divine right of kings and now children were challenging the divine right of teachers and of parents. It was parallel to Bonhoeffer's view of 'Man Come of Age'. Acland expressed what was happening in an equation. Children were being taught that Christianity = being good. But being good = learning to conform to the outlook and behaviour of respectable elders and betters. Because this was being rejected by sixties children as a view of goodness, Christianity was being rejected along with it. Acland welcomed the progress of this child emancipation as 'glorious' and felt that the social chaos these deeper challenges and changes were bringing about would be temporary. In this situation Christianity was called upon to find common ground with the other religions against the 'technological secularism that is now sweeping the world'[23] rather than in attacking or missionizing the other faiths. He therefore backed RE as concerned with religion rather than solely Christianity and used the phrase 'religious education' in the 1944 Act in defence of this. The passionate style of his book and its theology is best summed up the final paragraph:

> If, by the time they leave school, the adolescents know that the Church is not asking them to believe the impossible; if they are not waiting for a Proof; if they know something about themselves, and particularly that there is 'something wrong with us as we naturally stand'; if they have courageously looked at life in the world today with all its glory and horror, and answered with a heart-felt thankful 'Yes'; if therefore they stretch out in the hope of being aligned with whatever may be active at the heart and core of Life; if they have been given even an elementary insight into what may be involved in the quest for Christ Within; if they have often looked at verses, chapters and books in the Bible that are relevant to all this learning; and if the teacher then stands out of the way; is there not a fair chance that they will be found by the Truth of God?[24]

A sequel (1966) questioned how all the subjects within the school curriculum were being taught and raised the question whether teachers should abandon their role as acceptable servants of established orthodoxy and lead young people into constructive rebellion against its inadequacies. Acland had by then met History students who could claim that their college course had killed their interest in history[25] and discovered that teaching problems were not confined to RE.

Acland was by any measure unique, not least in that in RE he is the only figure to have been, albeit fleetingly, a classroom teacher, a theoretician and a politician involved in the legislative process that brought about the 1944 settlement. Although he left the Liberal Party, his was an essentially liberal view of education and religious education. Its philosophy was at least as old as George Adam Smith's teaching on Jonah. It assumed that social progress was automatically beneficial if occasionally painful. Acland was writing for the liberal sixties that were willing to hear this message again. But he was not promoting individualism, another sixties trend, as his new creed: 'Jesus did not say "Blessed are they who set the people free to promote their own self-interest." '[26] He brought to RE 'all the blazing assurance and simple sincerity of a man who, to many observers, appeared both maniac and mystic, fool and saint'.[27]

Madge

Violet Madge wrote (1965) after study undertaken during a year's secondment to Leeds University Institute of Education. She was a senior tutor at Rolle College, Exmouth, and her motivation was a personal interest in understanding the religious conceptions of children in the

75

primary years. She started with infants' wide-ranging questions to parents and teachers, such as:

> How do they make soap?
> How are tears made?
> Why do leaves fall off a Christmas tree so quickly?
> How do pips get into apples?

From this she moved to questions that implied meaning behind the expected answer, such as:

> How do babies come out of their mummies' tummies?
> How was God born?
> How do you die?
> If Jesus was God, who made Mary?
> Will Gran have one candle on her cake on her first birthday in heaven?

Other questions conveyed anxiety:

> What means a dead mother?

Some children seemed to put their question or search into a picture or poetry. Madge found that the 'search for meaning' of the primary children in her sample corresponded best to categories defined by Rudolf Otto (1917) in *The Idea of the Holy*: a sense of the mysterious, a sense of the numinous, and personal exploration of the world and relationships. Nearly half her text consists of comments and interviews from and with children, and while she did not take the development of 'child-centred' teaching much further theoretically, she produced vivid and compelling anecdotally-based evidence in its support. No-one who read her book could lightly go back to undiluted 'Bible-centred' teaching again.

Goldman

Ronald Goldman was to systematize the new approach. His name and influence in RE continued well beyond the sixties. He worked in the Education Department of the University of Reading. To him the problem was one of children's religious thinking. His view was that faced with complex problems of understanding, children tried to make sense of them but that they had serious limitations in attempting to make intellectual interpretations of experience. Although he chose to focus on developing the intellectual understanding of children—the teacher's main task as he saw it—he recognized that 'understanding may be emotional as well as intellectual'.[28] He doubted whether some types of religious experience were communicable at all.

Goldman assumed that religious thinking is no different in mode and method from non-religious thinking, that the Bible itself is a book for adults, that theology is a mature adult activity, and that a long period of 'apprenticeship' is necessary in childhood religion in order to graduate into adult religious thinking. Agreed syllabuses were quite blind to these insights and so were frequently unsuitable. He cited Loukes as evidence of school-leavers finding their RK to have been childish and irrelevant. Goldman turned to psychology to provide a frame of reference for what might be suitable. Psychology could not, he believed, throw light on religious truth claims, but it could provide research evidence about the conditions in which people become religious. This sort of evidence would be particularly applicable in the field of religious education.

The raw material of thinking is sensation which is selected, then perceptualized. A percept is a personal and immediate interpretation of a sensation or sensations. From that we move to categories or concepts about groups of objects. It is the only way to make sense of the world and reduce an otherwise bewildering complexity of experience. Thinking is then a process of sensation, perceptualizing and concept-formation. It also relates to ability. Concepts tend to change with age, becoming more numerous, more complex and more logical. He cited various psychologists from the 1930s onwards that suggest that there are stages in the conceptualization process of growing children. There are no definitive, separate, religious sensations and perceptions, but rather 'religious experience' consists of generalizing from various experiences, previous perceptions and existing concepts to 'an interpretative concept of the nature and activity of the divine'.[29] The opening lines of Psalm 23 are cited as an example. The concept of a caring God is based on an analogy derived from a shepherd and sheep. For a child to grasp it they must first have a concept of sheep and sheep farming in Palestine. Religious thinking is dependent on understanding the original experience on which the analogy is based.

Goldman used Piagetian definitions of levels of thinking: sensori-motor intelligence, co-ordinating basic perceptive and motor functions, elementary language development (the first two years of life); intuitive or preoperational thinking, internalization of actions into thought, but with little systematic thinking (from two to seven); concrete operations, inductive and deductive logic in concrete situations, classifying data, showing systematic thinking (seven to eleven); and formal operations, the capacity to think deductively and hypothetically. A child reaching one stage would not necessarily perform at that stage in all situations and regression is perfectly possible. Goldman proceeded to see how this Piagetian analysis could be applied to religious thinking in such a way as to help religious educators in the classroom. He was not the first to do this. Piaget's main books relevant to this area were written in 1929, 1930 and 1932. Griffiths (1935), Harms (1944), Mathias (1943) and others had studied the implications for religious thinking. But Goldman was writing in the sixties, when more people were ready to listen to why RK was failing and when the need for fuller work was apparent.

> The major problem posed by research is that about the time when more abstract thinking becomes possible, and so more religious insights can be seen, many adolescents appear to lose interest in religion or develop more negative attitudes . . . This appears to be less of a problem with brighter and girl pupils.[30]

He selected the age range six to seventeen and the clinical interview as research instrument, in the belief that questionnaires yielded limited results. Five 'simple' pictures, pen and ink drawings, and eight Bible stories were discussed with sixty young people individually and in small groups. Trials with another twenty-seven followed and again with a further twenty. There were variants of the pictures designed to be appropriate to the four age groups selected: six, nine, thirteen and sixteen years. The pictures were: a child entering church with a man and woman; a child sitting in church looking at an altar; a child looking at a picture of Christ; a child kneeling in prayer at a bedside and a child looking at a mutilated Bible. After trialling, these were reduced to the first one and the last two. The drawings attempted to make the features of the characters expressionless. The Bible stories were to be told in an abbreviated and simplified way and they were: Moses and the burning bush; crossing the Red Sea; the call of the child Samuel; Ahab and Naboth's vineyard; Jesus as a boy in the Temple; the healing of blind Bartimaeus; the temptations of Jesus, and the resurrection appearance on the road to Emmaus. They were selected on the grounds that they appeared widely in agreed syllabuses. Children were 'encouraged to voice difficulties about the stories and to explore points of interest'.[31] After trialling, these were reduced to the 'Burning Bush', 'the Red Sea' and 'the temptations'. The final test sample of two hundred excluded 'Roman Catholics, Jews, negroes [sic] or [pupils] of foreign extraction'[32] as a source of possible bias. Subsequent debate was to criticize this sample as limited. They were listed by age and gender, IQ, religious denomination and school/class distribution. Goldman then analysed the results under Paigetian categories and under concepts of the Bible, prayer and the church, the identity and nature of the divine, the holiness of God, God's concern for men, and Jesus and the problem of evil. He tried to distil the influence of church and home on religious thinking. Finally he addressed the implications for religious education.

He concluded that 'Moses and the burning bush' should not be taught before secondary school, that 'the Red Sea' was reduced to an incredible action adventure story in primary schools and should also be dealt with in secondary school with pupils aged thirteen or over, and that 'the temptations' should be postponed to post-fourteen owing to 'the limits of concretist thinking'.[33] In general he felt that the Bible was being taught too much, too soon and too often, that it was actually damaging and that a more child-centred approach was necessary. 'The child as a growing person . . . should be the centre of our concern.'[34] A sequel published a year later as *Readiness for Religion* outlined his plan for the content and methods of developmental religious education. At each stage of childhood an exposition of the basic religious characteristics of the child was followed by an analysis of its basic human needs, proposed content of teaching and recommended methods. Goldman wanted to move religious education on from the rejection it was experiencing by pupils and from their gross misunderstandings. He more than anyone exposed the failure of 'Bible-centred' teaching. But it was to be some time before the effectiveness of his own solution came under the same scrutiny to which he had subjected Bible teaching. During that time an almost reverse climate had arisen in many primary schools: that the Bible should not be taught because it was unsuitable for young children. It is possible that this was just as damaging an assumption as the earlier Bible-centred view of teaching. Meanwhile, Goldman exercised a direct influence on a new generation of agreed syllabuses.

The West Riding Syllabus

In 1966 the new outlook on RE was enshrined in a new agreed syllabus for the West Riding of Yorkshire, replacing and not revising a 1947 predecessor. One of the prime movers in its creation was Alan Loosemore, then Adviser in RE to the LEA, later to become Senior HMI for RE nationally. Chairman of the Agreed Syllabus Conference was Clifford Jones of the Leeds University Institute of Education who had himself written about children's attitudes to RE. The preface to the syllabus indicated its landmark status:

> The syllabus differs in many ways from all which have gone before it, but the main difference perhaps is that it emphasizes much more the

kind of things that children can be expected to understand and enjoy at each stage of their development rather than the things that their elders and supposed betters think they ought to know.[35]

This was over-optimistic, as their 'elders and supposed betters' had constructed the syllabus, but there had been more attention paid to the child than hitherto and the preface went on to acknowledge advice given by Goldman himself. Like the historic Cambridgeshire Syllabus, it began with an enunciation of principles: that the material in the syllabus must satisfy the religious needs of children and young people at all stages of their development, that the material in it must be related to life and experience and that the syllabus must provide opportunities for shared experiences to be enjoyed. The basic needs of growing children are defined as a need for security, a need for significance, a need for standards and a need for community.[36] It interprets this psychologically-based statement of needs theologically:

> From the Christian point of view these personal needs are religious needs, which are only satisfied by the growing discovery that at the heart of the universe there is a God who cares, a Spirit who seeks to enter into personal relationship with us. Ultimately it is this which gives us security and significance . . . He [Jesus] created a community where people could explore and go on exploring what is meant by this relationship.[37]

The syllabus content was an attempt to blend material from the everyday experience of the child, material from the Bible and material from other sources. The method was a thematic approach. So, for example, middle childhood (seven to eleven years) had as its stated principle the conviction that religion is not something separate from life, but is the essence of all life's experiences. Topics included Sheep and Shepherds, Wells and Water, Life in Bible times, Courage, Corn and Bread. When the Bible was presented it was presented as a collection of different types of literature: saga, myth, allegory, parable, history, poetry, letters etc. and not as monolithic literal truth. Detailed lists of book resources for teachers and pupils followed each section of the syllabus, including a thematic topic classroom series edited by Goldman. These topics and booklets came to dominate RE in some primary schools for the next twenty years. Also recommended was the latest paraphrase of the New Testament, *New World* (1966), by Alan Dale. This was 'child-centred' in its approach, deliberately produced with a reading age of nine to facilitate child access, and with pictures intended to lead the reader on to emulate them by painting, drawing, acting or other creative follow-up. Dale's own defence of Bible teaching (1972) came later (p. 105) but his most significant classroom influence was in the 1960s.

At the secondary school level the syllabus was dealing with personal relationships, home and family, leisure, friendship, material possessions, work, ambition and vocation, marriage and sex, class distinction and race prejudice, mass media, world hunger, politics, 'the colour problem',[38] refugees and world religions, albeit briefly. Most of the recommended books were written in the 1960s. There were sections for teachers with Jewish children in their class and on 'immigrant children and their religion', intended to promote tolerance and respect for their customs. A section on dealing with death with children was included, even though it was at that time a taboo area in education.

After this syllabus further content-based Bible-centred syllabuses still appeared in other LEAs, but in terms of the development of RE there was no going back. Child-related RE, which is perhaps a more accurate description of it than child-centred, was firmly established. Despite the major changes in the West Riding Syllabus which reflected the whole tradition of Loukes, Madge and Acland and especially Goldman, trendsetting was a more appropriate word for this syllabus than trendy. It caught the new mood among religious educators and it sensed the changing times. A *Times Educational Supplement* commentator summed it up:[38]

> Too often in the past we have tried to hand out theological answers before children had had time to formulate the questions. In discussion based on life and experience the fundamental questions underlying the human condition become real. It then appears that religion in general, and Christianity in particular, are not so irrelevant as is often thought, and that committal to a way of life is obligatory for human existence.

The Mid-Sixties Onwards

When the West Riding Syllabus appeared, the 1946 settlement and its assumptions were twenty years distant and the position of children in schools and society was quite different. If an Anglican report on the church and young people could say in 1955 that the residual Christian influence on the nation was 'not apparent',[40] it was even less so a decade later. In education the tripartite system itself was poised for steep decline with the growing numbers of comprehensive schools, sometime quite revolutionary, such as at Countesthorpe in Leicestershire. Staff–pupil moots appeared, to promote democracy and egalitarianism in a few schools. Authoritarianism and old ways of running schools seemed in decline. Religious instruction in the sense of Bible-centred instruction of the Christian religion was also declining, in favour of approaches that were beginning to take the personhood and learning processes of children seriously. In some classrooms these approaches preceded agreed syllabus change. Class text-books for primary school children that integrated study of Jesus as God's visible power at work with study of invisible rays of light, electricity and wind power seemed attractive by contrast with what had gone before. Mathews, in a book about RE for parents (1971) enthusiastically compared what was going on in RE with the shift away from phonetic teaching of reading, the abandonment of copy-drawing bowls of fruit in art lessons and the new emphasis being placed on discovery in the teaching of mathematics. The stimulus for these approaches in RE may have come largely from new educational and psychologically-based views of children rather than within RI or RK itself—Goldman translated these approaches into RK—but such views had a theological base, even if it was not clearly perceived at the time. Its roots lay in the parables of the Old and New Testaments in which the hearers are challenged to a personal response rather than instructed didactically what to believe and think. It was ironic that the parables themselves had been taught for many years in so unparabolic a fashion and that within the 'new RE', which drastically reduced the quantity of Bible teaching, they were rarely taught at all. For Cox (1966) the heart of the new development was the emphasis on readiness,[41] the recognition that there is an appropriate moment in a child's development to proceed to the next stage of learning. He found similarities in mathematical development in teaching number concept. Hyde (1969) argued for an integrated studies approach to teaching 'slow learners' on the grounds that it helped their difficulties but it also reflected a view that religion is co-extensive with life.

Mathews (1966) urged that another consequence of the changed situation was that the teaching of religion would now have to come to terms with the unquestioned sincerity of the humanist movement. This could be done by using common ground between religious believers and humanists such as the infant's sense of wonder, the junior's interest in the lives of inspiring people, and for seniors an induction into Christian–humanist dialogue. Mathews saw this as helping children in their final years at school make a responsible choice about their moral values and beliefs. His comments reveal a further shift in religious teaching, the awareness that the range of choices open to children is wide and that one corollary of a child-centred education is acceptance that children will exercise their right to choose and that a non-religious interpretation of life is a valid choice. The aim of religious teaching is no longer to promote religion, which in the UK is taken to mean Christianity. It implies a re-definition of the role of the RE teacher, and this was reflected in the Christian Education Movement's Christmas course title for 1967: The Secularization of Society and the Role of the Christian Teacher. Smith commented (1969) that traditional RE was answering questions adolescents had stopped asking.[42] Smart (1968) wrote about 'the present schizophrenia' in RE, reflected through the twin facts that Christian education was enshrined in the 1944 settlement, yet contemporary institutions of higher education were secular and neutralist in regard to religious or ideological commitment. He saw it again in that most parents supported some form of religious and moral instruction but those running schools were not so committed to the enterprise. Religious Education should be an open activity, which transcends the informative by being a sensitive induction into Religious Studies, with the aim of creating certain capacities to understand and think about religion. It does not exclude a committed approach, provided that (for pupils) it is open and does not restrict understanding and choice. It should help people understand cultures other than their own, thus breaking the limits of European cultural tribalism. While emphasizing the descriptive, historical side of religion it should enter into dialogue with the parahistorical claims of religions and anti-religious outlooks. Smart's analysis was to influence RE for the decade ahead and his ideas were developed further in The Phenomenon of Religion (1973). The study of religion is strategic to some of the human sciences. It has a broad base and does not make the truth assumptions made by theology. Its proper method is phenomenology, which can be traced back to Husserl and van der Leeuw. Religion, studied phenomenologcally, remains a present force in human affairs. Theology, according to Smart, is usually Christian Theology in disguise. In universities its spectrum of studies often ends in the fifth century, unless a Reformation course is offered. Theology expresses a world view and commitment. Religious study cannot affirm that people are sinful or that the Creator is good. It can show that understanding religion, including ideology, is a necessary and illuminating part of the human effort to account for the world in which we live.

The Sixties Classroom Scene

In some primary schools Goldman-related teaching books took over and held sway for another decade. In some schools no major change occurred. Good secondary departments with specialist teachers still tended to write their own syllabuses whatever the agreed syllabus said, as they had done before 1944. Some secondary schools had thriving examination option courses. Some did not even offer examination RE and when challenged, head-teachers pointed out the difficulty of recruiting and keeping good specialists. Hibberd (1970) visited infant, junior, secondary modern, comprehensive, grammar and independent schools between April 1968 and April 1969 to watch classroom lessons and school worship and talk to teachers and pupils. Her evidence is anecdotal and it is difficult to generalize from it. But she found a spectrum of RE in each age range.

In a Victorian infants school she saw a Goldman-type lesson on listening, integrated with music, and a pre-Goldman lesson on Joseph and his brothers, linked to rote learning and dramatic acting of the story by children. In a new nursery school she saw a lesson on family interdependence, which was said to be RE, and a reception-class lesson about the man lowered through the roof (Mark 2.1–12), which was then used as the basis for writing practice. Another school was using a story about hungry children in Hong Kong as part of the theme 'All God's Children'. 'What keeps us warm' was a prelude in another class to Goldmanic work on sheep and shepherds. A junior school based its themes on events during the week and linked RE in merely as 'caring'. Like the sheep, much of what she saw looked woolly and it is hard to think of it as intrinsically better RE than what had gone before. A church junior school had a weekly lesson on the Prayer Book by the vicar. Another had a dramatized version of the Good Samaritan. Another class were studying creation, with children encouraged to question and comment. Another had done pictures of heaven, based on a study of Michaelangelo and the Sistine Chapel.

Her secondary modern experiences included a lesson about Gladys Aylward, to which the children were resistant. Jonah and Ruth were more popular and in use as race relations material. General Booth, the crucifixion newspaper follow-up were also bases for lessons. Care was being taken in schools containing immigrant children to find parallels to Christian material in other sacred writings and to present Jesus as a prophet to be studied rather than the Son of God to be worshipped. Some schools were studying marriage, mass media and world hunger. One grammar school had direct Bible teaching until the end of the fourth year, then discussion. At times the level of pupil contribution was shallow and careless. Sometimes too many abstract questions were asked. Art, cartoon and poetry were encouraged as pupil responses. In one lesson a discussion between a visiting vicar and a pupil persistently asking awkward questions, with the support of his peers, broke down. Hibberd saw a sixth-form lesson on the Qur'an which provoked interested discussion, and in a different school part of a sixth-form course on Buddhism. At another school fifth formers were voluntarily visiting a Quaker meeting on the next Sunday; visits to other acts of worship had been made. In one independent school she saw a lesson on the Flood using an Old Testament wall map, in another lesson on St Paul. She saw sixth-form debates about the Maharishi and the Beatles. In a 'free expression', no punishment, 'progressive' school she found no evidence of RE teaching at all. Alves wrote about 'Recent Experiments in Religious Education'.[43] Gramophone records of dramatizations of of the New English Bible were being used. Alan Dale translations were being tested in secondary modern schools. Interactive learning via a book which offered readers different routes was being tried. One teacher had implemented the Loukes approach in a thorough- going way. Chairs were grouped in fives. Desks had been dispensed with. Walls and side tables were covered with displays, some produced by pupils themselves. On one wall was a large cardboard letter-box for questions pupils wanted to raise. In another corner were armchairs and a TV. The TV was devoid of tube and innards and was used to display roller pictures made by pupils. The whole corner was used to role-play scenes of home and family life. All the RE was discussion based, using work-cards derived from newspaper and magazine cuttings, or comics, with 'carefully graded' questions requiring oral or written response. A minority of these started from a biblical text or story. A large map of the local area was mounted on the wall and pins had been used to indicate places where the children had undertaken 'social work'.

May and Johnston (1968) attempted to assess classroom practice. In a chapter entitled 'The Lion's Den' they noted the difficulty for the RK teacher of constantly changing classes, the continual effort to remember pupil names, and for pupils to remember back to the previous week's lesson. They noted that repeating lessons up to four times over could be a burden and that the enthusiastic teacher who 'will tend to want to spend every lesson on his feet' will end the day in a state of physical and mental exhaustion.[44] They contrasted, perhaps unrealistically, the way in which children bow to the superior knowledge of the maths or history teacher but are quick to accuse the teacher of religion of dogmatism. They cited a secondary modern teacher following Loukes' methodology, who discussed the Great Train Robbery with his class, and decided that the train robbers were physically fit (PE), knew the best place for the attack (Geography), and the railway timetable (Maths) but somehow used their fitness and knowledge to harm others. The teacher used this as a device to introduce the Ten Commandments and RE into the discussion. Promotion of Millwall to a higher football division gave another teacher an opportunity to deal with prayer. A special needs child's linking of a hole in his sock and the word holy was used by a teacher with the child's explanation that just as the threads in the sock spring apart if a cut is made, so God and humans spring apart when a sin is committed. A nineteen-year-old school-leaver recorded that O and A Level RK had rid her, through discussion lessons, of a deep fear of death and funerals. Gordon (1965) wrote a general guide about education for parents, *What Happens in School*, seeking to present schooling favourably. RE teachers, she explains, are increasingly concerned in an age of material development to provide experiences for pupils of the good and the beautiful. Parents will recognize that knowledge of 'the ethics of Christian practice' are the child's right 'by virtue of tradition and historical truth'. This is linked to the act of worship and to RI lessons. Scripture [sic] will be supplemented by TV and radio, by outside speakers such as missionaries and social workers and visits from those who have travelled to the Holy Land. Older pupils will be introduced to the work of religious societies of a non-sectarian nature such as the Student Christian Movement and RI will be related to work in other subjects such as art via a study of religious art. In the secondary modern school Gordon did not expect to see RI as an external examination option but as part of the non-examination studies that she expected to occupy two-thirds of a week's timetable embracing PE and crafts as well. Hers is a bland presentation, which seeks to reassure.

Hibberd confirms that syllabus change and philosophical shift about the nature of RE and approaches to effective teaching were having a real effect at the chalkface. Her picture of RE makes it look varied and uneven in provision, in syllabus, in teaching method, in teacher commitment and in pupil response. May and Johnston's teachers, like experiments observed by Alves and the Plowden RE recommendations, are teaching in a much more child-aware manner than a subject-centred approach, so they confirm major classroom change. If the sixties in Britain were years of breaking the mould, dismantling received tradition and seeking new answers, then all this could be said to be reflected in RE.

Perhaps the mould was not broken but recast. A popular series for young pupils at secondary classroom level appeared from 1969 onwards with related volumes in geography, history, religion and science with the hope that pupils would follow the course in all these subjects. The first book on religion grew from the writer's experience teaching in a twelve form entry comprehensive school. There were lots of coloured pictures and many varied activities for pupils, including language and library work, art and craft, puzzles, discussion, deductive work and some Bible references to look up. It attempted to trace the development of religion *From Fear to Faith* as the title implied. Its basic supposition, that religion has evolved from primitive fears to developed faith, was highly dubious, but its determination to address religion rather than merely Christianity, to write for the comprehensive school, to relate RE to other classroom subjects, to break text up into less threatening sections than pages of continuous writing and to deal with themes that cut across religions—these were signs of practices that would remain important to religious educators. It was not all new in content and approach. Jesus still crowns the text as the high point of religious evolution, although pupils are required to 'think about' this,[45] not simply believe it.

Teachers' Groups

In 1965 the Christian Education Movement (CEM) succeeded the Institute of Christian Education and the Student Christian Movement in Schools. CEM in Wales was a separate organization. CEM was interdenominational and reflected a liberal Christian concern for education as a whole, not merely RE. It is a charity, with a tradition of voluntarism in some ways like a university settlement; some of its fieldworkers were young teachers who moved on after a few years to other positions in education. CEM cultivated dialogue and good relations with other faiths and it was later to prove liberal enough to be prepared to publish in its schools' packs multifaith materials. In the sixties it was funded partly through block grants from LEAs. Payment was per thousand pupils in the LEA. In return the LEAs received classroom support for their teachers and course provision by CEM's network of regional advisers. These were the precursors of LEA RE Advisers and as LEAs appointed more of these in the seventies, the CEM regional advisers declined in number. Some, such as Robin Shepherd and Ian Birnie, moved to LEA advisory work, becoming nationally known. CEM residential conferences offered support to lone specialist teachers in many schools at a time when LEA provision was patchy. They functioned as social and pastoral events as well as in-service training in the subject.

CEM was reorganized at a time when the Christian presence in education needed to be rethought, but when it was still assumed by the churches that they had a role in education—the British Council of Churches still had an Education Secretary. Members wanted to distinguish themselves from Christian education in the churches—Executive Committee Minutes show concern that the National Sunday School Union was proposing to change its name to National Association for Christian Education and asked the CEM General Secretary to make representations about the matter.[46] CEM was more than an organization, almost 'an ethos'.[47] It developed a tradition of initiatives in sponsoring groups which would be encouraged to become autonomous. Christians Abroad and the Churches' Commission on Overseas Students were examples of this.

It was not merely the specifically Christian groups in education that reformed themselves. In 1969 a conference for those interested in the development of world religions in education was held at Shap in the Lake District. Participants came from different religious backgrounds and represented the full range of educational provision from reception class to university. This conference led to a stream of publications, courses, further conferences, study tours, advice to examination boards and the Schools Council, regular Shap mailing to members and articles in *Learning for Living*, and the Shap Working Party on World Religions in Education Limited. Donald Butler, a Newcastle-on-Tyne head-teacher, wrote 'A Shapstyled Syllabus of Religious Studies'[48] arguing that RE should provide opportunities for pupils to understand what it is like to be religious, or committed to a particular way of life, and they should hopefully leave school 'with an open mind' on religious matters and perhaps the beginning of a personalized commitment of their own. While accepting Christianity as the 'home culture', Butler wanted it to be taught objectively 'with no preconceived notions about its truth or otherwise.' Even in the West Riding, by the end of the decade, it could be claimed that world religions were being widely taught, strongly supported by teachers, and that such interest was likely to expand (Hinnells in Macy, 1969).

The decade had seen massive change. But some things were constant. In 1968, rather reluctant parents at St Paul's Junior School, London, were treated to an afternoon premiere of a twenty-five minute musical. It was called *Joseph*. It was revised and expanded, finding national and international fame within a few years as *Joseph and the Amazing Technicolor® Dreamcoat*. Despite its depiction of the Pharaoh as an Elvis Presley figure, the inclusion of a Chevalier sound-alike nostalgic song and other strongly sixties themes (notably that 'Any dream will do') the storyline was one of the oldest favourites of primary school RE.

Chapter Four

Controversies in RE: The 1970s

[The teacher] should not be asked to pretend that he is above all
commitments, that he has a stance above all stances from which he
can 'critically' assess them all. What will ultimately be communicated
to the pupils is the commitment of the teacher, and therefore this must
be open and explicit.

Lesslie Newbigin (1977)

Society

Decimalization of British currency took place in 1971, temporarily
masking the alarming inflation. Entry to the EEC opened opportunities,
in theory, for British business in Europe. But the final terms were so
poor and the benefits so less than obvious that despite a referendum
held in 1975 endorsing British membership by 67 to 33 per cent, British
politicians and people retained a damaging ambivalence to Europe.
British industrial relations remained bleak throughout the seventies.
In one decade the British economy had fallen to half the strength of
West Germany's from a position as equal in the mid-1960s. Sterling
depreciated by over forty per cent against the major world currencies.
The Ford workers went on strike, an occupational rhythm, and were
eventually awarded a 17 per cent pay rise. Then came firemen (22%),
bakers (14%), heating engineers (30%) and long-distance lorry drivers
(20%). More workers were on strike than at any time since the General
Strike of 1926. Suntanned Prime Minister Jim Callaghan returning from
a foreign holiday to strike-ravaged Britain was misreported as saying
'Crisis—what crisis?', but the public relations image was still wrong.
January 1979 saw selective local strikes by health service workers,
refuse collectors and cemetery staff. They achieved rises of more than
9 per cent. This was the 'winter of discontent'. Even in schools a
self-styled pupils' union was urging its members to resist school

uniform, punishments and general oppression by teachers. There was talk of Britain becoming ungovernable.

Unemployment continued to rise relentlessly. By 1980 it would reach two million and only one year later three million. There were closures, bankruptcies and take-overs; fishing, steel, coal and ship-building entered steep decline. So did rural life: some rural railway stations, village schools, shops, public houses and sub-post-offices disappeared and along with them a sense of community. The all-devouring motor-way, causing many thousands of trees to be felled and the landscape re-written, was another sign of deep and permanent social change. The motorway and the out-of-town superstore were convenient for car owners. The car-less were becoming disadvantaged.

The spectre of racism remained. In 1971 the Police Federation Conference spoke of the police in some communities as being on top of a pressure cooker. In 1979 a National Front meeting at Southall Town Hall, the heart of a predominantly Asian area, was targetted by 3,000 anti-Front demonstrators and policed by 4,000 officers. A young teacher, Blair Peach, was killed, some said by a member of the police. There were other race troubles, e.g. in St Paul's, Bristol, and Notting Hill. The 'troubles' in Northern Ireland continued. The first soldier was killed in Ulster in 1970. Bloody Sunday followed in 1972. Terrorism struck mainland England in 1974, with IRA attacks on the Tower of London, army barracks at Guildford and Woolwich and the horrific Birmingham pub bombing (twenty-one dead, 162 injured) after which the authorities promptly arrested and imprisoned what took sixteen years to demonstrate were the wrong men. In 1979 the IRA assassinated leading Conservative MP Airey Neave. Violence appeared in industry in the 1973–4 miners' strike at Saltley, Birmingham.

If the sixties had appeared to erode respect for authority, including that of the schoolteacher, the seventies saw a series of police corruption trials which damaged public perceptions of the police. In the five years that Sir Robert Mark was Commissioner of the Metropolitan Police, 478 members left the force following, or in anticipation of, disciplinary procedures. It was an annual departure rate about six times higher than usual. It was part of an unsettling process in which the public came to believe that those in high places were not what they seemed, which continued until the mid-nineties with royal affairs and divorces.

Skinhead and Punk were contrasting youth fashions. By the end of the decade average TV viewing hours per person per week were sixteen in summer and twenty in winter. Since the adverts clearly influenced viewers to buy products, the programmes could be assumed to have some influence too. Sociologists and psychologists could not agree how much this was and whether, for instance, violent programmes promoted violent behaviour. But royal occasions, major sporting events and specially popular films topped the viewing charts. Christmas for years in the seventies was dominated by the television show of comedians Eric Morecambe and Ernie Wise and many families planned their Christmas Day to allow for viewing it.

Divorce continued to rise after—some said because of—the Divorce Law Reform Act of 1971. There had been 23,000 in 1963 and by 1980 the number had risen to 150,000. In the 1970s as a whole over one million couples were divorced. Many had children. The trauma in the lives of some of those children began to be reflected in their behaviour in school and the job of the teacher became gradually more difficult. There were more problems and fewer sanctions. By the mid-decade there were 750,000 one-parent families. Abortions by 1980 were running at almost the rate of divorce, 140,000 in one year, and more than one million lives or potential lives had been destroyed or terminated, according to one's view of it. To stem the tide of social collapse came the Nationwide Festival of Light (1971) supported by Mary Whitehouse, Malcolm Muggeridge and Lord Longford. Periodicals could still be charged with blasphemy, as happened to *Gay News* in 1977.

A decade of radically different political and social life was heralded with the arrival in Number 10 (1979) of a 'conviction politician', Margaret Thatcher. She later wrote:

> I quoted a famous prayer attributed to St Francis of Assissi, beginning with the words 'where there is discord, may we bring harmony.' Afterwards a good deal of sarcasm was expended on this choice, but the rest of the quotation is often forgotten. St Francis prayed for more than peace; the prayer goes on: 'Where there is error, may we bring truth. Where there is doubt, may we bring faith. And where there is despair, may we bring hope.' The forces of error, doubt and despair were so firmly entrenched in British society, as the 'winter of discontent' had just powerfully illustrated, that overcoming them would not be possible without some measure of discord.[1]

Education

In communities with high unemployment, demotivation among pupils could lead to truancy or classroom disruption by those who saw formal education as irrelevant to their world of no jobs. School uniform blazers increasingly gave way to sweatshirts, or no uniform, as the cost of formal clothing became unaffordable for some families. Free school milk was abolished by the education minister, Margaret Thatcher, in

1970. She considered her principal contribution as minister in education (1970–74) to have been arguing for the right structures and resources for education, replacing out-dated primary schools, expanding nursery provision, raising the school leaving age and beginning to come to grips with 'our suddenly limited resources' in the economic crises. She later regretted not addressing the content of education during this period. The Wilson government policy had been to remove bias towards the City and the professions and to try to encourage a new generation of engineers, technicians and managers, but in Wilson's term from 1974 schooling was not a priority. James Callaghan presided over the last years of so-called Butskellism and consensus politics, but was weakened by the decline of the Labour right wing and an inability to deal with rising industrial action. When he took over as Prime Minister in 1976 he already had a strong and genuine interest in education. But Labour lacked an education policy and as a consequence Callaghan unveiled the so-called Great Debate on it, drawing the media into the process. Tory right-wing thinkers were able to gain ground in this, partly through the lack of Labour policy but also because the Education Secretary herself, Shirley Williams, appeared irresolute. She did, however, ask all LEAs what their local arrangements for determining and overseeing their school curricula were. This was to be the start of a search for the source of the curriculum river. The answer seemed to be that there wasn't one. Thus seeds were being sown for co- ordination or reform, moving towards a common curriculum. The roots of this stretched back to the Council for Curriculum Reform (1945). The notion of entitlement curriculum appeared in the HMI document Curriculum 11 to 16 (1977). These did not anticipate the centralized national curriculum that was to come. Other HMI reports showed variance not merely in quality but in content between curricula in schools within the same LEA as well as LEA differences.

Meanwhile, responsibility for Welsh primary and secondary education was transferred from Whitehall to the Secretary of State for Wales, to be administered by the Welsh Office Education Department. A separate schools' inspectorate was established. But the educational quangos that were to arise in England over the next decades were simply replicated in Wales. In the eighties the National Curriculum Council (England) would be matched by the Curriculum Council for Wales. Its successor, the School Curriculum and Assessment Authority would be matched by the Curriculum and Assessment Authority for Wales. But there was no permissible variance in policy. Gareth Elwyn Jones (1982) describes educational policy in Wales as a strange mixture of centralization and decentralization simultaneously.

In the decades that followed, the dominant Labour education themes were to become sixteen to nineteen education and training, and the abolition of 'A' Levels, the latter a ready target for Tory claims that Labour would lower standards, just as comprehensive schools were portrayed as a levelling down process. The right-wing *Black Paper* themes included an attack on the dangers of socialist education; the use of schools for social engineering by means of peace studies, anti-racism and ideologically-based mixed ability teaching; 'progressive' teaching methods that allowed children to decide whether or not to bother to learn to read; and the lack of discipline among young people and the general collapse of 'standards'. Against this they wanted to strengthen the 'voice of parents' and to redress the balance in an education system dominated, as they saw it, by producers rather than consumers. The concern against social engineering did not prevent the 1988 Local Government Act inserting a clause to prevent LEAs from promoting 'teaching in any maintained school of the acceptance of homosexuality as a pretended family relationship'. Some social engineering was apparently acceptable.

> The right wing feared that schooling had ceased to be a means of promoting order and obedience, and had taken on the role of encouraging the young to be critical of authority and disrespectful. And pupils could not spell.[2]

In the eighties an increasingly right-wing government was to be pitted against a minority of increasingly left-wing LEAs. The seventies saw the first rounds in this campaign, but they were not years dominated by educational debate.

Religion

Anglican baptisms fell from just under half of live births nationally to forty per cent. Marwick argues[3] that England was permeated by a secular Anglican tradition which permitted a peaceful accommodation to consumerism, youth culture and feminism, and that the process led eventually to a form of self- congratulatory conservatism. The 1970s saw the arrival or rapid growth of new forms of spiritual experience for those in search of something: Transcendental Meditation, the Divine Light Mission, the Children of God, Krishna Consciousness, Scientology etc. All were concerned in some way with improving the 'self'. Perhaps they created a sub-conscious feeling of relativism among many people, i.e. that since all religions couldn't be right, there must be a reasonable chance that they might all be wrong.

The continuing decline of the Free Churches, both the greatest and the most predictable church decline, now became the most noticeable. Redundant chapel buildings either became carpet warehouses, Sikh or Hindu temples and mosques, or else curio residential conversions. Methodist closures were running at more than a hundred per annum and Methodist membership declined by more than twenty per cent across the decade as a whole. Even within itself Methodism was divided and historic Victorian controversy about the role of Conference and of people like Jabez Bunting and the Fly Sheets controversy arose again in dispute over whether the vote by Conference—Methodism's governing body—to take the church into union with the Anglicans was consultative or representative. The Voice of Methodism Association thought Conference handling of the matter was not representative of the Methodist people. The successful organic union in 1972 of Presbyterians in England and Wales with many Congregational churches to form the United Reformed Church did not halt their loss of members, 60,000 in ten years, nor did it enlist all the churches of the former two denominations. The new church took what to those ignorant of the Reformed tradition was an incomprehensible name, continually misspelled ever since as United Reform. But Free Church Christians were now a clear minority among Christians in all but a few pockets like Cornwall, which had a Methodist and Bible Christian legacy.

Even the Church of England was closing buildings, roughly one every nine days, many in the depopulated inner cities. It was also closing theological colleges as the number of ordinands dropped. Perhaps symbolically a late Victorian cathedral in architecture was completed and opened by the Anglicans in Liverpool in 1978. Not all local churches were in decay. When David Watson moved to the almost redundant York church of St Michael-le-Belfry (Guy Fawkes had been baptized there) he turned it into a thriving evangelical congregation, using house groups and lay ministries and organization that resembled early Methodism, drawing in people from other churches as well as those who had not attended a church before. Such churches were exceptional and often characterized by Pentecostal or charismatic renewal features. Such renewal generated an ecumenism of its own and the denominational label began to matter less than at any time before. There were other Anglican changes. General Synod was opened by the Queen in 1970 and became a growing and more open, if to some frustratingly bureaucratic, collective approach to Anglican government in England. It had a membership of 560 divided into three houses: bishops, clergy and laity. Membership was by election, except for diocesan bishops and the two archbishops. It had a permanent staff headed by a Secretary General and its measures were subject to parliamentary approval in the Ecclesiastical Committee of fifteen MPs and fifteen peers. The Anglicans in Wales, as a disestablished and autonomous church, were organized and governed separately, in a similar three-house body of 345 members, not responsible to Parliament. English General Synod did not achieve the majority required to approve Anglican–Methodist reunion (the House of Bishops gave the scheme sufficient votes; clergy and laity, though achieving majorities, were insufficient to carry the measure), nor did it agree to the ordination of women in 1978. It rejected the re-marriage of divorced people in church in 1973 and again in 1978. The role of the state in the appointment of bishops in the Church of England was reduced in 1974 when it was agreed that the selection committee, appointed by the church, should be attended by the prime minister's appointments secretary as an adviser and that the committee should send to the Prime Minister two names for a vacant appointment in order of preference. She or he would send one of these names to the monarch. Despite the advances in secularization and the reduction of the Church of England to an internally self-governed church, a denomination among other denominations, there was still little real pressure to disestablish it. Perhaps Thomas Gray's 'Elegy Written in a Country Churchyard' was too powerful a part of the English national psyche.

The fewer buildings and larger congregations of Roman Catholics made them less susceptible to the process of building closure, but their conversions were down, from 12,000 to 4,000 in roughly a decade, along with marriages and numbers attending mass. Anglican–Roman dialogue looked promising. Joint statements on the eucharist, on ministry and ordination and on authority seemed encouraging, if rather irrelevant to society outside the fold. The climax of this real advance, however, occurred in 1982 when Archbishop Robert Runcie and Pope John Paul embraced in Canterbury Cathedral. The Anglican roots of this reconciliation went back to Bishop Charles Gore a century earlier. It was as well that in the New Testament II Peter offered the thought that with God a thousand years are as a day.[4]

Immigrants and their UK-born descendants continued to be seen by some as a problem rather than an enriching dimension in a changing society which historically was ethnically diverse. In the TV series *The Comedians*, jokes about Pakistanis were top of the list, followed by jokes about the Irish. A new Race Relations Act was passed and the Commission for Racial Equality was set up (both 1976) to work towards a society free of racial discrimination. Ethnically diverse groups continued to arrive, in restricted numbers. These included Vietnamese 'boat people' in 1979. Fears that immigrants were 'taking our jobs' did not match the facts that they were creating employment as their own commercial enterprises began to prosper. The response of indigenous Christian groups to new or growing religious neighbours varied from offering settlement help, entering into dialogue and joint enterprise, seeing 'other religions' as mission targets or ignoring them altogether.

Religious Education

The 1970s in RE opened with two convergent strands of concern: concern about indoctrination—whether RE was an activity of integrity or whether it was indoctrinatory and therefore morally questionable in its current form. The other concern was to emphasize and develop RE within the context of education rather than religion, in the sense of religious nurture. As well as critics of the subject, it was also shared by some who still took the view that RE should be essentially Christian education. Hubery (1972) argued that it was a function of education to transmit culture from one generation to another while allowing individuals to reach self-fulfilment; Christian education was about a search for truth and about discovery, not evangelism. Hilliard (1966) had argued that the task of RE was to bring Christianity to the attention of young people. They should then be left to decide about it. He criticized some first steps in world religions teaching, on the grounds that much remained superficial, even after considerable study, and that to understand deeply what being religious meant one had to study the religion of one's own environment. But against Hilliard in the UK of the 1970s one could legitimately ask what the religion of the English and Welsh environment actually was.

Joan Dean (1971) suggested that judged by the standards of church attendance, compulsory RE was a failure. But in a changing and uncertain world, where the study of psychology and sociology had called into question underlying motivation and values, materialism had led to a simplistic assumption that science was the only way to measure and describe truth. Changes in RE had to not only take into account these factors, but also that a large proportion of members of the teaching profession did not practise Christianity. In many primary schools the class lesson, assumed to be the base for RI in the 1944 settlement, had been largely replaced by individual or group learning. The whole of education was less authoritarian, less concerned with transmitting 'answers', than it had been in 1944. Dean argued that RE should be honest in the light of these changes. She offered a view of RE based on the mystery of life. Religion in the broadest sense is concerned with every aspect of life, but life itself is mysterious.

The Fourth R

Growing concern to develop RE within the context of education as a whole, rather than to see it as a legally protected arm of the church in school was demonstrated best in a report, *The Fourth R* (1970), commissioned by the Church of England Board of Education and the National Society 'to inquire into religious education' (Foreword). The committee was chaired by Ian Ramsey, Bishop of Durham, a distinguished philosopher of religion. The report (380pp) considered the origin and development of RE in England, theology and education, RE and moral education, county schools, independent and direct-grant schools, church schools, and RE within other Western societies. It tried to show the complex historical and political background against which RE in the UK had developed and which had shaped its character. It also sought to take into account Christian concern about education as a whole, not just RE. It argued for replacing the concept of Religious Instruction by Religious Education, but for retaining school worship as 'an essential component of "religious education"'.[5] It wanted to see RE acknowledged on educational grounds, not merely grounds of legal compulsion, admitting that the cultural climate was so different from that of 1944 as to make the 1944 settlement no longer appropriate. But it wished to retain some measure of statutory acknowledgment for RE,[6] suggesting that in any new education Act it might be stated that all pupils shall be provided, according to their ages, abilities and aptitudes 'with education in the arts and sciences, in religion and morals, and in physical and practical skills.'[7]

The fashionable words child-centred, relevant and open-ended were criticized. Alternatives were suggested: pupil-related teaching; the notion that it is the teacher who makes material relevant and not the content itself, and that open-ended need not imply 'an orgy of relativism where the teacher pretends that any opinion is as good as any other'[8] or that one operates in a cultural vacuum.[9] It should mean that RE is conducted as an exploration where no one viewpoint is considered automatically as invariably correct and pupils' sincere views are treated with the utmost seriousness. The report recommended for RE a minimum timetable allocation of two periods per week, though it did not specify period length. It also recommended that cumbersome legal procedures for agreed syllabuses should be abandoned, that the DES and the Schools Council should provide supporting publications for RE, that LEAs appoint advisers in the subject, and that there should be RE provision in all institutions catering for the 16 to 18 age range. It recommended further research into RE for children with special needs, for the 5 to 13 age group and for the needs of 'immigrant children',[10] extra courses for teachers provided by LEAs, the use of all modern available teaching aids, research into applications for RE of newest technologies—notably closed circuit TV and video-recording. Stress was laid on properly structured use of discussion as a technique.[11]

The committee had consulted widely, not always with people who could be assumed to have a sympathetic view, using a questionnaire and media appeal for response. Statements and evidence were received from church and educational groups and from hundreds of individuals. The National Secular Society[12] conceded that school-leavers should know what members of different religious groups believe, wanted arrangements for children withdrawn from the subject to be humane (not leaving them in draughty corridors) and stated that: 'We do favour complete secularization, but prohibition of religious teaching of all kinds would be wrong. We want teachers of all religions and none to be able to express their opinions, and to compare and contrast views in an atmosphere of freedom'.[13] The National Secular Society had, perhaps unwittingly, written a brief for how RE was to try to develop in the decade ahead. In similar vein the British Humanist Association affirmed the importance of understanding Christianity as part of the European tradition; the freedom of all teachers to express their beliefs or rejection of religion; and the options of Christianity, humanism and other unnamed positions as part of the search by young people for a way of life.[14] Professional religious educators were already building on this common ground and it was to become the dominant theme of RE in the seventies.

The Report rejected the view that non-Christian religions might be dismissed as heathen[15] and offered a rationale for world religions teaching.

> It would be idle to pretend that, even if time allowed, teachers and pupils brought up in a Judaeo-Christian religious environment could expect to aim at or attain a depth of insight into the attitudes, beliefs and religious experiences which lie behind the religions of the Middle and Far East comparable to that which they could hope to reach from the study of the Christian religion. Even so, acquaintance with some basic facts about other men's religions and the social and cultural contexts within which they find expression can itself broaden not only the pupils' religious but also their international understanding[16].

Once again the submerged theme of citizenship application of RE, present in the 1944 settlement, had resurfaced. *The Fourth R* even envisaged that pupils might share in a limited way in the worship of religions not their own, and accepted that pupils might legitimately decide against the claims of the Christian faith.[17] This was a radical view for an Anglican report of its time. But it did not receive the support it merited from government or the extra resources it called for at LEA level to make RE more effective and to move it towards 'Fourth R' status. Perhaps the report was seen as partisan by virtue of its church base. Or perhaps the political will was not there to strengthen or rewrite the provision of 1944 in a more secular society. Or perhaps its view of RE was simply too radical for the establishment in education to countenance.

At practitioner level there was more concern to demonstrate that RE was not indoctrinatory than to endorse an Anglican report about it. The idea that the RE teacher should be neutral was gaining ground. At staffroom level the issue raised stark questions like whether teachers should suppress their own beliefs and disbeliefs and simply not state them to children, teaching the syllabus in an 'objective' way and conducting children through the various religions under study, leaving them to draw their own conclusions. Some said that perhaps agnostics might make better RE teachers than committed Christians or members of other religious groups, since the agnostic teacher would be more detached, more neutral. If these views seem naive now, they have to be set in the context of the attempt to shed the image of Religious Instruction in a society which had seen massive change since 1944. The concern of some teachers about Christian indoctrination was matched by those of some parents and politicians about political or atheistic indoctrination via RE.

The Bath Agreed Syllabus

When the City of Bath LEA attempted to revise its 1953 agreed syllabus in 1970 it included at draft stage a reference to humanism and communism. The *Bath Chronicle* reported the draft[18] with an emphasis that it was now religious education, no longer instruction, and quoting its statement that RE should be open in its selection of material, methods of enquiry and respect for the integrity of the child. The references to humanism and communism were not mentioned. But a City Council meeting on 3 November 1970 was reported as sparking a 'row'[19] over the proposal to include an insight into communism. Councillor Dr George Kersley was reported as saying that communism was almost atheism and 'if they want to teach atheism in schools, why not just call it atheism?' He proposed deleting both communism and humanism from the syllabus. Councillor Laurence Coombs welcomed 'comparative religion' but opposed teaching communism and humanism as 'we are giving carte blanche for any teacher to inject his own views during the time dedicated to religious instruction'. But others present warmly welcomed the whole syllabus. The *Bath Chronicle* letters columns took up the Council debate on both sides in *Lessons that make me see red*.[20] Humanism, Buddhism and communism should be excluded from RE as 'it must be difficult enough to the teacher . . . when there are hundreds of Christian sects to confuse the child's mind, without adding secularism in any form'; 'all children must be informed about all religions and philosophies so that they can freely make up their own minds, rather than raise them [children] in hatred'.[21] The section objected to was published:[22]

> Because of the Christian tradition in this country and limitations imposed by time available and the extent of the field, it is appropriate to examine the Christian faith more closely than other faiths, but in a more pluralistic society there must be an attempt to understand views other than Christianity (e.g. Humanism, communism, Buddhism etc.).

Donald Whittle[23] rejected the notion that 'children of tender years will be reciting the thoughts of Chairman Mao'. He reminded readers that the 1944 settlement provided for religious rather than specifically Christian instruction and that the syllabus had been drawn up in agreement, by proper process of law, that the spectrum of parents' views within a school might include Christian, humanist, agnostic and others. Finally he contextualised the offending suggestion: it was in parenthesis, at the end of a paragraph, simply exemplars of beliefs other than Christian. A letter challenged him the next day suggesting the real issue was that humanism and communism cannot form part of a 'religious syllabus' and that if they appear as philosophies to describe how our lives should be lived neither Nazism nor communism could fill the requirement adequately.[24] But the Education Committee endorsed the syllabus without any change. At classroom level the reality was that children of the seventies were not going to be told what to believe or disbelieve and would react to attempts to do so either with open hostility or with polite indifference. The Bath debate, though less widely publicized than the later Birmingham debate, illustrated identical issues.

Working Paper 36

Into this growing debate *Schools Council Working Paper 36, Religious Education in Secondary Schools*, appeared (1971). In Lancaster a new—for the UK—approach to the study of religion in higher education had emerged with the appointment of Ninian Smart to a professorship not of Theology but of Religious Studies, from a job advertisement inviting applicants of any religious persuasion or none. If it was not a typical theological job, he did not possess a typical theological background. The travels of his early career were redolent of the itinerant experiences of Rudolph Otto. During war service in Intelligence, Smart had studied Chinese. Based at Sri Lanka he had studied Buddhism. He later taught in places as diverse as Birmingham, Wales, Yale and India. Partly through his person, Religious Studies was presenting itself with a fresher, less confessional approach than Theology, whose concerns with church history, compulsory Greek and Hebrew courses, Christian doctrine, Old and New Testament studies etc. were replaced by studies in the psychology, sociology and anthropology of religion and by major emphasis not just on comparative religion but on the study of non-Christian religions in their own right, in degree structures in which the study of Christianity might not be the major component. *Working Paper 36* stemmed from this approach: 'the world is changing faster than most theological faculties'.[25] In the early seventies it seemed as if a rival discipline to Theology had arrived, more suited to the needs of students of religion of its time and which might relegate theology to the seminary. Smart's work on the religious experience of humankind and on world religions was internationally known.

Endemic to this new approach as it affected school RE was rejection of what became labelled confessional teaching. Fear of it was to haunt RE for the next two decades. 'Confessional' was assumed to be the opposite of 'educational'. It was taken to mean teaching which was intended to produce, or which assumed as the norm, a particular view of life (usually Christian) and whose whole purpose was to increase or produce commitment on the part of the child. *Working Paper 36* called it intellectual and cultic indoctrination,[26] equating it with 'dogmatic'. It was seen as the principal cause of pupil resentment of RE. Its opposite was defined as the anti-dogmatic approach, such as that of the National Secular Society, which conceived of RE as a dispassionate, objective exercise, part of the History syllabus.

Working Paper 36 commended a middle way, the phenomenological or 'undogmatic approach'[27] which 'sees the aim of religious education as the promotion of understanding. RE uses the tools of scholarship to enter into an empathetic experience of the faith of individuals and groups. It does not seek to promote any one religious viewpoint but it recognizes that the study of religion must transcend the purely informative.'[28] The passionate commitment of religious belief is arrived at by inner recognition and personal dedication and religion cannot be understood except through such subjectivity. However the objective study of religion, which is the only appropriate educational study of it, must concern itself with the subjectivity of commitment and, using the human capacity for self-transcendence (to participate in the experience of others through the power of imagination), can actually achieve this. In the primary school this might mean being a Jew or Muslim for a day or an hour by witnessing a sacred festival or acting out an imagined ritual occasion. This capacity for self- transcending awareness was seen as the basis for all objective scholarship. It is not the main function of the scholar to express personal beliefs and feelings but chiefly to expound and interpret the beliefs of other people.

> This ... is the foundation of all scholarly objectivity and the presupposition of any intellectually responsible education. The objective study of religion is only a special case of the objective study of any subject whatsoever. There are ... features of religious inquiry that differentiate it from the study of other matters. Still, the same fundamental canons of sound scholarship apply in the field of religion as in other fields of investigation.[29]

Interpretation, for example of scripture, was accepted as inescapable, objectivity depending on the uses made of it. 'Objectivity is the willingness to admit the possibility of alternative patterns of interpretation'.[30] It requires critical teaching and academic freedom, although secularizing schools will not per se make teaching more objective. The Soviet Union is cited as an example of secular indoctrination by means of a school system. Such an approach towards interpretation may have appeared to be novel, but it was not. As distantly as 1939 W.R.Niblett in 'Concerning the Objective Teaching of RK' had argued that all teaching is interpretation and that Religious Knowledge is not simply a knowledge of 'facts'.[31]

Working Paper 36 sought to break with the past. Previous RE writings—Plowden, Newsom, Loukes, the West Riding Syllabus—were seen as confessional 'because they remain Christian documents written by Christians and aiming at Christian education'. Loukes was commended for clearing away 'a great deal of the wishful thinking that blinded teachers to what was happening in their own classrooms'[32] and for his view that good teaching is a process of dialogue about experience. Together with Acland, Loukes' approach is labelled 'implicit religion' as it starts from 'life' and the religious dimension is implicit in that. Goldman, despite his commendable analysis of religious thinking in childhood and of children's religious needs, writing that 'Christianity must be taught because it is true' yet also arguing against RE as 'a pew fodder, citizenship fodder and democracy fodder device' is presented as 'neo- confessional'.[33] 'Explicit religion' is the term for the approach of Smart, Cox and J.W.D.Smith, although Cox's admission that Hyde 'might' have been right in suggesting that only sincerely religious people should teach RE is seen as evidence of neo-confessionalism.

RE should emphasize the descriptive, historical side of religion and can play a part in dismantling 'European tribalism' by providing an understanding of history and cultures other than our own.[34] Teachers should be ready to portray sympathetically and without bias any viewpoint they are called upon to teach and there is no need to sanitize RE by keeping controversial teaching out of school. Religion should be presented in Smart's six interrelated dimensions: doctrinal, mythological, ethical, ritual, experiential and social. Religion cannot be understood simply from the outside. The report likens it to stained-glass windows in cathedrals. From the outside they are drab, grey, colourless. From the inside they are full of life and colour. The paper's suggested teaching units for RE include: creation and evolution; the poetry of religion; the mystery of suffering; the religious community; enlightenment; and personal relationships. Moral knowledge is seen as autonomous, not dependent on religious knowledge and therefore moral education is seen as outside the responsibility of the school RE department. Gower and some primary head-teachers provided practical examples (Gower et al., 1982) of the implications for infant RE: explicit religious experience includes the baptism of a child, passing by a church, a visit from a minister, meeting people of other faiths, nativity plays; implicit experience includes death in a family, kicking leaves, illness, sharing with others, birthdays, praise and nature tables.

It is hard to over-emphasize the influence of the approach embodied in *Working Paper 36* on RE in the next two decades. Many teachers felt it provided a key to more interesting materials—their pupils were always asking to learn about 'other religions'—and therefore to solving problems of pupil motivation. It supplied the anti-indoctrination movement with a manifesto and inspired many in RE to a view of the subject that could survive the apparent disintegration of a Christian society. It enabled many teachers to feel that they could at last teach RE honestly without pretending to Christian or religious views they might not possess. It sustained the element of curiosity by making RE world-wide in its range and study of religious practice, and lifting it out of its base in predictable biblical study in many schools and syllabuses. As examination syllabuses changed, it enabled self-consciously atheistic children to take an interest in RE, and in many schools the composition of the Advanced Level group became less a coterie of devout Christian sixth formers, resembling the biblical remnant, and a more comprehensive group of all shades of religious commitment and none. Dennis Bates (in Tickner and Webster eds. 1982) assessing the impact of the Working Paper's approach argues that it cast RE into an academic mould, defining itself as the achievement of the understanding of religion based on the systematic study of world religions. In school it was seeking to model itself on Religious Studies approaches in colleges and some universities. Bates saw another effect as the mutual recognition between RE and moral education that they were autonomous areas best treated separately at school level.

Wedderspoon (1966) had already noted a serious failure of communication between the work of theologians in universities and the work of RE teachers in schools, and that there was growing criticism of current theological qualifications as excessively historical and linguistic and unrelated to contemporary intellectual concerns. *Working Paper 36* was an example of academics in religious studies engaged in dialogue with educators. But Smart did not strictly have a partner in education; rather he had educators who were prepared to test and develop his ideas in the classroom. Webster's criticism of religious educators went further[35] for failure to engage in dialogue with theology and the churches. By not doing RE fails to understand itself, to create a taxonomy or to promote sound research. Netto[36] argued the opposite, that RE in its agreed syllabuses, Shap documents, the Christian Education Movement and the RE Council were 'dominated by theology' and that the hegemenony should be broken, but he seems to be confusing theology with Christianity.

Working Paper 36 spelt the end, although not immediately, of a generation of agreed syllabuses. When Lancashire reissued their 1968 *Religion and Life* syllabus in 1973, statements that the function of RE was 'to bring children and adults into an encounter with God'[37] were archaic and even embarrassing to many RE teachers. The new Birmingham syllabus (1975), within the spirit of the Working Paper, was to lead future syllabus development. But the new movement created unintentionally a new orthodoxy in RE in which the labels confessional, neo-confessional and crypto-confessional became terms of abuse when applied to individuals and their work. Teachers were sometimes asked in job interviews whether they favoured the implicit religion approach or the explicit one, as if there were no others. Nor did the Working Paper explore the question of syllabus selection: on what basis should material be selected in a multifaith society, and how should religions be weighted in terms of syllabus time and demand on pupil attention? It strengthened theme teaching across religions: sacred buildings, rites of passage, sacred writings etc., an approach that was later to lead to right-wing attacks on the grounds of what the media came to call a multifaith mishmash. The label might be pejorative, but it was quite proper to question whether the way in which some children were actually taught the themes left them just as confused as children of an earlier generation had been by indiscriminate Bible teaching. Some of the supporters at classroom level of the Working Paper were more hot-headed than the report itself and embarked so enthusiastically on an 'objective' and 'neutral' approach to teaching that they ceased to be aware that in religion no-one is neutral and that the report itself had placed various restraints on the use of the word objective. Kincaid (1991) comments that the report was subsequently mistakenly quoted as simply exemplifying a phenomenological approach when it actually commended both a study of religious phenomena and a concern for personal relevance. Ironically it was a Christian commentator (Brown, 1991) who dared to raise even more basic questions:

> What kind of person do we wish to enable to develop through our educational provision?

and

> What is our vision for society?[38]

The Last Stand of Bible Teaching

The last clear defence of Bible teaching as a centrepiece in RE appeared in 1972. It seemed somewhat out of place in the new mood. But Alan Dale did not try to put the clock back to the fifties. He saw the difficulties in Bible teaching as much more than 'a matter of language and comprehension. It was a matter of reading and understanding the Bible as a book worth reading and understanding today . . . Doesn't even Jesus sound remote and ineffectual in the massively changed and changing world of the twentieth century?'[39] Dale held to the view that the Bible remains 'one of the great public documents of the world . . . not the private possession of any community',[40] a book in which we can see our human predicament in miniature. Dale's own Bible paraphrases were planned for a reading age of nine (New Testament) and twelve (Old Testament). He belongs to the new age in RE in that he defends Bible teaching philosophically and pedagogically and his aim is theologically Reformed: to empower children to read the Bible with understanding for themselves. Teachers of the Bible are referred by Dale to Auden's six functions of the literary critic: to introduce us to authors and writings we did not know; to suggest that we may be undervaluing books we had not read carefully enough; to show relationships between works from different ages and cultures; to provide an interpretation which increases the reader's understanding; to throw light on how the book was made and to relate it to life, ethics and religion. But Dale was swimming against the seventies tide.

Webster[41] was critical of the emergent dichotomy between Bible-centred RE, which collapses through its irrelevance to children and 'life-centred' RE which collapses through lack of definition, ambiguity and loss of direction. He argued that RE should be addressing education for serendipity and wonder; reverence and mystery; a sense of the divine milieu; a capacity to be surprised by the Other; and self-transcendence.

The Decline of CEM and the Rise of the RE Council

Significantly the rise of the new post-Working Paper orthodoxy co-incided with the decline of the Christian Education Movement. The professional advisory services and the networking of those services, for which CEM and others had successfully campaigned, were now in place in many LEAs. This led to an identity and a cash crisis for CEM. LEAs with their own advisory services were now less willing to subscribe to CEM. The whole concept of a Christian Education Movement began to look increasingly outmoded within an open-ended, phenomenologically dominated RE, which was no longer perceived as requiring Christian teachers in order to function. CEM continued to address the problems of resourcing RE, especially at primary school level, but the late seventies and early eighties were years of contraction and uncertainty in the Movement. Experiments of shared appointments with colleges of education of 0.5 time between CEM and the college ended in failure as the college tended to draw the appointee into more than 0.5 of their paid working time.

There was also an alternative and in some sense rival organization. The Association for RE (ARE) had been formed (1968) by Peter Lefroy-Owen, as an attempt to express the religious independence and professionalism of teachers in the subject. Although its membership was never large, some 400 at its height, some of whom were also CEM members, ARE produced a regular bulletin and provided a focus and lobby for the growing professionalism within RE. It was later to merge with the CEM Teachers' Department—itself formed to respond to the concerns that had led to ARE—to form the Professional Council for RE (PCfRE). But that was more than a decade away (1985). The year 1973 also marked the founding of the RE Council. Membership of this was open to organizations, not individuals. Representative groups were the main UK religions, organizations concerned with RE, and organizations concerned with RS and Theology. Over the years the RE

Council encouraged mutual education between the religions and the professional groups in its membership, encouraged member religions to encourage their own young members into teaching RE and acted as a persistent lobby to government and the DES on the question of specialist teacher supply. That it was not heeded is no reflection on the statistics and publications it produced over the years in support of this cause. After the 1988 Act it was to develop a more sophisticated parliamentary lobby. CEM was to come into its own again after the 1988 Act, when the weakening of the LEAs led to the collapse of some of their own RE support services and the new in-service culture moved towards buying in outsiders for a fee rather than maintaining local services. But despite retrenchment in the seventies, the unobtrusive contribution of CEM was maintained through its sponsored publications, *Learning for Living*, later *The British Journal of Religious Education*. BJRE was a 'wholly owned subsidiary' of CEM. The editor is appointed by the CEM Executive. By 1995 the overseas readership of the BJRE was almost equivalent to the UK readership and two other complementary journals had joined it. Nobody could call it confessional.

The Birmingham Syllabus

Birmingham had been using a 1950 syllabus expanded in 1962. But Birmingham had changed more than many cities with its plural communities and the role or potential role played by RE in community relations. The Religious and Cultural Panel of the Birmingham Community Relations Committee had been meeting from March 1969 to discuss the sort of RE appropriate to the city in the 1970s. The panel included Sikhs, Jews, Muslims, Hindus and all the major Christian denominations. They recommended that all children should know something of the 'traditional religion of the land, namely Christianity' alongside something of the major world religions. They recommended that a deeper study of one religion should be undertaken, normally the religion to which the child adheres and in consequence that in a multi-religious school RE options would have to be provided to allow for this. Children would also be expected to study at least one non-religious stance for living such as humanism or communism. The syllabus, which was kept deliberately brief to reduce prescription to a minimum, together with an accompanying large advisory handbook for teachers, was complete late in 1973 and approved by the four committees of the conference. It went to the Finance and General Purposes Committee of the City Council early in 1974. They expunged references to communism from the text but accepted the rest. This decision hit the local and national press with headlines such as *Happy Marx* and *Communist Textbook*. The Education Committee and the City Council over-rode this, accepting the full syllabus, communism included, but the Council split on party lines, the minority Conservatives opposing the inclusion of communism.

Legal opinion was sought and in 1974 the Council was advised that the syllabus did not fulfil the requirements of the 1944 Act, since included within their syllabus of 'religious instruction' were 'non-religions' to be studied in their own right. There was also some Anglican opposition within the city which sought independent legal advice from the National Society. Under Section 10 of Schedule Five of the 1944 Act appeal could be made to the Minister of Education where a conference could not agree or where an LEA failed to adopt a syllabus that a conference had agreed unanimously. The Minister in question was Reg Prentice (Labour). Meanwhile on the basis of legal opinion it had itself sought, the agreed syllabus conference decided that it had not finished its work, so no definitive legal judgement could be made about an unfinished piece in the hands of the Minister. A sub-committee was charged with making the very short syllabus statement more specific. It added some headings, included items for study which had previously been placed in the draft handbook and clarified the outline of the intended approach. Crucial was the inclusion in the syllabus that 12 to 16 year olds should study a minor course in one of the non-religious stances for living, but it did not specify any particular one. The advisory handbook included sections on humanism and communism, but neither was prescribed. In the end the revised syllabus appeared in 1975 without further opposition. John Hull (1984), a member of the sub-committee, defended the inclusion of non-religious stances in a religious education syllabus on the grounds that it is perfectly proper to make excursions into non-religious areas, provided these are related to religions in such a way as to advance knowledge and understanding of religion and provided they were taught in the same spirit of critical sympathy or tolerant understanding that should be accorded to religions. This did not go far enough for Harry Stopes-Roe, who as a humanist regretted that the phrase 'stances for living' in the 1974 draft had been replaced by 'religions' in 1975, describing the 1975 syllabus as 'dominated by religion.'[42] John Hick countered[43] that the teaching unit on humanism had been retained.

Hull (1975) interprets the whole process as a sign of the bankruptcy of the old approach to agreed syllabuses that saw them as ecumenical Christian documents whose purpose was to 'teach' Christianity. Naylor and Krejci (in Cole, 1978) defended the teaching of Marxism on the grounds that it was a mode of coping with the human predicament and a vision of a new civilization embraced in varying forms by about half the world's population, adducing that if it seemed not to fit religious education it might well be because in the West religion had become conceived too narrowly as something that was both automatically theistic and concerned with a person's private life, and hence not essentially a public activity. They conceded the difficulties in their case, however, in that Marxism explicitly claims to discredit religion and to provide an entirely satisfying alternative. If Marxism were to be taught, Naylor and Krejci suggested that the social and intellectual background to Marx, his synthesis and message, historical developments such as reformist and revolutionary Marxism, Lenin, Stalin and Mao, and 'comments' on lifestyles in selected communist countries could be included.[44] But there would have to be 'objectivity' and 'true professionalism' on the part of the teacher. They concluded 'it would be misleading . . . not to admit that the handling of potent forces like Christianity, Buddhism and Marxism is like poking crocodiles; there is always the possibility of someone getting bitten'.[45] Harris (1976) suggested that one might even teach about Nazism or existentialism. But many religious educators and the more ephemeral public opinion were less convinced that Marxism should be taught as part of RE, or whether it should be taught at all. That proposals to teach it in RE arose was part of the desire by religious educators to demonstrate that they were being honest and open. Marxism was a potent and apparently threatening anti-religious way of life. Could one pretend in RE lessons that it did not exist? Gates wrote:

> It is not the business of teachers to insist that a child decide for this faith or that . . . Religious education is a continuing process of personal development which involves both teacher and pupil in a continuing quest for truth.[46]

Gates's remark would have found ready support among RE professionals, but it begged the question of what syllabus content should be provided. Cole[47] argued the priority of Christianity on cultural grounds, comparing this with natural priority given to Islam in Pakistan and Judaism in Israel. He contended that a pupil should gain 'a similar knowledge' of one other religion and a general knowledge of a number of religions. The pupil should also understand how people with no religious beliefs interpret life and their contribution to human welfare and knowledge. His preferred example for this was humanism. Cole argued that pupils should gain a general knowledge of the main questions with which religions deal and their proposed answers, finally achieving attitudes and skills to equip them to study some other belief system in adult life that they had not even heard of in school, should they wish to.

That the debate took place at all was a sign that religious instruction had disappeared some time before and been quietly replaced in all but the law by religious education, in which no particular religion or 'non-religion' were being 'taught' in the sense of imparted to pupils as true. Cox[48] wrote that in this new situation even the revelation of the Bible is a special sort of belief-based knowledge, not a universally accepted fact, and has to be presented in the classroom as such, 'a book which some people use in a unique way and in which they, but not others, find a truth that they believe'.

The debate about issues raised by Birmingham did not permeate all schools. Harris (1976) presents an anecdote from a Church of England VA village primary school where the head-teacher told a student on teaching practice that in RE they were 'doing missionaries'. The student's atheist tutor encouraged her to interpret the concept of missionaries liberally, as missionaries to Mars, with associated art work, costumes and drama. The tutor advised that if the vicar were to turn up, as was his right, he should be asked to play the part of the missionary. This cameo illustrates the conflicts that could arise between trendiness, change, and half-digested approaches to RE.

Although it made little immediate impact on classroom RE, 1977 marked the founding of the International Seminar on Religious Education and Values. It was based on a realization that RE, although widely different in different countries, was facing some common issues which were in the West part of a reconsideration of culture and cultural values. By means of annual conferences and papers the members of ISREV, most of whom were engaged in RE at higher education level, were able to engage in dialogue and search for a perspective above or beyond the purely national. That RE might have an international dimension at all had not been obvious to everybody engaged in it within the British scene.

From Mid- to End-Seventies

Jean Holm, Principal Lecturer in Religious Studies at Homerton College, Cambridge (1975) attempted to provide working definitions of religion, noting that the common denominator was that religion has always been an important phenomenon of human experience, expressed as a need to make sense of the world, to affirm that there is purpose not of human making, that the structure of reality is something that humans belong to rather than something that belongs to them. Religion, she argued, provides a coherent interpretation of the whole of human experience and involves a way of life based on that interpretation, suggesting answers to the ultimate questions raised by humankind. Religions are varied within themselves, according to their cultural setting; they exist in time and are subject to change. They find expression in sacred writings and ethical codes, in individual lives and in corporate groupings. They also have traditions, customs and rituals. Although we cannot isolate something called religion and study it, since religion can only take the form of a particular religion, we can study specific religions and must do so to go beyond Christianity and the 'scandalously distorted picture of Judaism' which presents it as merely part of the story of Christianity. But the key words for Holm are 'understand' and 'study'. This includes imaginative entering into the situation of others. Implicit and explicit elements should be used in a balance. Her chart of teaching units includes human experience themes such as Barriers, Fear, What is Man?, and Conflict. Her explicit themes include Creation Myths, Signs and Symbols, What is Belief?, Sikhism and Buddhism. The life of Jesus is still taught.

> If primary schools have tended to present Jesus as kind and gentle and loving, secondary schools have tended to present him as the upholder of conventional morality, as the ally of authority, and as the opponent of change.[49]

Holm is an example of ·the mid-seventies situation. World religions teaching has arrived, largely uncontroversially, at least among teachers. The controversies were concerned with teaching non-religious stances for living as part of RE. But the seventies did not 'invent' world religions teaching. G.E.Phillips had written 'The Study of Other Religions in Schools' as distantly as 1939,[50] arguing that 'other religions' should be taught, that the teaching should not be 'competitive', that other races should not be presented merely as 'natives', nor at the other extreme should everything Eastern be presented as mysterious and wise. With older children Phillips argued that one should teach via the classic literature of the religion in question. He argued that teaching world religions will demonstrate the interesting character of religion in general and the uniqueness of Christianity. Those religious educators who believed that teaching world religions had been 'discovered' as a new approach in Lancaster in the seventies were wrong. Phillips and others were exploring the area before the war, but the war largely obliterated world religions teaching from the view of religious educators.

The dominant book for RE teachers in the seventies was, however, *What Can I Do in RE?* by Michael Grimmitt. Grimmitt was then Director of the Regional RE Resources Centre at Westhill College,

Birmingham. A number of such centres had been set up on DES initiative, under the umbrella of colleges of education. Others were at London and Bangor, with the National Society for RE, an Anglican charitable foundation, having centres of its own at London and York, also college-based. Collectively these centres provided not merely access to resources but also in-service education for teachers, not least in the field of world religions, which had not been part of the original training courses of most teachers of that time. Grimmitt's book went through two editions (1973 and 1978) and two reprints (1976, 1977) during the decade. He gave voice to the new ideas in RE that now seemed unstoppable. In the past, he argued, the connection between the legal status of religious instruction and its classroom status constituted a major problem. Associated with this was the teaching of beliefs as if they were facts. He argued that the justification for RE must be educational rather than religious: it is worthwhile for the understanding of the human situation it promotes; for its potential to develop the child's cognitive perspective and aid in personal development; it can be taught in such a way to help children think for themselves.[51] Grimmitt proposed 'depth themes' to replace the confessional life themes of Goldman and the sixties. Depth themes were intended to help children to look at their own existential development in depth, based on the supposition that insight into religious concepts arises from the process of reflecting at depth on our own life experiences and those of others. Pupils should learn how to '"step into the shoes" of, say, a composer or a poet and see and feel what he sees and feels . . . Only when we can "bracket out" ourselves, our pre-conceived notions and our particular values and concentrate on what, for example, a Muslim feels when he prays to Allah . . . will we begin to appreciate and understand the essence of Islam.' It was a definitive guide to the new mood in RE.

Some of the issues in RE in the seventies were hardy perennials. Benfield, analysing RE in Lancashire[52] noted that out of 700 teachers involved only 20 per cent had a specialist qualification in the subject. At school level the subject was heavily dependent on the attitude of the head-teacher. Yet even sympathetic head-teachers were being discouraged by the difficulty in recruiting suitable teachers. Twenty per cent of schools had 'absorbed' RE into Humanities courses, yet where History or Geography teachers and/or material dominated course planning, the RE element of such courses tended to be contrived or non-existent.

In Holm and Grimmitt there is not yet an emphasis on Christianity as a diverse world religion. Thematic teaching has continued as part of the diet of RE, despite the unnoticed danger that dissolving religions into themes can give a distorted view of them. There is also an underlying humanist base, partly introduced so that Buddhism can be taught as a non-theistic religion, partly to avoid the taint of confessionalism, but with the danger that taken further by others in the decades to follow, God, the transcendent, awe and mystery, could remain outside the RE syllabus and classroom, leaving the resultant religious education courses less distinguishable from a tour of the sociology of religion. Newbigin glimpsed this,[53] writing that religion, like science and history, is an attempt to understand and respond to 'what is really the case'. RE is 'self defeating if it is only concerned with the study of "the religious dimension of human experience" and not with the realities which religious experience tries to grasp and respond to.'

Grimmitt[54] produced an analogy for the role of the RE teacher, which many were happy to espouse:

> If RE teachers could adopt the attitude of a shopkeeper with wares in his window which he is anxious for customers to examine, appreciate and even 'try on' but not feel under any obligation to buy, then many of the educational problems connected with RE would disappear.

It was not to prove an entirely felicitous image in the next decade. Cooling[55] commented that such a picture implies that all the wares are equally valid and worthy of 'trying on' and conceals that there may be other wares under the counter, such as fundamentalist Christianity or Islam, which the 'shopkeeper' deliberately conceals from the customer. Later criticism of world religions in RE as a pic-'n'-mix drew on the problems in this image. But it was an analogy of its time, developed against what had gone before. Cooling's own substitute, a comparison between the RE teacher and a doctor, had hardly fewer problems. Was religion the illness? Cooling's doctor allowed patients choice while providing clear advice, but how much choice do patients really have in the face of strong medical advice?

The seventies saw a discussion beginning about what skills, attitudes and knowledge a 'religiously educated' person might be expected to have. Holley (1978) lists the primacy of spiritual insight, spiritual awareness, and scholarly insight into religion. The task of RE is to promote understanding and to provoke. An educational curriculum which ignores the spiritual dimension of personhood was in Holley's view incomplete and necessarily fragmentary. RE is logically central to all educational activities as it is about the discernment of ontic values. The best skills for the RE teacher are a love of learning, the skill of prescient questioning and to recognize the level of insight at which one's pupils have arrived. Despite Holley, not many schools were prepared to see RE as central to all educational activities. The problem emerging was that as the territory of RE appeared to extend, the teaching time allocated remained static and often inadequate.

Not all those who wrote about what RE should be dealing with wrote realistically in view of timetable allocation available. A short book by two classroom RE teachers (Copley and Easton, 1974), which was likened, in an editorial in the *British Journal of RE*, to children playing tick in a graveyard, provided what could be seen, despite its publication date and relative unconcern with theoretical considerations, as a comment on the entire seventies debate in RE. It suggested that whatever the theory of religious education and whatever the syllabus adopted, much classroom teaching of RE could be, from the child's point of view, a worthy but dull business. They proposed teaching strategies intended to make the RE lesson unpredictable, memorable and enjoyable as a weekly or twice-weekly event in the life of the child.

Meanwhile there was a changing educational world beyond RE. The secondary curriculum in particular was becoming complicated and diffuse with a proliferation of 'subjects' and courses and, between LEAs and individual schools, many syllabuses. Moving house to a new area at a critical time of life could cost a child a year's schooling to re-start different CSE or O Level syllabuses. There was growing pressure to simplify and give coherence to what had hitherto been ad hoc growth. On the horizon, in a cloud no bigger than a person's hand, was an approaching political whirlwind which would take up the entire curriculum, and with it RE. Education would never be the same again.

Chapter Five

A New Deal for RE: The 1980s

The fact that since 1944 the only compulsory subject in the curriculum in Britain had been religious education reflected a healthy distrust of the state using central control of the syllabus as a means of propaganda. But that was hardly the risk now: the propaganda was coming from left-wing local authorities, teachers and pressure groups, not us . . . But it would be no easy matter to change for the better what happened in schools . . .

Margaret Thatcher

Society

In 1982 Britain went to war, causing the re-election and strengthening of Margaret Thatcher as prime minister. The attempt to recapture the Falklands was, militarily speaking, a gamble, with over-stretched supply lines, antique aircraft carriers and pressed tourist liners for troop carriers. The Argentinian invasion might never have happened if the British government had acted on earlier intelligence reports, but this was forgotten in victory. Mrs Thatcher instructed the nation to 'Rejoice, rejoice' but Archbishop of Canterbury Robert Runcie fell from favour as a result of his muted address at the victory service in St Paul's, by emphasizing thanksgiving rather than victory.

Wales at last attained its Welsh language TV channel, Sianel Pedwar Cymru (1982). It was a long way from 1945 when Welsh had no public status and could only be used in court if the speaker would be disadvantaged by using English. Pressure for a new Welsh Language Act built up in the late eighties and led to an Act (1993) that still disappointed many by providing for equality between Welsh and English only 'where appropriate in all the circumstances and reasonably practicable'. But by 1990 there would be hundreds of Welsh-medium schools catering for thousands of pupils. From 1980 a Welsh-medium external degree was offered by the University College of Wales,

Aberystwyth. The Welsh language culture had passed from the control of the chapels into the schools and the education system. If the legal provision was still not ideal, Welsh had indisputably risen from the dead. The shift out of the chapel culture was important, for in Cardiff as in English cities, redundant chapels were becoming business premises and mosques. Thatcher believed that the hard left's power was entrenched in three institutions, the Labour Party, local government and the trade unions.[1] Having defeated Labour, Thatcher resolved to bring the trade unions to boot and end the free-for-all situation of the seventies. The Tebbit Act of 1982 on strikes and other industrial practices was to be much invoked. The National Graphical Association in dispute at Warrington was among the first of many unions to be broken by this Act. In 1984 an IRA bomb at the Conservative Party Conference at the Grand Hotel, Brighton, neither destroyed the Prime Minister nor broke her will. The 1984–85 miner's strike showed that no union was able to break the government where mere terrorists had failed. Thatcher referred to it as Mr Scargill's Insurrection[2] but miners were themselves divided over the refusal of their leader, Arthur Scargill, to call a ballot before the strike and a new union, the Union of Democratic Mineworkers, emerged as a moderate rival to the NUM. It was too late. Within ten years most pits were closed and those that remained were privatized.

The government continued in a non-consultative style to ride roughshod over more liberal groups who, unlike the miners, had been nurtured on the principles of consultation and dialogue. These included the teachers' unions, universities, the medical and legal professions, even the BBC—which was subjected to criticisms of unpatriotism for critically reviewing the bombing of Libya (1986). Government intervention seemed universal; even museums, hardly seen as traditional profit centres, were to move towards self-funding. There was a change in Conservative attitudes to the Church of England that would have amazed earlier English generations. The Church was accused of being left wing and castigated for interfering in social and political issues.

The eighties were an era of superficial prosperity: growing house and share ownership, soaring investments, foreign holidays on a scale not seen before, new high-tech industries along the M4 corridor all the way to Newport, Gwent. In Wales the 'Valleys Initiative' attracted investment from the Far East. But the Thatcher government imposed the community charge or poll tax in 1988, without the safety nets, transitional period and low initial rates demanded by some Tories. With interest rates at 15 per cent by 1989 and unemployment on a scale not seen since the thirties the decade did not herald prosperity for all. North Sea oil revenues totalling $100 billion financed benefit payments for the millions out of work.

Religion

Set against a society which appeared to be dominated by materialism and scarred by poverty, Bruce (1995) noted an inarticulate spiritual quest, recording that in the twenty years from 1970 to 1990 the number of books on the occult published increased by nearly 150 per cent[3] and as one example cited Waterstone's bookshop in Aberdeen, where seventy metres of shelving were devoted to 'Body, Mind and Spirit' against five metres devoted to Christianity. The eighties saw the rise to prominence of the New Age—in reality a very wide range of differing beliefs and practices involving 'new' science, ecology, psychology and spirituality, with wide-ranging examples from magno-therapy, Gaia, the Age of Aquarius etc. Some spiritual resurgence carried strangely materialist consequences: Exegesis weekends cost $200 at 1984 prices. Tabloids identified the New Age with 'New Age travellers', scruffy itinerants often encamped illegally on the land of others, sponging benefits off a society they affected to despise.

If there was a New Age, an older set of undefined religious or spiritual attitudes surfaced in April 1989 after a disaster at Sheffield Hillsborough football ground in which over ninety Liverpool supporters died during a crowd surge at a match. Within days the Kop end of the Anfield ground at Liverpool became a shrine. Floral tributes, scarves, written messages, filled the ground, which was visited by one million people in the first week alone. At the official memorial service John Newton, a Methodist and Moderator of the local Free Church Council combined part of the twenty-third psalm and the unofficial Liverpool anthem, when he referred to God's promise that 'even when we walk through the valley of the shadow of death, we shall never walk alone'. Examples of this semi-articulate mass spiritual emotion were to appear again, notably after the Dunblane Primary School massacre of 1996 when even the sacrosanct Sunday busy- ness of superstores paused for a minute's silence on 17th March; they did not stop for Remembrance Sunday.

In 1988 an author who was not then a household name appeared on radio's *Desert Island Discs*. His choice of one luxury to take to the fictitious island was an ex-directory mobile phone so that he could ring up other people without them being able to ring him. Within months he was castaway himself as a result of a fatwa from a distant Shi'ite leader in Iran, the Ayatollah Khomeini. Salman Rushdie's crime was to write an offensive and provocative novel, to anyone who knew anything about Islam, *The Satanic Verses*, in passing uniting the British Muslim community as no Muslim leader had been able to do. Muslim opposition to the book led to tabloid media pillorying of all Muslims as potential murderers, made easier by the public burning of the novel in Bradford. To many within the British Islamic community there seemed a double standard: the government would ban a book like Peter Wright's *Spy Catcher* but not *The Satanic Verses*. Much less publicized was that Khomeini's fatwa was not universally recognized in the Muslim world, nor was it interpreted as a literal death sentence by all who supported it. The *Star*[4] denounced as 'misguided and . . . potty' the followers of Khomeini adding that 'the terrifying thing is not that a lot of these crackpots actually live here among us in Britain, but that we are actually becoming frightened of them.' From the point of view of community relations—and those RE teachers who had been working patiently to promote tolerance—the fatwa was a disaster.

The churches seemed as weak as Islam seemed strong. Norman Tebbit, one-time Chairman of the Conservative Party, wrote:

> The church—particularly the Church of England . . . seems to have lost certainty and authority on moral issues as it has gained certainty on political and economic issues. Having thrown out the baby of the authority of the scriptures it seems now to ask its dwindling followers to worship nothing more than the bath water of ephemeral sociological policies.[5]

The Church of England Report *Faith in the City* was denounced as Marxist and the Bishop of Durham, who had criticised the government's handling of the miners' strike, was pilloried as 'the first cuckoo of spring'. Robert Runcie, Archbishop of Canterbury and David Sheppard, Anglican Bishop of Liverpool met the Environmental Secretary, himself an Anglican, Kenneth Baker. Baker's view was that the report was more secular than spiritual and that the philosophy behind it was too collectivist, failing to recognize the role of individuals in improving their own communities (Baker, 1993). The Pope's visit to Britain (1982) was less controversial, except to extreme Protestant groups who tried to protest at it. His sharing in worship at Canterbury Cathedral and his meeting with the Moderator of the Church of Scotland showed signs of growing closer together, as did the initiation of the *Revised English Bible* (1989 successor of the *New English Bible*) which included Roman Catholics as full members rather than observers on its committee.

Mrs Thatcher's appearance at Anglican, Methodist and Church of Scotland assemblies had a ring of papacy about it: she condemned their unease over material gain, their support for black nationalism in South Africa and their 'SDP' (Social Democratic Party) tendencies. But the church's support for racial harmony was stronger than its practice; in 1986 only about fifty out of some 11,000 Anglican clergy were black. Thatcher found church opposition to the creation of grant-maintained schools on the grounds that they were or would become divisive 'unexpected'[6] and she set up the GM School Trust to publicize their benefits. Wealth creation was commended as a Christian act. Christianity too, it seemed, had been taken over by 'wets', liberals and lefties. Politics could become a substitute religion; Thatcher talked of 'believers' and people who were 'one of us', as opposed to the rest.

Education

Lawton (1992, 1994) distinguishes various types of Conservative attitudes to education, two in particular applying to the eighties: privatizers, who believe that parents should choose what they want and pay for what they can afford, a view encompassing the abolition of LEAs and the privatization of each school under its governors or parents or private limited company (plc) status; the second group are 'minimalists', believing that the state should provide basic schooling as cheaply as possible, with parental rights to buy extras. The Assisted Places Scheme where the state paid for selected able children to go to private schools is an example of this.

A sign of the political times appeared when the Education (No 2) Bill of 1980 reached the House of Lords. This was intended to introduce the assisted places. It also contained cost-cutting clauses including empowering LEAs to charge parents for school bus services in rural areas. The cost-cutting was attacked on two occasions by a Conservative peer. First, on the grounds that the money saved by not implementing assisted places could pay for the threatened school buses. The second attack came in committee, on the grounds that the proposed charges breached the undertakings given to religious denominations, especially Roman Catholics, in negotiating the passage of the 1944 Act, and also a commitment made to the churches in 1950. It would, his Lordship argued, go back on a double promise and he cited Luther refusing to recant in his attack on his own party's proposals: I can do no other. It was the veteran Lord Butler in his last full public speech. Aided by the Duke of Norfolk, Earl Marshal of England, speaking for the nation's Roman Catholics, by the (Anglican) Bishop of London and the Methodist socialist Lord Donald Soper, Butler knocked the clause out in the division by 216 to 112. *The Times* called it the first important defeat for the government since they had taken office. But it did not prevail against the tide; Butler resembled Canute rather than Luther. He died two years later. It escaped comment that he and Baker had overlapped in Parliament, albeit in different Houses and with (at the time of overlap) different interests.

Meanwhile moves towards a national curriculum were part of the centralizing of control that was symptomatic of the Thatcher era. The way was paved during the Secretaryship at the DES of her friend and ally, Keith Joseph (1981–86). Joseph moved there from Industry, where he had been fighting what he saw as the anti- enterprise culture which had so damaged Britain's post-war performance. He was quick to see the same culture in education, for example in drab mediocrity in comprehensive schools. His other concerns were the bottom forty per cent of pupil ability range, which led to the apocryphal remark that he longed for the day when all pupils would be above average in maths and English. Joseph wanted a good, cheap, state-run system of education. He was one of a growing number of Conservatives to see themselves lining up for an apocalyptic battle against the combined forces of Directors of Education, socialist teachers, teacher trainers, DES civil servants and 'ideology'. Labour's commitment to abolish independent schools helped Joseph greatly in his perception that they were driven by socialist dogmatism. Thatcher herself referred to the ethos of the DES during her years there as 'self-righteously socialist'.[7] She noted with horror at an official dinner that the leaders of the NUT and a large number of DES senior civil servants were 'on the closest of terms', evidenced by in-jokes, unstated allusions and body language.[8] Joseph wanted to introduce a common examination at 16 plus, the GCSE, to replace separate GCE O Level and CSE examinations, the latter having suffered the same fate at the hands of parental and employer esteem as the secondary moderns. His Technical and Vocational Initiative (TVEI) introduced more than a curriculum initiative; there were cash bonuses for co- operating schools and a new power in school curriculum, the Department of Trade and Industry, to break the monopoly of the DES. Through the medium of a DES paper, *Better Schools* (1985) Joseph even included a statement of intention for RE. Its aims were:

> to help pupils to develop personal moral values, respect for religious values, and tolerance of other races, religions and ways of life.

Changes to the external examination system included Advanced Supplementary (AS) Levels, the so-called 'half A Levels', and the National Vocational Qualifications (both 1987) intended to bring coherence to training qualifications. In theory a national curriculum would eliminate massive local curriculum variation and establish a base-line for assessment, which was quickly admitted to conceal a simpler intention, testing, which in turn was to lead to league table results for school performance. All this masked continuing lack of cash investment in school plant, school resources and teachers themselves. The mythology arose that 'trendy leftist teachers of the sixties' were being dragged into the glorious gospel day of higher standards, accountability and guaranteed lesson content.

Religious Education 1980–88

While the political storm clouds of radical structural and curriculum change in the education system were gathering, without any of the public debate and consensus that characterized the 1944 settlement, religious education was going through a period of quiet but significant consolidation. Hull could write (1982) of the recent history of RE as an attempt to be faithful to its own natural content, which would be 'impartial but not arid, personal but not proselytizing'.[9] Its focus would no longer remain 'far-off lands of long ago but in the teeming religious life of the towns and cities in which we live'. Religious educators had not been so quick to consider the implications for the less changing and remote villages, many of whose inhabitants considered themselves Christian but whose children were bored with the old RE. Agreed syllabuses seemed to be reducing in influence compared to Schools Council curriculum development projects, materials published by the Shap Working Party on world religions, materials for the classroom produced by the Christian Education Movement and at local LEA level. Hull had foreseen this[10] in September 1971 when he noted that educators are 'less and less willing to consent to a situation which allows the churches to prescribe and to veto what is taught in the classroom'. In the *BJRE* editorial for spring 1981[11] he was able to write of world religions presenting opportunities for RE rather than problems. He noted that the Welsh Christian Teachers' Association and the Association of Christian Teachers in England wanted world religions teaching but via a Christian interpretation and the Welsh Christian Teachers' Association remained opposed to the teaching of non-religious philosophies in RE. But there was at least a consensus that world religions should be taught. The debate on skills appropriate to RE continued with Eric Johns suggesting classification, evaluation, self-examination, empathy and epoche (the ability to suspend judgement) as crucial ones.

Hulmes (1979) had already questioned whether neutrality by the RE teacher was an obvious and simple position. He suggested that the first requirement for a teacher in RE was to be aware of their own commitment, attitude and prejudice with regard to religion. Second is an awareness of the commitments, attitudes and prejudices of others. Third is the ability to use these two areas of awareness to resolve potentially conflicting situations caused by a clash of commitments. Hulmes noted that while most people agreed that one essential task of RE was to help children to understand religion, it was less easy to define what religious understanding consisted of.

Hull defined the question for the next development phase of RE as: how can the descriptive study of world religions engage the pupil's own life and concerns?[12] Marvell commended again the phenomenological approach to RE as presuppositionless, essential and unique to the essence and manifestation of religion. Newbigin was less sure: we would not want to see 'pretty stories about the personal behaviour of Adolf Hitler' or racism within any revised Birmingham Handbook.[13] Latent value judgements in syllabuses were being acknowledged.

The teacher's own value judgements were considered by Hull. In the 1987 Shap Handbook he noted that commitment had by then become seen as a prison: restrictive, closed, anti-innovative, anti-questioning, redolent of the old certainties that led to wars. RE teachers were anxious to emphasize that they were not teaching for commitment on the part of their pupils but for understanding. But 'if commitment is a prison, apathy is a betrayal'.[14] Once 'set free' from commitment, modern young people discover that one cannot live without values of some sort. Yet to have values is to be committed to values. Commitment is not monochrome. There is a kind of commitment which makes one ready to listen and there is a kind which makes one deaf. Commitment can be a stimulus to discovery and exploration. If the RE teacher has a religious commitment it is the style of commitment that will make or break them as religious educators. But if they have no religious commitment they should not at the same time reject values. Moreover, commitment and objectivity are not opposing options for the RE teacher. 'If commitment is a prison, life without values is a desert. Can religious education become a garden?'.[15] Cooling[16] warned that there was a danger that unacceptable conservative theological dogmatism was in danger of being replaced by an equally unacceptable educational dogmatism posing as 'objective'.

Grimmitt (1987) stated clearly that there was no possibility of any rationale for RE that is ideology and value-free. Despite their job title, religious educators are essentially secular educators concerned with the educational value of studying religion and religions. The educational principles governing their work are those that govern all educators, irrespective of their subject. These include the development of cognitive perspectives or rationality, understanding the structure and procedures of the subject and recognizing the integrity, autonomy and voluntariness of the pupil. Education should be the 'first-order activity' of the religious educator, not religion. Their concern for religion is with its instrumental worth—the contribution which the study of it can make to the achievement of educational goals. RE should therefore resist domination either by religious nurture or theology. Grimmitt compared domination by the latter over RE to courses in school on Christian Geography, Christian Chemistry etc. He recognized that theology could offer a perspective on education as a whole and on the human condition. But it cannot provide a rationale for RE which would legitimize its place in the curriculum or support for education in religion as a first-order activity.

Grimmitt also warned about the serious threat to secondary school RE posed by the recent rise in courses in Personal and Social Education. Most of the outcomes were in his view unfavourable to RE: reluctant teachers were drafted into it; RE was often subsumed as a one module 'grace and favour' unit within PSE; and it led to the demise of RE in the upper years of many secondary schools. It subverts the real truth, that the study of religions itself makes a contribution to pupils' personal, social and moral development and that to do this best requires a separate identity for RE. When religious educators are enlisted into PSE courses they should take every opportunity to initiate debate about the value-assumptions that underlie them, especially those that make content subservient to process, or warn teachers not to 'teach' or in any way threaten the 'self-esteem' of pupils. The debate about assumptions widened to include assumptions about gender in RE. Christine Trevett in 'The Lady Vanishes'[17] highlighted sexism by omission in RE in such exercise-book or text-book entries as telling a Sikh by 'his' beard and turban. She noted that gender-free terms like believer and worshipper were being used infrequently in RE.

Religious Education and Religious Studies

There was a tendency to distinguish between Religious Education and Religious Studies. Hull (1984) defines Religious Studies as the study of the religions, and the term became favoured for external examination syllabuses. Religious Education was seen by Hull as a cluster of subjects, in which things like sensitivity training (in many infant and junior schools), social and political studies, moral education, personal relations, current affairs, social and community service, study of the 'non-religions' are set outside RS, as the periphery round the core. Of course it could simply have been that, in an effort to establish relevance to the lives of children and the rest of the curriculum from the sixties onwards, RE had become sloppy in its self-awareness and definition, a sort of utility bin for what were considered to be issues of meaning that did not fit obviously anywhere else in the curriculum. Hull maintained that Religious Education can be seen as a quest for meaning by the pupil; Religious Studies is the search for other people's meanings. Among teachers still haunted by the fear of confessionalism, RS became the rapidly preferred term. Some children were still missing out on RE and RS. The HMI survey *Aspects of Secondary Education in England* (1979) showed that RE appeared in the non-examination subjects for all older (4th and 5th Year in pre- 1988 National Curriculum language) pupils in 58 per cent of secondary schools but noted[18] that it was often omitted for pupils in the top stream due to pressure of examination studies. The cleverer a child was, the less likely they were to receive RE in some schools.

Priestley (in Tickner and Webster eds), 1982) applauded the new Humberside agreed syllabus' assertion that religious education should help children to understand religion. But he stated the paradox that religion can never be understood. Within the English religious tradition Priestley went back to Coleridge as a philosopher able to provide a confident critique rather than a retreat or denunciation of the contemporary German rational and sceptical approach to the study of religion. Coleridge taught the importance of self- knowledge as against the mere absorption of facts, affirmed the religious value of doubt and the discovery of wholeness. Priestley held that transcendence is a necessary condition of any inquiry which claims to be religious. Any education which engages in this dimension is fulfilling the minimum requirements of what RE might mean. Merely to require RE by law does not guarantee that transcendence will be addressed. If RE draws on the depth of religious experience in a merely superficial way it will actually negate understanding of transcendence. Story, festival, liturgy, ritual are expressions of religion closely allied to drama, music, poetry and art. All lack the closed-endedness which is characterized by finiteness. The world's greatest teachers, among whom is Wittgenstein as well as Jesus, have not just brought their disciples from confusion to clarity but towards mystery and unknowing. That is the heart of the parabolic method. RE may rise, Phoenix-like, from the ashes of the empiricism it has often sought to embrace. Priestley, as a philosopher of education, was anxious to uncover enduring roots for RE. He feared it had too often tried to meet the demands of the age by acceptance of notions such as objectivity, by emphasizing the empirical and communicating through the language of description. He challenged the educational norms on which these trends had been based.

There was growing unease about theme teaching. It had dominated the primary school RE scene and lower secondary years from Goldman onwards. Hull (1984) defended it, conceding that some theme work was 'running to seed'. He defined a theme as a unit of work organized around a topic which is known to the child from first-hand experience, e.g. homes, food, holidays, rather than something arising in a 'subject' slot such as History or Mathematics. Themes could produce idiosyncratic RE, e.g. the theme of Flight used to provide RE work on angels. Hull cited an example of one theme 'All work and no play' which was divided into thirty-two topics from how to avoid travel sickness, the Egyptian creation myth, bank holidays and the advantages of mid-week travel! Disciplined interrogation of a theme was vital and Hull concluded 'A theme which is consistent with almost anything contains almost nothing.'[19] But he argued that good theme work still had advantages: it related the sacred to the secular; it could still be a vehicle into relevant biblical material; and it could be a way of exploring the religious experience of children. It was a measured defence, but it did not address theme teaching within religious material, e.g. producing a unit on Sacred Writings describing scriptures within five or six religions. This could cause confusion and might encourage teachers or pupils towards the concept of equivalence, a misleading tendency in the study of religion: a synagogue is a Jewish church, an imam is a Muslim vicar etc. Wintersgill was more cautious about themes, arguing (1995) that theme categories might emerge from Western religions that distort Eastern religions, that themes sometimes exclude an individual religion's distinctiveness and that common headings distort. They can remove knowledge and understanding from the primary context of the religion itself. She countered the idea that themes relate more easily to pupils' experiences, questions and interests than 'straight religion' teaching by pointing out that it is the teacher's task to demonstrate relevance. If it is claimed that themes deal with 'religion', what is the nature of 'religion' in a world that sees only specific religions?[20]

While theme teaching was being modified, the importance of RE was being stressed by outside bodies and commentators. The Swann Report (1985) stressed the importance of non-dogmatic RE to help pupils to understand the nature of religious belief, the religious dimension of human experience and the plurality of faiths in Britain.[21] Robinson wanted RE to engage with the sorts of experience of transcendence being examined by the Religious Experience Research Unit at Manchester College, Oxford. He held that the child could be a resource for RE and that part of the role of RE might be to enable children to explore the dimension of mystery within themselves. He felt that the education process might be stunting an intuitive feeling in children about the mystery of life and quoted Sean O'Faolain:

> What end is there anyway to child education except to learn a few necessary things and after that to shock the intelligence, stir the sensibilities and warm the imagination into some sense of the mystery, horror and beauty of life?

The Shap Handbook went into its third edition in 1987, making it one of the last publications in the field before the Education Reform Act. It could speak of RE having disappeared in some schools. In most schools where RE existed, world religions teaching occurred, but often in a condescending or patronizing way. Teachers could be divided into those who emphasized the explicit dimension (the study of religions) and those who emphasized the implicit (the pupils' search for meaning). It recorded some vociferous objections to world religions teaching within the nation rather than the RE profession. But RE in a plural society should integrate pupils and respect and affirm diversity. The undenominational teaching required by the Cowper-Temple clause looked 'rather bland and emaciated'[22] but when teachers abandon proselytization as their aim for RE, the clause is no longer needed. This would mean that the distinctive things that give religion its shape can be taught. RE should help pupils to 'take seriously' religion. 'Take seriously' is something less than practising it, but it is the only style which is educationally viable. It may be that the inner sancta of faith may only be understood by its devotees.[23] But if humankind is therefore condemned to living in mutually incomprehensible groupings, there is little hope for the future.

Professional Associations and Management of RE

Professional RE teachers made a significant regrouping in 1985 when the ARE (see p. 106) merged with CEM Teachers' Department to produce the Professional Association for RE (PCfRE), a 'wholly owned subsidiary' of the Christian Education Movement. It was intended to be a professional association for RE teachers who might come from any religion or none (and as such might be unwilling to subscribe to CEM's broadly Christian remit), and for those evangelical Christian teachers for whom CEM was perceived to be too liberal or those who found the curriculum concerns of local CEM groups, where they existed, too broad. Such local groups had concerned themselves traditionally with the role of Christianity in education as a whole rather than in RE. PCfRE quickly moved to produce a magazine for RE teachers, *RE*

Today, which reviewed new materials and presented articles about curriculum development in the field. By 1988 PCfRE had a membership of about 700; it was to rise to more than 2,000. A second magazine, *Resource* was later adopted by CEM from Warwick University. The CEM Development Plan for 1992–3 notes that 'a professional subject association is needed both for development purposes and to sustain morale'. Independent of CEM on policy and with its own chairperson, PCfRE was serviced by CEM staff and the General Secretary of CEM was ex officio General Secretary of PCfRE. The PCfRE chairperson was ex officio on CEM General Council. PCfRE has its own officers, programmes and publications. The process of professionalization continued within CEM itself when it moved out of 'grace and favour' accommodation in London to a twenty-five-year lease of a new base in Derby (1989), selected for its central road and rail position. The appointment of a publications director further upgraded output. CEM continued its unobtrusive support of RE by helping to generate local projects which could quickly become self-sufficient. An example of this was a grant to support an RE Centre at Great Yarmouth. This was to provide a curriculum reference point for teachers working in eastern England and not easily able to access material elsewhere by virtue of distance. Not everyone hailed these developments as advance and during the 1988 Act debate CEM was referred to as the 'so-called Christian Education Movement' by Hart and others who wished it to provide a more vocal Christian presence within RE. Stephen Orchard, the CEM General Secretary at the time, distinguished the 'Christian–humanist' approach to RE from the 'Christian fundamentalist' one.

Marrat (in Felderhof (ed.), 1985) made one of the last pre-Reform Act statements about RE and its title to exist in schools into the 1990s. He argued that it is neither the philosopher of education, nor the expert in curriculum development who legitimate RE, but society, whose consensus is reflected in national legislation on the matter. The cynic might argue that such legislation is a cultural hangover, but education cannot be divorced from its social context. Examination boards, employers, universities all legitimate religious education, which is essentially a study of religion(s) and what religious people say and do.

Alongside continuing debate about the nature of RE, the first book on the management and organization of an RE department in a school appeared (Copley, 1985), dealing with issues specific to RE like building up the examination option groups, the head of RE within the total curriculum, raising the subject profile in the secondary school and coping with the problems faced in many secondary schools by lone specialist teachers with a heavy case-load of pupils to teach each week. The case-load of the RE teacher was compared to the maths teacher.

In a secondary school with a forty period teaching week the maths teacher might teach only six classes per week, for five periods each, excluding Advanced level work, whereas the RE teacher might teach fifteen classes for two lessons (or one double period) each. That might mean the RE teacher's case-load would be 450 pupils (30 x 15) compared to the Maths teacher's 180 (30 x 6). This would reflect in end-of-term reports, homework, examination and test marking and parents' evening appointments. Only in Advanced Level work could the RE teacher expect smaller teaching groups than the maths teacher. The book tried to help the head of the RE department to develop strategies to manage this sort of situation.

Consolidation in RE was confined to the ranks of the teaching profession and to professional religious educators. It was interrupted by direct intervention from outside which was to change the whole face of education. These resulted from initiatives instigated by the Prime Minister herself. When Richard Acland as Liberal MP for Barnstaple made his dramatic gesture of crossing the floor of the House in the 1943 education debate (see p. 71) his passionate speech stressed four points about education as a whole which he made by number. These were:

1 Things have gone wrong in a big way.
2 There have got to be fundamental changes.
3 There are great forces that will resist these changes.
4 I wonder if we are going to be led up the garden path again.

By a supreme irony the first three were to be taken up as the Conservative rallying cry for their reforms of the system in the eighties. Observers were left to ponder the aptness of the fourth.

The Education Reform Act (1988)

A letter from a concerned Tory supporter citing a question about gender stereotyping from a course for intending teachers was the basis for Thatcher's attack on standards at Brighton Polytechnic[24] and her trigger for action to reform education. The nation's children were going to be given what they deserved. The teacher training monopoly of higher education was to be broken. At least half of new entrants to the profession were intended to come via routes like articled teacher or licensed teacher status, being trained on the job, ironically by those same classroom incompetents that other reforms were to berate.

I had always been an advocate of relatively small schools as against the giant, characterless comprehensives. I also believed that too many teachers were less competent and more ideological than their predecessors. I distrusted the new 'child-centred' learning techniques, the emphasis on imaginative engagement rather than learning facts, and the modern tendency to blur the lines of discrete subjects and incorporate them in wider, less definable entities like 'humanities'.[25]

She also had convictions about curriculum content.

I had a very clear—and I had naively imagined uncontroversial—idea of what history was. History is an account of what happened in the past. Learning history, therefore, requires knowledge of events . . . a clear chronological framework—which means knowing dates.[26]

Her will became law, but not without some debate in Cabinet. When Kenneth Baker arrived at the Department of Education he came from Environment. But he had already intervened in education as Minister for Information Technology in 1981. This was through his scheme to get a computer into every secondary school (later all schools) by means of the government meeting fifty per cent of the cost. It was a laudable initiative, less obviously an omen for future action—the direct intervention in education at classroom level; Baker admits that the DES resented it.[27]

Baker's two watchwords in education were standards and choice and his intended to achieve them by city technology schools, grant-maintained schools and a national curriculum with testing. But first he had to assert himself in the DES. It was a department with some 2,000 employees but no local or regional offices, unlike Employment, with which it was later to merge (1995). Baker compared his move from Environment to a two division drop by a football team. The DES was based at Elizabeth House, a sixties tower block built by architect John Poulson, later jailed for corruption. The Secretary's office overlooked the Charing Cross railway line and the noise drowned conversation. Double-glazing lessened the noise but increased the sauna effect in summer. Successive Tory Secretaries believed that there was a DES conspiracy by civil servants to scupper their plans to reform education. They viewed the Department as in the grip of sixties ideology and 'progressive schooling' methods. To Baker the DES represented the theory of producer-capture, whereby the interests of the producer prevail over those of the consumer. Walter Ulrich, Deputy Secretary in charge of the Schools Branch is presented in Baker's memoirs as a formidable presence, capable of bullying secretaries of state. Baker had to make it clear 'there was only room for one boss in my departments'.[28]

Baker was prepared to be the strong-arm boss, but he was no cultural boor. His recreations in *Who's Who* included collecting books and he had edited volumes of poetry. His deep interest in English literature and history had been nurtured in his own school days at St Paul's. He moved to Education in 1986, the year in which he was fifty-two, writing later (1993):

> Of all Whitehall Departments, the DES was among those with the strongest in- house ideology. There was a clear 1960s ethos and a very clear agenda which permeated virtually all the civil servants. It was rooted in 'progessive' orthodoxies, in egalitarianism and in the comprehensive school system. It was devoutly anti-excellence, anti-selection and anti-market . . . Not only was the Department in league with the teacher unions, University Departments of Education, teacher training theories [sic], and local authorities, it also acted as their protector against any threats which Ministers might pose.

If the DES appeared to be in league with these groups a less sinister explanation than that put forward by Thatcher and Baker is equally plausible. It lies within the Department's structure. A department like Employment had 50,000 staff and regional and local offices. Its local officials knew local situations, people and places. It had eyes and ears on the ground. With only one central office and 2,000 staff the DES did not have the structure to give it a direct entry into schools. Its officials rarely visited schools. Its advice could legally be ignored by LEAs. It was dependent for its eyes and ears on those who did have the entry to schools: LEAs, professional associations, teacher trainers and Her Majesty's Inspectorate, which until privatization was part of DES structures. Moreover, for more than twenty years the DES had been given no Permanent Secretary from within its own ranks—the resultant effect was demoralizing for its senior staff. The evidence for a conspiracy theory to block reform is therefore patient of another interpretation. Such an interpretation also gives credibility to the view by some in the RE profession, shared by Baker and by senior civil servants in the Church of England, that the DES had developed an implicit secularism that viewed RE as unimportant. This was not so much a view, as a non-view, i.e. that RE was not considered.

Geoffrey Holland, one-time Permanent Secretary at the DES, described Ministers as transient (he worked for twenty-three Ministers in thirty-two years), stating that the constant is the party and its policy, not the person.[29] At the same time, 'because the average tenure of a

Minister is so short, all want to make their mark'. Ministers have no standard induction or course and have to work at speed, taking complex decisions. Holland described them as wearing called various 'hats': their individual persona, their party loyalties, their role as constituency MPs, their role within the parliamentary party and the Commons, their department role and then their Cabinet role.[30]

Rapid and significant change in education was in store but not, like its 1944 predecessor, based on national or cross-party consensus. Thatcher wanted a simple national curriculum, 'a basic syllabus for English, mathematics and science with simple tests to show what pupils knew'. Baker was working with a group of right-wingers whose own aims for education were diffuse. He had to try to keep them—and the PM—happy. Thatcher later stated that she thought that Baker had been over-influenced by teachers' unions and Her Majesty's Inspectors of Schools, another group the Tories intended to break up and privatize. HMI were, as we have seen, part of the DES information networks. That Baker should have been influenced by teachers' unions was laughable. But his sin was to endorse a report (TGAT on testing, 1987) which was also welcomed by Labour, the National Union of Teachers and The Times Educational Supplement. Different pressures within the Conservative Party, all more influential than the writings of the experts and professionals they derided, simply underline that there was never a monochrome Tory view of education. Less publicized was Neil Kinnock's sympathy as Shadow Education Secretary in the early 1980s with the idea that education was too important to be left to local councils. Ironically, the idea of panels of experts determining curriculum and taking over failing schools had been dismissed by Labour jokingly as 'the Romanian model'.

Lawton argues (1994) that the dominant value in the Education Reform Act was consumerist parental choice, with its corollary of differences in quality and selection, not by eleven-plus examination, but by middle-class parents playing the system effectively. Watkins detected a deeper flaw, that the National Curriculum had no architect, only builders (1991). If it had a philosophy it was an ad hoc mixture of Joseph, Thatcher, Baker and others. Watkins was another cast-off, as former deputy chief executive of the National Curriculum Council. His comment went further:

Many people were surprised at the lack of sophistication in the original model [for the new national curriculum]: ten subjects, attainment targets and programmes of study defined in a few words in the Bill, that was all. Indeed such design as there was seemed to be retro-spective.[31]

The ERA introduced testing alongside the National Curriculum. Thatcher wanted 'objective outsiders' [32] rather than professional teachers to do the testing. She personally intervened in the proposals for history teaching.[33] She wanted more emphasis on British history and on political events rather than 'social, religious, cultural and aesthetic matters'.[34] She then involved herself in a personal response to proposals for Maths, English and History in the National Curriculum, an astonishing performance from a busy prime minister who had a Secretary of State in the post she had once occupied to do that very job. It was the act of an old-style headmistress, summoning to her study Ken Baker, the teacher who had not delivered what she wanted with the unruly yobs of the teaching profession during the last lesson on Friday.

Politicization and the GM 'Solution'

Thatcher argued that grant-maintained status could help a school 'escape from the clutches of some left-wing local authority keen to impose its own ideological priorities'.[35] Derbyshire was seen as one of these bête noire authorities. Official school letter-headings were over-printed with 'Derbyshire County Council Supports Nuclear-free Zones'. There was a curious policy on school uniform. The County Council allowed school governors to recommend a uniform for their school, but ruled that parents could exercise their right for their child not to wear it. In other words, 'uniform', which by definition is uniform, became optional, on the basis of a confused ideology of personal rights and freedom. There was a county appeal tribunal for parents who felt their children were being pressured into uniform, 'victimized' by teachers. Disciplinary action against such teachers could result if the tribunal found against them. The result was the immediate disappearance of uniform in some Derbyshire schools and in others the odd situation that some children were wearing uniform and others were not. From 1988 as an implementation of equal opportunities policy, application forms for Derbyshire jobs did not allow candidates to state their sex (sexism), age (ageism) or marital status (privacy), but shortly afterwards did ask candidates to declare whether they belonged to a Masonic Lodge. Derbyshire LEA began to axe its school sixth forms on the principle or dogma that tertiary colleges were better. When one comprehensive school, the Ecclesbourne School, secured an Adjournment Debate in the House of Commons on 31 March 1987, as part of a fight by parents, sixth formers and friends of the school to retain its sixth form of more than 300 students from an LEA bent on destroying it, the incident was a sign of how politicized education had become.

The Commons debate was called at the behest of the Conservative MP for West Derbyshire against the intended action of the Labour county council, themselves acting against the expressed wishes of the vast majority of parents and pupils at the school.

It was to break this apparent left-wing LEA tyranny that GM status was launched, but behind it was an equally ideologically-based right-wing intention, to weaken and destroy LEAs altogether. Schools could become grant-maintained, i.e. directly DFE funded and beyond LEA control. It was a logical development of LMS, local management of schools, a system which allowed schools direct control over a much higher proportion of their budget, previously managed by the LEA. GM school governors appointed staff including the head, agreed admissions policy (subject to the Secretary of State), and owned the school with its assets. FE colleges were removed from LEA control during this period. Religious Education was to remain the one subject that was still controlled at local level. The results of disempowering the LEAs rendered RE politically isolated and therefore vulnerable, but also protected it from centralized control in the same move. The danger would be that all the LEAs might be left to control after a process of attrition by central government would be school buses and RE.

The 1988 Act in Outline

The first twenty-five sections were devoted to the National Curriculum. There were three core subjects: English, Maths and Science. In schools in which Welsh was the main medium of instruction, Welsh became a fourth core subject. Then followed foundation subjects: Art, Music, History, Geography, Technology, modern foreign languages, Physical Education and (in schools in Wales in which Welsh was not the main medium of instruction) Welsh as a second language. Then followed a confusing requirement: first that Religious Education should continue to be compulsory, including in key stage 4; second, that together with the National Curriculum it would be known as the Basic Curriculum. This Basic Curriculum was not further defined.

Sections 26 to 32 concern open enrolment to county and voluntary schools. All schools were required to accept pupils up to their maximum capacity rather than to a target set by an LEA area plan. The intention was that good schools would expand and bad schools would close. The Roman Catholic bishops were one group who criticized this on the grounds that it might lead to 'sink' schools. The publishing of school league tables was intended to help parents to choose schools.

Sections 33 to 51 of the Act concern LMS, the local management of schools. LEAs were required to delegate various staff management responsibilities to schools and had to pass on funds to schools on a per capita basis. Discretion to plan regionally was severely limited. Moreover, as experienced teachers were higher on the pay scale, it became cheaper to employ inexperienced teachers on fixed-term contracts. The quest for higher standards was making some of the best teachers redundant or, when they retired or moved, irreplaceable. The power of the LEA to lay down a staffing establishment for each school was removed. By attaching formula funding to schools, they were brought into competition to attract students and therefore cash. Primary school class sizes rose in consequence as heads packed classes to avoid teacher redundancy.

Sections 52 to 104 created grant-maintained school status. These schools opted completely out of LEA control and into a direct financial relationship with the DES. Cash bonuses were awarded to such schools and many governing bodies and parents, not entirely convinced about the philosophy, still voted for the status in order to acquire buildings they had long been seeking unsuccessfully from their LEA. The power to opt-out rested entirely with parents by secret ballot. School staff had no vote. Schools that opted out took with them their proportion of the LEA budget, so every opt out weakened the LEA further. It put overall planning in LEAs and dioceses (voluntary aided schools could become GM) seriously at risk. It also made schools remaining in LEA control more independent. They could threaten to opt out if, for instance, closure of an unviable sixth form was threatened by an LEA trying to work within its budget. There was no mechanism for opted-out schools to opt back to LEA control, however many parents might wish to reverse the decision. It was not unambiguous parent power.

Section 105 introduced City Technology Colleges (CTCs). These aimed to involve business investment, to provide technological emphasis, to blur the distinction between state and independent school and to provide inner-city areas with centres of excellence, preferably at little cost to government. CTCs like independent schools are exempt from the National Curriculum but have to have regard for 'its principles'. But it was not an auspicious time after the erosion of the country's industrial base under the same government, to launch schools like this.

Sections 120 to 138 brought higher education under much tighter government control. Polytechnics and colleges of higher education were removed from LEA control. Higher education institutions would no longer receive formula funding but contracts to carry out teaching and research on a per capita basis. Academic tenure was ended amid furore and attempts in the House of Lords to dilute these clauses, but the real sea change was financial control. The much-vaunted and internationally admired independence of UK universities was seriously eroded, possibly ended.

There were other clauses: the Inner London Education Authority was abolished. The length of the school day was detailed. In total 366 new powers were added to the Secretary of State for Education. The low status job Butler had taken up as President of the Board of Education was distant history.

The Politics of 1988 Act Settlement for Religious Education

Different and conflicting strands of feeling about RE and its importance were present in the debate about the Act. The resulting legislation has to be seen as a compromise between these forces. Baker's political shadow opposites in the House of Commons in Education were Jack Straw (Labour) and Simon Hughes (Liberal Democrat). Hughes was an Anglican and a one-time member of General Synod. But there seems to have been no specific position taken on RE by the opposition parties as revealed either in *Hansard*, in correspondence with them in 1995 or in interviews with politicians. Baker felt that the opposition had no interest in RE, apart from some members who were Roman Catholics and had interest as individuals, and that opposition thinking had become unconsciously secularist in its assumptions that RE was of no particular importance, hence did not merit a specific policy. Nancy Seear (Liberal Democrat) stated that Liberal views on RE were left to the conscience of individuals; there was no collective view.

Labour members who supported the Swann Report had implicitly accepted the integrative role of good RE in community relations, but that was less than a clear policy. A 1989 Labour document on multicultural education continued to stress Britain as a plurality of cultures and traditions and the desire for a national curriculum 'free of cultural bias', but again this carried only an implicit view of RE. There was no Labour whole-party forum on education. This meant that anti-church schools views by pressure groups such as the Socialist Educational Association were not countered within Labour.

Although she had very clear views about the content of History in the National Curriculum, it seems that the prime minister had no specific view of RE, except that it mattered.[36] In this field at least, Baker had a free hand without prime ministerial guidance. But it does not seem to have been high on Baker's horizons at the start of the curriculum reform proposals. His memoirs relate simply a concern that certain aspects of the Butler settlement had fallen into disuse, notably 'in many schools' the provision of RE and daily worship. 'I strengthened the 1944 Act by making it a duty for Heads, governors and LEAs to provide religious education.'[37] But this duty was already laid upon them. In other words Baker was not concerned to reform RE provision, merely to enforce it. This may have had a very damaging long-term effect on the settlement for RE within a curriculum which was in every other way about to be radically reshaped. Before the bill was enacted Hull attacked this in a BJRE editorial:[38] all the government seemed to be offering RE was a law requiring people to obey earlier laws. But if the earlier laws are being disregarded, what confidence can we have that this requirement to observe them will produce any better results?

> For many years the subject has been a little uncomfortable in its isolation as the only required subject. Now religious education is to become even more uncomfortable in its isolation as the only required subject not really required.[39]

When the bill came into the Lords from the Commons in April 1988 the only direct reference to RE was in clause 6(1):

> It shall be the duty of the local education authority and the governing body to exercise their functions with a view to securing, and the duty of the head teacher to secure, . . . that section 25(2) of the 1944 Act [compulsory religious instruction] is complied with.

It was hardly a formula for radical change or one that showed recognition of the need to improve the position of RE within the new legislation. Prior to this, the RE Council was one of the delegations lobbying Baker on the issue. CEM Executive Minutes[40] contain a report of their visit. The DES 'had obviously expected a church-centred group concentrating on the old quarrels of 1944 and before, rather than a group interested in RE for its own sake.' Baker's advice to them was to liaise with the proposed National Curriculum Council. He then left to attend another meeting and Angela Rumbold as junior minister took over. When RE Council members pressed for better specialist provision for RE, civil servants present 'countered with assertions about the number of teachers with main qualifications in RE. It was clear that the government expects pressure groups to lobby for their subjects and press them on LEAs and governing bodies.' Neither of these was good news for RE: to be told that there was no real teacher shortage and to be told that unlike other subjects they would have to lobby at every level for effective provision. It was to lead to a satirical novel (Copley, 1991) which suggested that employed in the DES basement was a powerful civil servant dedicated to the obstruction or destruction of

RE. Certainly no-one could claim that the framers of the original bill had sought to strengthen RE.

The Lords' Debates

The real political controversy about RE burst when the bill reached the House of Lords, when a group of peers saw an opportunity to raise their concerns about children not receiving their entitlement to RE. The bill had already arrived with proposals for change in the RE provision from the Commons. Baker had expected some alterations. The churches had lobbied for compulsory Standing Advisory Councils for RE. The Lords group was to add another set of proposed amendments to the list. At this time the upper House had a regular attendance profile, i.e. peers who attended a third or more of sessions, composed as follows (Griffith and Ryle, 1989): 168 Conservatives, 88 Labour, 27 Liberal, 24 SDP, and 73 Independent. The different Christian views—and others—were well represented among these groups but it came as a surprise to many RE professionals to find their role being debated and defined by people largely outside RE and education altogether. On 2 February 1988 a warning came when Lord St John of Fawsley tabled a question about collective worship. He viewed the teaching of RE without collective worship like the teaching of astronomy without the stars. Baroness Hooper, replying for the government, re-stated government commitment to a daily act of worship, indicating that the whole area of religious education was 'of course' separate. Baroness Seear for the Opposition agreed emphatically on this point: worship and RE were quite different activities. The 'of course' was very significant.

The Second Reading of the Education Reform Bill was debated on the 18th and 19th April, 1988. After the customary prayers, read by the Lord Bishop of Salisbury, Baroness Hooper introduced the bill for the government, speaking for twenty-two minutes. Baroness David, opposing, made a twenty-six minute speech, concentrating on the short consultation period of only two months for the bill and the 366 new powers the Secretary of State was taking. She also attacked what she called the arrogance of Baker's claim to have produced a new religious settlement analogous to Butler's. She had a strong case, since at this point Butler's settlement had simply been re-proposed. The churches had already expressed deep concern that if RE were outside the proposed National Curriculum it would be marginalized. They would have much preferred RE to be part of the national curriculum, but with local determination in syllabus making, 'a national curriculum for RE, locally agreed' (Alves, interview). Baker stated[41] that the churches did not want RE to become part of the formal curriculum determined by a secular body, the National Curriculum Council and that he 'satisfied' them by making RE part of the Basic Curriculum of the school. While fair to the churches' wish to see local syllabus determination, this statement was not fair to their wish to see RE within the NC. They were not satisfied. The Lords' Committee stage commenced on 3rd May.

The Role of Graham Leonard

Central in the Lords' process was the Church of England spokesperson on education, Graham Leonard, Bishop of London. Previously he had been Bishop of Truro and before that Willesden. His role in education stemmed from his position as a senior bishop with a seat in the Lords. He was also chair of the Church of England Board of Education. In the 1950s he had been diocesan director of education for St Albans and General Secretary of the National Society. He established himself in these roles as energetic, clear-minded, diplomatic but also single-minded and unafraid of opposition. He had produced the church response to the 1959 government proposals on education that had led to increased funding for church-aided schools. In some situations he was seen as a combative Anglo-Catholic: his trenchant views on the invalidity of ministerial orders in the Free Churches, his firm opposition to the Anglican–Methodist unity proposals of 1964, his support for what many saw as a renegade Anglican community in Tulsa, USA, in the mid-eighties, and in opposing the ordination of women. It was the 'whole question of authority' (Carpenter, 1996) which was to lead him to join the Roman Catholic Church in the mid nineties. For many years he had entertained a great admiration for John Henry Newman. Leonard like Newman challenged the view that openness and questioning might be the appropriate attitude for a modern believer. These reduced the gospel, in his view, to a mere option people have in trying to make sense out of life and create the misapprehension that the gospel ought somehow to be modified to meet the needs of modern thought. Leonard endorsed Frederick Temple's view that the danger of individualism was that it led people to think that they could judge what the church should be. His Green Lecture at Westminster College, Missouri (1987) was significantly entitled 'The Tyranny of Subjectivism'. It was an attack on the view that principles and values are in essence no more than statements about the likes and dislikes, desires and aversions of those who hold them. If humankind is to survive, he argued, a sense of authority needs to be recovered. Even Feuerbach appreciated, unlike some modern liberals, that to believe in God demands obedience to him.

It was to fall to Leonard to calm and defuse pressure for the inclusion of the most overtly and aggressively Christian amendments to the bill in the Lords. While the bill was going through its various stages, the teacher associations were mounting a 'campaign for local education' to counter the centralist tendencies in the proposed legislation. Leonard, conservative as he was politically and religiously, supported this campaign. He believed in a counter- weight to central government control and that in education this should be the LEAs. If they were further weakened, he believed that the church would be the only opposition left. For this reason he was very committed to agreed syllabuses. Leonard also represented a wider Christian constituency. His formal parliamentary statements were drafted by Colin Alves, General Secretary of the General Synod Board of Education and General Secretary of the National Society. Alves was one of the Church of England's senior civil servants and well experienced in diplomacy and RE. He was assisted by Alan Brown, Schools' Officer (RE), himself an authority on the subject. Alves was an ex officio member of the British Council of Churches Education Committee. Alves and Brown attended the Churches' Joint Education Policy Committee. They were also in contact with Anglican diocesan directors of education and with the Archbishop of Canterbury's public relations officer. So the context within which Leonard's contribution was made was both wide and ecumenical. He also had some limited contact with other religions.

In his Second Reading speech Leonard asserted Anglican concern for education as a whole, not just RE. He affirmed the importance of the spiritual, expressing pleasure that the position of RE had been improved from beyond a mere mention in Clause 1 of the bill. He expressed approval of two named agreed syllabuses: Hampshire, by then in use in twenty-two LEAs, and the 1975 Birmingham Syllabus in its require- ment that all pupils should study Christianity. But he doubted the wisdom of legislating for RE teaching to be predominantly Christian. Within this debate it was entirely consistent with Anglican tradition running back to The Fourth R and earlier for Leonard, as education spokesperson for the established church, to argue that children should be entitled to hear the claims of faith without a monopoly by Christianity on syllabus content.

But the Lords process exposed a dangerous assumption by some that RE was still essentially a voluntary activity. Even Leonard asserted that the churches should supply good men and women as RE teachers and not expect the government to do their job for them. RE was still seen as an area in which good Christian women and men should offer themselves for service and the same reluctance shared by the 1944 Act for the state to take over entirely the responsibility for RE was present.

It was assumed that the basis for RE was the nation's broadly Christian base. This principle of voluntaryism was soon to apply to funding. The National Curriculum subjects would be flooded with government cash to launch their new schemes, while RE would be left to individual LEA initiatives and funding by agencies such as church college trusts, ironically with their own funding base founded on the demise of church colleges. The partial collapse of one Christian base in education —church colleges—was being used to finance what was seen by government as part of the remaining edifice. This was part of the wider issue about the relationship between religion and English and Welsh identity and the continuing debate about whether and in what sense the country was Christian.

The 'Tribe'

Leonard was faced on the one hand with government tokenism—despite Baker's statements about enforcing 1944 RE provision no-one was taking it very seriously—and on the other hand the 'Tribe'. The 'Tribe', a nickname used by Leonard both in Church House and in meetings with staff at the DES, and quoted by Baker in his memoirs[42] included Baronesses Blatch and Cox, and Lords Boyd-Carpenter, Buckmaster, Elton, Renton and Thorneycroft. Rodney Elton had been a history teacher who had taught some RE while on the staff of Loughborough Grammar School. He had also been a lecturer at Bishop Lonsdale College, Derby. The 'Tribe' were concerned to assert the Judaeo-Christian base of national culture and hence RE, which in their view needed Christianity written explicitly onto the face of the Act. They raised the public profile of the debate about RE but at the cost of diverting the Lords' debates into damage-limitation of their own strongly pro-Christian proposals from what might have flowed from the earlier amendments. In his attempts to broker an acceptable settlement Leonard met Peter Thorneycroft and others on 29 June 1988 and again on 4 July.

Another key member of the 'Tribe' was Baroness Caroline Cox. She appeared to be an indefatigable protagonist inside and outside the House of Lords for a vociferous right-wing Christian lobby. This does not entirely do justice to her stated position when interviewed in December 1995. She was a deputy speaker in the Lords and had been created a life peer in 1982. Her background lay in nursing, including time as a staff nurse and later as director of the Nursing Education Research Unit. Her own academic specialism was sociology, in which she not only had a First but was a published author and one-time Head of Department at the Polytechnic of North London. She was well known for her work with the Parental Alliance for Choice in Education and the Freedom Association, both right-wing pressure groups. The crisis in RE, as she saw it, was that children were not receiving their entitlement.

> I wanted them [children] to have a grounding in the main spiritual tradition of the land.

In her Second Reading speech she declared:

> Developments since the 1944 Act show how the spirit and the letter of the law have been grossly violated . . . Many pupils have no RE. And what passes for worship and RE is often a shallow dabbling in a multifaith pot-pourri, doing justice to no faith, and possibly destroying all faith; or a secularised message, sometimes amounting to little more than political indoctrination. What has happened under the present dispensation . . . is a betrayal of our spiritual heritage in many schools . . . Many people believe we should now rectify the omission of the 1944 Act which failed to specify the predominantly Christian or biblical nature of RE and worship . . . There must be an opportunity for all to learn about other major world religions . . . But we are still a predominantly Christian country and we need to ensure that our young people do not grow up ignorant of the faith of their forefathers or of the great Christian influence in the nation's spiritual heritage, culture and history . . .

Other speakers endorsed her theme. Baroness Blatch wanted to see Christianity as the core of RE and to have this written into the bill, but she did not wish to see RE as a national curriculum subject or to be subject to national tests. Lord Orr-Ewing accused the government and the churches of subverting the 1944 Act by encouraging multifaith RE. He cited the statistic that 85 per cent of the nation were said to be Christian, as sufficient grounds for mainly Christian RE. Lord Northbourne argued that no child can be given a real idea of the religious view of life by being taught comparative religion:

> Religion is about commitment . . . betting your life that there is a God. I cannot accept that religion can be adequately taught by an atheist or a teacher who has no religious commitment. Which of your Lordships would condone the teaching of swimming by someone who has never put a toe in the water?

Like Baker, the basic intention of these speakers was to apply the 1944 Act, not essentially alter it in regard to RE. Lord Elton raised the issue of morality, urging that 'right' and 'wrong' have meaning only within a system of morality and that in this country the system is based on the Christian religion and Christian literature. 'We must not, in our enthusiasm to protect the cultures of our minority societies, neglect the culture of our majority society.' He welcomed the promotion of RE from 'the bottom of the third division of subjects to its present position as a compulsory subject' ending by saying that he was anxious that the syllabus for RE should be principally Christian 'for the valid secular reasons that I have already given'. Lord Milverton wanted Christian teachers, but fully intellectually trained for the task:

> It would be of little comfort to be assured before having a tooth pulled out that the dentist, although unqualified, was a good Christian.

He supported compulsory assessment in RE on the grounds that not to assess RE formally like other subjects would soon be treated would relegate RE to nominal status after all. On the first day of the debate the House rose at 12.25 a.m., late by Lords standards. The bill was called again at 3.10 p.m. the following day.

Day Two of the Debate

Ex-Prime Minister Lord Callaghan stated that the reason the 1944 settlement lasted so long lay in the massive effort by Butler and Chuter Ede to ensure that all the issues had been dealt with before the bill came to the House. Ex-Prime Minister Lord Home, attacking the permissive society as 'not the happiest or most creditable period in our national story' argued that a heavy price was now being paid in its legacy. In pre-war Britain the mother, the minister and the school master gave children the Christian story and a Christian code of values. He supported the case for strengthening Christianity in the bill. The Earl of Stockton referred to his own 'far from distinguished' career at Eton but was grateful for the standards of 'Christian morality' he was taught there. Lord St John of Fawsley, former junior education minister under Margaret Thatcher and a leading Roman Catholic layman spoke in support of academic status for RE. He wanted to see testing introduced and teacher supply improved. He commended RE in these terms:

> It is to transmit the fundamental, moral and spiritual values on which our society is based, and the preservation of which constitutes the life of our society and the loss of which constitutes its death. These values include self-control, loving kindness, care of neighbours and moral responsibility, among others. Where do they come from? On what do

they ultimately rest? In this country the answer must surely be on religion in general and Christianity in particular . . . Therefore the case for teaching religion is not primarily theological; it is cultural, social and historical. The moral values in this country must be principally, although not exclusively, Christian, because that is the foundation on which our house is built and you cannot take it out of the foundations without the house falling down.

Few speakers differed. Lord Dormand of Easington urged that as we live in a pluralist democracy we need education managed and controlled according to pluralist democratic principles. 'Every clause in the bill negates that objective.' But he did not specifically mention RE. It was significant that the perspective on RE in the debate was almost entirely British, more often English. Christianity as a world faith, rather than an English one, and religions as world phenomena, were largely ignored except by Baroness Seear (Liberal Democrat).

Nancy Seear summed up for the opposition. She herself had been a personnel officer at Cyrus Clark Shoes (1936–46), originally a Quaker firm based at Street, Somerset. She became Reader in Personnel Management at the London School of Economics where she had worked from 1946 until her retirement in 1978. She had written various books about women at work. Welcoming the agreement between the government and the bishops on RE and speaking as an Anglican she hoped that the result would not simply be Christian education. One of the reasons for the importance of religion was its global expression. No subject is 'more explosive and more important'. 'Religion is not always a force for good, but it is undeniably a force.' RE needs to be tackled in a rigorous way, not marginalized. The fact that it will lie outside the National Curriculum ten subjects which will swallow time, does not encourage thoroughness. She noted that it was strange preparation for the future that, with the exception of Latin being replaced by Geography, the foundation subjects in the new National Curriculum for the twenty-first century were the same ones she had studied sixty years earlier.

Committee

The Committee stage embraced a crop of proposed amendments in which collective worship figured as prominently as RE. Two (Nos 2 and 11) linked RE to the concept of a 'basic curriculum'. Two (93 and 94) required local education authorities to establish SACREs. The Cox amendment (No. 28) required RE in all maintained schools to be 'predominantly Christian' with further provision being made 'for the religious education of children of other faiths, according to their own faiths'. In the light of the discussion about this, Leonard offered to introduce an amendment of his own to try to win more general acceptance and it was this undertaking which persuaded Cox not to press her own amendment to a vote. She withdrew it 'on the clear understanding that any subsequent amendment [from Leonard] must enshrine the spirit and substance of this amendment,' i.e. her own. When amendment 93 (compulsory SACREs) was moved, Thorneycroft attempted to introduce a further amendment (93A) which sought to ensure that a SACRE would be so composed 'that it will at all times contain a two-thirds majority of members representative of the Christian churches'. Leonard responded that this would impose unacceptable religious 'tests' upon SACRE members. Leonard undertook instead to explore further how a veto imposed by a particular college within a SACRE might be avoided. In the end Leonard presented a complex package of thirteen linked amendments. Baker later wrote that Leonard had the Prime Minister's support in this[43] as Thatcher felt that 'the Tribe' had gone too far in their demands for explicitly Christian RE and worship. During consultations in late May and early June it had been agreed to replace 'religious instruction' with 'religious education' but to add the phrase 'religious worship' to keep the new Act within the 1944 framework of religious education, which had embraced the classroom subject and school worship. When Lord Sefton moved his amendment (No. 8) calling for 'education which does not promote a particular religion or belief' he was defeated by 120 to 31.

Third Reading

Such was the need for rapid progress that the Third Reading debates took place on 7th and 8th July, 1988. Two hours into the Third Reading a fifty-minute debate on the more contentious provision for collective worship led to agreement without vote. During the time between the Report and the Third Reading, Leonard had brokered a solution to the vexed question of how far Christianity should be present explicitly in the bill either within the framework of RE or the requirement for collective worship. Recalling this, Lord Elton wrote to me:

> The passage of the bill through our House was rendered particularly interesting to me by the large numbers of meetings which took place between the stages, of people of differing views on it. They gradually achieved *something like a consensus* [my Italics] which was only complete when the then Chief Rabbi, Lord Jacobovitz, arrived

back from America minutes before the final debate on one of the issues.[44]

On the 8th of July the House sat after prayers read by the Lord Bishop of St Albans. The bill was called at 11.30 a.m. and, apart from a forty-minute adjournment for dinner, did not rise until 11.15 p.m. Much of the Third Reading in relation to RE was taken up with congratulations to the Bishop of London on his success. Baroness Cox commended him for gaining 'explicit recognition' that RE and worship should, in the main, be Christian, 'thus enshrining Christianity as the main spiritual tradition of this country and providing young people with opportunities to learn about Christianity . . . which have too often been denied in recent years. There is also *enshrined a respect* [my Italics] for the other major faiths and opportunities for those of other faith communities to teach and to worship according to those faiths if parents request that and teachers find it feasible.'

But this interpreted the wording in a particular way. It was less unambiguous than she perhaps imagined. Lord St John saw the ambiguity in Leonard's solution, noting that 'the amendments [by Leonard] are to a certain extent obscure . . . unless one is, as he is, an expert in exegesis. My noble friend Lady Cox expressed the hope that a DES circular would make everything crystal clear. Speaking as a former education Minister, I can say it will be the first time in history that has happened.' He went on to thank Baroness Cox, 'a heroine of this particular area'. Leonard was also commended by the Chief Rabbi, for 'enormous skill, ingenuity and persistence'. Jacobovits himself had argued against 'a cocktail of all the faiths' which would do none of them justice. But he too found the Leonard amendment perplexing and expressed the hope that 'by promoting respect and tolerance of other faiths as part of our national commitment, we may succeed together in restoring the fatherhood of God in all of us, through whom alone we can establish the brotherhood of man.' Alves took the view that Cox's interpretation of the result itself contained an inconsistency between her phrase 'teaching and worshipping according to those faiths', which implied a form of separate religious nurture for the different religions and 'opportunities to learn about Christianity and to experience Christian worship' which to Alves seemed to carry 'a clear educational purpose'.[45] Asked seven years after about the ambiguity in Leonard's solution, Baroness Seear wrily noted that where very strong and divergent views are held a 'fudge solution' [her phrase] is sometimes desirable and right.

Lord Campbell of Alloway withdrew his own proposed amendment on the understanding that the substance would go into a DES circular. It had stated that the governors of a maintained school shall use their best endeavours to ensure that RE, Christian or otherwise, shall promote respect, understanding and tolerance for those who adhere to other faiths and a spirit of social unity within the realm subject to the rule of law. It reflected a very British view of the place of religion. Insofar as RE as understood by professional religious educators was protected in the 1988 Act, it owed more to a liberal Anglican view of education and RE within it than to government or the DFE concern for the subject. The Church of England was still a potent lobby. The 'Tribe' had at least seen that RE needed strengthening. The RE professionals were, politically, less important.

The Final Provision for Religious Education

The Act confirmed unchanged certain elements of the 1944 settlement: there must be provision for all pupils; RE provided in county schools should be non-denominational (the Cowper Temple clause 126 years on) and taught according to an agreed syllabus; parental rights for withdrawing their children; the right of teachers to decline to participate in RE.

There were changes: the classroom subject was now legally referred to as Religious Education, no longer Religious Instruction; new agreed syllabuses from 29 September 1989 'must reflect the fact that religious traditions in this country are in the main Christian, whilst taking account of the teaching and practices of other principal religions; whilst RE in county schools must be non-denominational, it was made clear that teaching about denominational differences is permitted; the establishment of Standing Advisory Councils on Religious Education (SACREs) was now compulsory; SACREs could now require, not merely request, that their LEA should set up a conference to review the agreed syllabus; in a grant-maintained school the syllabus for RE should be that of the LEA the school was in before it became grant-maintained (GM schools were later given freedom to chose any agreed syllabus) unless it was formerly an aided school, in which case RE could be provided according to the trust deed, i.e. in a church GM school, denominational RE could continue; RE was placed outside the National Curriculum but within the Basic Curriculum, defined as the National Curriculum plus RE.

Immediate Reactions

There were mixed feelings about this provision at the time by RE professionals and faith communities. First there was relief and even pleasure that the Act had not been hijacked by the Christian right and turned into an attempt to Christianize the nation via the county school classroom. This would simply have led to mass parental withdrawal of children and undone decades of work in RE. Professionals were concerned to see RE as an integrative activity rather than an exclusive activity. There was also pleasure that at last the law recognized that the subject was part of a process of education, not instruction, rather late recognition of what *The Fourth R* had argued as distantly as 1970. Moreover while affirming the importance of the position of Christianity in the UK, the law required that the principal religions represented in the country should be taught, which was seen as an affirmation of the place of world religions within RE. But there was also considerable unease. Once again, RE had been assigned a unique and potentially inferior position, outside the National Curriculum, lacking NC high finance, high media profile, and a high status position in the forthcoming national tests, and without national attainment targets, centralized syllabuses, free literature to parents, and well-publicized inspections etc. RE was left to LEAs, a group that the same Act deliberately sought to undermine by allowing grant-maintained status and 'opting out'. The stated intention was that RE should have 'equal standing in relation to the core and other foundation subjects within a school's curriculum', but one cannot legislate intention. During all the training for the new curriculum with its new jargon including PoGs, ATs, SATs, EKSS and Year Group numbers (4th years in secondary schools became Year 10 etc, not a compulsory change, but one which was immediately widely adopted), the RE teacher would alone in the staff-room lack finance, training, change, and new status. These fears had been articulated very clearly, to the surprise of some in government circles, by the Roman Catholic bishops before the bill was enacted. They had strongly attacked proposals for grant-maintained status for schools and raised objections to the proposals for RE. These objections were that the Act plays down the importance of RE by failing to include it as a core or foundation subject, forcing it to compete with a number of optional subjects for very limited classroom time, and reducing its status, making it less attractive as a career for specialist teachers. They were blunt:

> Religious Education is not simply a body of knowledge co-terminous with Religious Studies, nor merely to be 'fitted in' after time and resources have been allotted to the ten Core and Foundation subjects . . . Rather it stamps the Catholic school in every aspect of its operations with its distinctive Catholic character.[46]

They also opposed the failure of the Act to represent RE on the National Curriculum Council and on the Schools' Examinations and Assessment Council. The early refusal of the National Curriculum Council in York to appoint an officer for RE alongside other subject staff confirmed fears that RE had been handed Cinderella status again, though this was redressed when Barbara Wintersgill, an RE advisory teacher from Essex LEA and experienced chief examiner who also written books for secondary RE, was brought into the York team. From then on the NCC gave advice about RE and after demands from the profession published a digest of annual SACRE reports, but could not by law give the direction to RE that it could provide for other subjects. The comments of the Roman Catholic bishops were indeed prophetic.

On the other hand, against the centralization of all the National Curriculum, RE alone as a subject retained a genuinely local, consultatively agreed syllabus, within the broad guidelines laid down in the Act. The first controversies after the Act concerned the teaching of English grammar and the amount of British history that should be taught in the new National Curriculum, not the content of RE.

Unnoticed at the time was the failure of the Act to grasp the nettle of the withdrawal clause. In a system of religious instruction the notion of a withdrawal clause is both obvious and protective within a free society. But although this existed for RI there were other areas in which parents lobbied for something similar: teaching of history by openly Marxist teachers, the 'celebration' of Hallowe'en, or even the use of computers. But in a system of religious education, which affirms the involvement of pupils and their right to question, discuss and reach their own conclusions, the retention of a withdrawal clause is an anomaly. Logic suggests that in such a situation it should apply to all subjects or none. However, the removal of this clause could easily have been portrayed as potentially a human rights or civil liberties issue, so the matter was never raised. Its unquestioned retention confirmed the legacy that there still was or might be something evangelistic or proselytizing about RE. One militantly atheistic parent withdrew his child from RE and collective worship (but could not from History when monasteries were being studied), openly admitting that he locked away any book at home which mentioned religion so that the child should not encounter it. In such a case, unusual as it was, the child needed protection from the withdrawal clause.

The limitation of the role of SACREs to advise was also an inherent weakness. Although three of the four SACRE committees using their votes could compel the fourth (LEA) committee into LEA revision of an agreed syllabus, SACREs could neither command cash, nor guarantee an advisory service for RE, nor in-service training, nor press for more specialists in school other than to request. In the immediate post-Act years many LEAs did increase their adviser and advisory teacher staffing for RE to help to implement the Act, especially as new agreed syllabuses were devised in its wake, but these gains were soon lost as the government siege of the LEAs via increased promotion of GM schools, led to gradually reducing financial support at LEA level. Many advisory teachers on fixed-term contracts, in other subjects as well as RE, were not renewed in post. They had two or three years.

Another result of RE remaining under local control, unlike other subjects, was the continuing vast duplication of effort in producing agreed syllabuses. One cannot examine large numbers of them without finding the different styles, formats, lengths and language confusing, masking as it does so many common aims and so much common content. A great many person-hours were duplicated. Of course, that allowed local input and involvement which was clearly beneficial in some syllabuses, but the existence of the RE Council was itself evidence that interfaith consultation and co-operation can work at national level. Welsh LEAs were advised to send their SACRE reports to the Curriculum Council for Wales to help in its monitoring of the whole curriculum process; English LEAs sent theirs to York to the National Curriculum Council. The NCC and later SCAA were at first unclear on how to use the new syllabuses they received. Analyses were later undertaken to see how far they conformed to the Act and subsequent Circulars.

While taking an overall cautiously optimistic view of the Act, Cairns (Cox and Cairns, 1989) saw it as leaving unresolved the issue of inability to define the nature and roots of our society. Citing an Independent Broadcasting Authority survey of 1986 she noted that 47 per cent of the population said that they would describe themselves as very or fairly religious, that 42 per cent said they were 'certain' that there was a God, while 65 per cent thought that religion was the proverbial 'good thing' because it provided a set of rules to live by. Yet only 9 per cent in the same survey went regularly to church. The inference Cairns made was that a strong element of religious belief in society does not wish to be involved with institutionalized religion, yet was sympathetic to religious teaching. Cairns noted that it was an interesting matter for speculation how these adults thought their children would acquire Christian or religious attitudes without encountering the doctrinal teaching that underpinned them and how they would have come upon their own beliefs and ideas if they had not been subjected to such teaching in the past. What was presented in the Act was in her view too narrow and seemed to reflect more the hopes of government that they might revive a Christian culture. This might actually impede the use of the Act as entitlement for pupils in a search for personal meaning, beliefs and values[47] She did not raise the equally valid question why, if religion in some form meant something to so high a proportion of the public, it did not receive a better deal in the 1988 Act. Perhaps despite the religious connections of so many leading politicians noted in the Introduction (p. 5) the legislators, like so many teachers, had become secularized to a far greater extent than they were aware and that it was in this vortex that views about reviving a Christian culture were heard, tamed and adopted.

If Cox and Cairns could be cautiously optimistic, the interim research report *A FARE Deal for RE* (FARE was an acronym for Forms of Assessment in Religious Education) was less cautiously pessimistic. It regretted that RE had been isolated outside the core and foundation curriculum and left to local rather than national debate. It noted that this was inconsistent with the attention paid to the subject in numerous government reports—Crowther, Newsom, Plowden and especially Swann—over the years. It publicized the 'strange decision by the DES' not to publish the Curriculum Matters Discussion Document, which had been ready since February 1987, revised five times by December 1989, and still unpublished. It deplored the failure to publish more recent HMI findings on RE. It pointed out that although government monies had supported national debate and development for all other subjects, none had been forthcoming for RE. Deprived of proper resources it had fallen onto individuals, LEAs and charitable trusts to attempt to press forward the work in RE in a dangerous repetition of the tradition of voluntarism. FARE itself had been funded by three Anglican college trusts, a fourth independent Christian trust and smaller subscriptions from the seven participating LEAs and the States of Guernsey. No other curriculum subject had been left to beg for cash to develop its assessment schemes and procedures.

However, at the time, whatever impact the Act made upon the teaching profession in regard to its provision for RE was overshadowed by the negative reaction to the provision for collective worship. The tightening of the daily observance clause, made less avoidable by new flexibility as to time of day and size of group (whole school assemblies for worship were no longer mandatory) was matched by a specifying of content, that taking a term as a whole collective worship should be mainly or wholly of a broadly Christian nature. Large secondary schools could no longer use their inability to assemble all the pupils in one hall at the same time as a reason for collective worship only once or twice weekly. Tutor group collective worship was now legally acceptable but personally unacceptable to many tutors. Head-teachers saw the potential divisiveness of these requirements in their staffrooms and among their pupil populations, especially in multiethnic schools. It seemed as if years of work to make school worship a community occasion had been challenged by attempts legally to enforce Christian observance on school children. Christian commentators were divided about the wisdom of this. The debate falls outside the scope of this study, but it is important to note that it diverted the attention of senior school staff from implementing the RE clauses of the Act in its immediate aftermath. Dealing with collective worship was perceived to be more controversial and certainly more urgent.

Hull[48] argued that the Act gives no support to a Christian supremacy in education but merely reflects curriculum development in RE over several decades. The principal religions represented in Great Britain are now required to be taught. Moreover, they are required to be taught throughout England and Wales even in communities in which they are not locally present. Hull was also angry about the political attacks on 'mishmash' and in the summer 1990 editorial of the BJRE[49] attacked what was being presented as the alternative: separation of religions, no mutuality, no mixing, no dialogue. Such a view was 'deeply Protestant',[50] 'a kind of Sunday School system', taking us nearer to Belfast and Beirut that to 'the life of love'.[51] The next step would be to have classes in each religion instructed by leaders of that religion. Historically religions have influenced each other. RE has a potential to integrate. The difficulty was that pressure for separation did not come merely from the Christian right but from some sections of British Islam. By 1994 there would be more than forty Muslim schools, pressing their case for the same rights enjoyed by Jewish and Christian schools of state funding.

But it was the ambiguity of the curriculum position occupied by RE, so damaging and yet so characteristic of the British attitude towards religion, which would preoccupy professionals in RE and politicians into the opening years of the nineties. Bates took the view that 'the notion of "Christian England" [which lay behind the Lords debates] . . . derives from nostalgia for England experienced by mainly elderly middle and upper class peers during the first half of this century'.[52] This analysis might explain some of the debate about collective worship, but in relation to RE it is too simplistic for three reasons: 'diffusive Christianity' as a presence and influence extended well beyond elderly middle- and upper-class peers; diffusive Christianity may have been less potent than institutional Christianity but it was more than mere nostalgia; also among the peers' concerns, albeit not articulated in the language of professional religious educators, was that the provision for RE should not be tokenistic.

Circular 3/89

The DFE Circular which some peers hoped would bring clarity to the situation for RE appeared in January 1989. It perpetuated the notion that the government had convinced itself of, that RE 'has equal standing in relation to the core and other foundation subjects within a school's curriculum'. This homely fiction could relate back in part to DES officials not visiting schools (see p. 130). It pointed out that RE is 'not subject to nationally prescribed attainment targets, programmes of study, and assessment arrangements'[53] but that locally-determined attainment targets, programmes of study and assessment arrangements were legal and binding if adopted by an agreed syllabus standing conference. Again it entered the realm of pious hopes when it stated that an agreed syllabus conference 'should assume that there will be a reasonable time available for the study of RE.' The specious basis for this assumption was not explored. As far as making clear the clause in the Act about the position of Christianity in RE the circular simply requoted it verbatim.[54]. A section on GCSE RE[55] noted that a GCSE syllabus could be adopted as the local agreed syllabus for key stage 4 pupils taking it, exempting them from the requirement for further study outside their examination option to meet the needs of the agreed syllabus. The same could be done for A or AS Level RE.[56] Outlining the complaints machinery[57] further optimism was expressed that 'the new arrangements will give parents and others a better opportunity to make representations locally if the law is not being met' but no clear guidance was given except to refer to Circular 1/89 'Local arrangements for the consideration of complaints'. In short, 3/89 did nothing to help RE. In defence of the Circular it has to be noted that Circulars are non-statutory and 3/89 could not itself provide strength for RE that the Act had failed to supply. If those who had spoken to defend RE in the Lords read 3/89 quickly they might have been content; if they had visited schools and seen what was happening in the implementation, many of them they would have been horrified at how far RE was still at risk when their good intentions to support it met the combined forces of the National Curriculum, national attainment targets, programmes of study and assessment, and the time and resource demands they swallowed up.

Chapter Six

RE after a New Act: 1990 to 1994

> Geographers speak of a rock deposited by the Ice Age perhaps hundreds of miles from its place of origin as an erratic boulder, and it often seems to me that that is how RE appears in the landscape of today's schools. What is it doing there—strange, alien, even threatening?
>
> Brenda Watson

The End of the Thatcher Premiership

The year 1990 began with Britain entering the Gulf War and ended with the resignation of Margaret Thatcher as Prime Minister after eleven and a half years in office. Thatcher's political demise was a blow to Labour. 'She had been an easy target with her poll tax and the savagery of her social policies'.[1] Under Thatcher had served as Education Secretaries Mark Carlisle (1979–81), Keith Joseph (1981–86), Kenneth Baker (1986–89) John MacGregor (1989–90) and finally Kenneth Clarke, who survived in post into John Major's premiership, serving from 1990- 92. With the exception of Keith Joseph, Margaret Thatcher found all these Secretaries wanting. Joseph was regarded as a co-founder of Thatcherism, 'my oldest political friend and ally, indeed mentor'.[2] Thatcher and Joseph shared many mutual enthusiasms about education including the use of vouchers as a means of parental choice of school.

Society and Religion

Religion was in the news when the Archbishop of Canterbury's envoy, Terry Waite, was released after 1,763 days in captivity in Lebanon (1991). If returns such as his excited comment, so did disappearances. The mysterious death at sea of media magnate Robert Maxwell brought to the surface allegations of corruption and mismanagement of monies.

The arrest of one of his sons was itself a media event, with a film crew conveniently outside the house. Crime itself could be said to have become an industry with an estimated UK turnover of £14 billion (Campbell, 1994) and the active full-time involvement of at least half a million people, including police, prison staff, judiciary and career criminals.

Archbishop George Carey succeeded Robert Runcie in 1991. Carey had grown up in Dagenham, attending a secondary modern school at Barking. He went on to attain the degrees of BD, MTh and PhD and to lecture in several Anglican theological colleges. Archbishop was still a position of some standing, with access to royalty, politicians and a prominent part in state occasions. He headed a church in which 28.5 per cent of English babies were still baptized, 66.1 per cent of religious marriages took place (34.3 per cent of all marriages in England and Wales) and Sunday attendances averaged about 1.2 million out of total church attendances of about 3.7 million.[3] His stipend was £43,500 (the national average income was then c.£16,000). Most suffragan bishops at the time were paid £19,410 and most Anglican clergy £12,800, with what were said to be housing benefits. In 1992 Carey withdrew his patronage for the Church's Mission to the Jews, opting instead for mutual recognition and dialogue. It was symbolic of a mood that was shared by many Christians, to live and let live in their approach to the members of other religions. In 1993 General Synod condemned the government's pit closure programme by 190 votes to 0, with two abstentions. Established church and government were no nearer consensus. By 1996 *The Times* front page banner headline could suggest that the Church of England was now the LibDems at prayer.[4] In 1993, figures released by the Church Commissioners, the body which handles the Church's finance and investment programmes, revealed that bad investments in property had taken almost a third off the Church's assets, which had shrunk from £3 billion to £2.2 billion since 1989. There was a £50 million shortfall between income and expenditure in the clergy salary and pension account. It was perhaps the economic finale of the idea of a national church with a real presence in every English settlement. In 1995 it could still claim 900,000 regular attenders at Sunday worship.[5] But they could not provide the upkeep for all their ancient buildings. The government had already made £11.5 million available for repair of cathedrals and comparable buildings over three years (1991). By 1996 some large churches were seeking money from the National Lottery. But the Church Urban Fund established in the wake of the *Faith in the City* report (1985) had raised more than £21.3 million, supporting 451 inner-city projects. *Faith in the Countryside* was published in 1990.

In Sheffield the Nine o' Clock Service started as a liturgical attempt from the evangelical and charismatic tradition to attract those not normally enticed into churches. It quickly acquired a growing congregation of more than two hundred and its leader, a former Christian rock group member, Chris Brain, was ordained to the Anglican non-stipendiary ministry hurriedly after a reduced training period. Using forms familiar to nightclub-goers—disco dancing, special lighting, projected images—the Planetary Mass attracted national and international ecclesiastical attention and was visited by international spirituality guru Matthew Fox who pronounced it good. But in 1995 Brain was accused of sexual impropriety with as many as forty women members of his congregation, causing his resignation and the collapse of the Service amid recriminations.

The ordination of women (1993) to full priesthood in the Church of England (but not until 1997 in the separate Anglican Church in Wales), led to different but equally publicized resignations, occasionally of Anglo-Catholic priests and their entire congregations, sometimes by individuals, including the former Bishop of London, Graham Leonard. Numerically Anglican losses to Rome were small, perhaps 100 clergy out of more than 9,000. Much publicized 'flying bishops' were appointed by the Church of England to have care of those across dioceses who objected to the ordination of women, but wished to remain in the Church. It was a uniquely Anglican compromise: you could in theory remain a loyal Anglican and oppose the ordination of women and equally remain a loyal Anglican and support it. Such compromise was not helpful to newly ordained women, who found jobs much harder to acquire than ordained status. Another less public split of Anglican opinion arose in connection with grant-maintained schools. Articles for and against continued to appear in *The Church Times*. The Major government added to the bribes or incentives to opt out, according to which view one took of them, the possibility for governors of an aided school to opt the school out without recourse to parental ballot. This was withdrawn as a result of church opposition. The churches were still a force in education: in 1992, 7,712,200 children were estimated to be attending some 26,956 church schools with a combined teaching force of 432,100.[6] The breakdown of school numbers then was as follows:

nursery 560
primary 18,926
secondary 3,867
special 1,352
independent 2,271

Estimating the influence of these church schools on those who attended them and on wider society is difficult. Bruce argues that in the Britain of the 1990s the decline of the churches is part of the modern lack of faith in institutions of any sort, including football clubs. Churches still retained the status of icons, in his view, visible symbols of history and tradition, albeit nostalgically viewed and certainly not sociologically meaningless.[7] Thompson[8] argues that symbols, including those originating in religious communities, seldom die out and that study of the sociology of religion need not lead inexorably to pessimism about its future. Hastings[9] set the apparent decline of Christianity within a context of centuries, rather than decades, and ended optimistically for Christians:

> Within English history there have been waves of religious enthusiasm, of attempts to convert and truly Christianize a rather nominally Christian England. We see such waves in the tenth century and the thirteenth, the seventeenth and the nineteenth. Hitherto, at least, ours has not been such an age. It is far more like the sixteenth century—one in which, after a period of close integration of the religious and the secular, an integration which left religion rather secularized and society with an over-heavy burden of dated religion weighing on its structures, society thrusts religious things away from its functioning to a quite considerable extent, thus in fact enabling religion itself to stand once more on its own ground, desecularized . . . Our age seems one of that sort . . . It is one of the secularization of society and the desecularization of religion, one more act in the ever continuing drama of a wrestling match between the two.

In Wales the decline of Christianity seemed to be not so steep. D.P. Davies (in Cole (1990)) suggested that although membership of Protestant churches had fallen (from 743,361 in 1905 to 393,500 in 1982) one in four of the adult population was still formally affiliated to a mainline Christian church. Even religious broadcasting had falling viewing and listening figures. The television 'God slot', Sunday from about 6.40 to 7.10 pm (on BBC and ITV simultaneously), was switched out of its protected time space after pressure from ITV programmers, who found it was attracting the wrong audience, often elderly and female, with little or no money to spend on the foreign holidays and expensive cars of the adverts. The emphasis changed from religious programmes to programmes about religion like *Everyman* or *Heart of the Matter*. A traditional programme like *Songs of Praise*, essentially an outside broadcast of a church service with cut-away shots and interviews interspersed, went from seven million viewers (1987) to five and a quarter million (1992). Radio 4 still found support for its

Thought for the Day, whose most popular contributor was Reform Rabbi Lionel Blue. The more explicitly religious *Prayer for the Day* was reserved for early risers, transmitting at 6.25 a.m. If people were turning away from institutional religion, it did not seem to be as a result of knowledge and understanding of what they were rejecting. A Gallup poll carried out in 1993 suggested that 49 per cent of sixteen- to twenty-four-year-olds did not know what Good Friday com- memorated and that 71 per cent did not know what happened on Palm Sunday. Had Loukes et al. laboured in vain?

The 1991 census included for the first time a question on ethnicity. It revealed that 5.5 per cent of the UK population was black and that nearly half of them lived in Greater London. 7.3 per cent of the population had been born outside the UK, the largest groups being those born in the Republic of Ireland (592,000) and those born in India (409,000). By 1996 the Commission for Racial Equality could cite about 23% of doctors, 10% of nurses, 15% of pharmacists, 16% of professors, and about two-thirds of London's small shops as staffed by people born overseas. The CRE reported signs of optimism as well as of continuing racism and employment disadvantage.

National pessimism was the mood in 1993, the year of the murder of toddler James Bulger. His abduction was shown on national TV in the search for the killers. When the killers were found to be children themselves, in primary school Year 5, an orgy of theorizing followed about their motive. Investigations by reporters included their experience of RE. The boys were in fact pupils at a Church of England primary school at Walton, Liverpool, but their own record of family problems, 'sagging' (truancy) and previous behavioural disorder meant that any school would have little chance to change them. The school ethos was one of tolerance to different races, religions and ways of life, of responsibility, of working co-operatively and being sensitive to others, treating them as you would wish to be treated yourself. The class teacher, experienced with special needs children, had offered them firm, structured support. But the inquiry into RE and school ethos was en passant a reminder that however RE professionals interpreted their work in the 1990s there were those outside education who still saw RE as part of the moral undergirding of the country, necessary to teach the Ten Commandments and the difference between right and wrong. The media did not ask whether the boys who committed the murder did know right from wrong. Yet during recorded police interviews Thompson was asked:

> I shouldn't really have to ask you this, but what do you think of those things? [the details of the abduction and murder]

The answer was

They're terrible. I was thinking about it, all the time.[10]

Andrew Brown in The *Independent*[11] saw in the murder not only evidence of something profoundly wrong in human nature—'we knew that already'—but also signs of something rotten in British society and that as a partial response church leaders were being listened to by politicians as they had not been for a very long time. The *Daily Telegraph* leader[12] chose to blame education:

> Will any of our educationists have the intellectual courage to open their minds to the possibility that they have been captives of a false doctrine . . . giving primacy to the child's anarchic desires? . . . Could the Church [of England] not put aside its obsession with sexual politics long enough to pronounce unambiguously on the dangers of the one-parent family? Or to take a stand against the mixture of moral relativism and social studies that passes for religious education in our schools?

The *Telegraph* did not question its own view, namely that if unambiguous authoritative pronouncements had been made, who would have listened? Or that the boys who committed the murder knew that they were doing wrong, but still did it. It seemed good enough instead to castigate the education system and commend the Commandments.

But whose morals and whose commandments? The 1991 census had confirmed the plural nature of religious life in the UK. The Muslim community alone could be reckoned at between 900,000 and 1.3 million, with countries of origin Pakistan (highest number), the Arab countries, East Africa, India, Bangladesh, Iran and Turkish Cyprus. It was one of the smallest contributor countries, Iran, which continued to dominate the media image of Islam and Shi'a images (only ten per cent of British Muslims) held sway over Sunni. The Hindu population (400,000) had similarly diverse origins (some from Gujarat via Kenya, Uganda, or Tanzania, others from Uttar Pradesh, Bengal and the southern Indian states). The Sikh population roughly equalled the Hindu but comprised the largest Sikh community outside the Punjab. UK Jains (20,000) originate from East Africa and India in the ratio 3 to 1. These groups were experiencing problems of culture collision with the increasingly secular host culture. Not all religions experienced collision. Nearly all Britain's Buddhists were ethnically English, Welsh, Scottish or Irish, and Buddhism has roots in the UK that date back to *c*.1900 and the work of Alan Bennett (Ananda Metteya). Judaism had been anglicized in Victorian times under Chief Rabbi Adler. Parsis had been coming to Britain for business or education for some two centuries.

A persistent campaign of law breaking by large stores opening on Sunday, coupled by a well-orchestrated chorus from members of the public filmed in these stores on Sundays, indignantly insisting that although the stores were already open on six days, often for eleven or twelve hours, they 'couldn't possibly manage without being able to shop on Sunday'. It was presented by the media not as profiteering but as a human rights issue, the freedom to shop when you want. The opposing Keep Sunday Special Campaign was doomed from the start. By a strange irony a Conservative government, traditionally the party supportive of church and state alliance, dealt the final blow to the protection of Sunday as an option for national religious observance. In doing so it removed one of the last traces of Victorian evangelical influence on English and Welsh national life. What the customers gained in freedom the shop-workers lost. But the latter were a minority.

Education

In February 1995 the Free Church Federal Council Education Committee issued a press release including the following:

> Ways must be found to increase respect for teachers, as a major step towards relieving the pressures they face in today's society . . . The main reasons [for teachers being at breaking point] were an increased workload through the need for more administration, assessment, the demands of a new curriculum, OFSTED inspections, budget cuts, and poor pupil behaviour and violence.[13]

The immediate post-war image of teaching as a comfortable, if not well paid, rather pleasant job for life, was dead. Compared to the relative pay, status and image of teachers in some other cultures, Britain could qualify as a real contender for bottom place.

> The market looms large as a god-like dominating force. Morality has become more a question of individual beliefs (even taste) than consensus or community norms . . . [Tories prefer] to look back and seek inspiration from traditional culture, but since 1979 the culture of Conservatism has itself changed.[14]

The Thatcher era had kept education constantly in the news and hastened the process of politicization. Education Secretary became a high-profile job attracting media attention. A Secretary like John MacGregor survived in post for a mere seventeen months (1989–90).

He was seen by many education professionals as a consensus seeker who might repair some of the damage they believed had been inflicted on the system. Perhaps for that very reason he could not remain there. He had the reputation of a good listener. But the media fastened on his conjuring expertise and his membership from 1989 of the Magic Circle, making wry comparisons with his work in politics.

He was replaced by the more combative Kenneth Clarke, described by Thatcher herself as an energetic and persuasive bruiser. He shared the Tory orthodoxy that officials at the DFE were obstructing his reforms. Within six weeks of being in post he had introduced a system of teacher appraisal for the 440,000 teachers in England and Wales. Clarke's main achievements were to make mandatory the growing practice of providing school-leavers with a record of achievement for potential employers, and the introduction of school league tables based on examination results. He introduced more flexibility into the National Curriculum in key stage 4: the core subjects would be taken at GCSE by all pupils; all would take Technology and a modern language, but not necessarily to GCSE level; they would choose History or Geography or a mixture of the two; Art and Music were to be completely optional; all would do PE (not necessarily as a GCSE subject).

Clarke also continued the Conservative attack on LEAs. In *On the Record* on BBC TV[15] he declared that

> until we started on the reforms . . . if you wanted a window repaired, you had to ring up County Hall to get them to do it. Some councils employed more people in the head office than they employed in all their classrooms put together . . .

But he did not name any. All colleges for 16+ age students were removed from LEA control. In 1991 Clarke issued a press release, without telling the GCSE boards, that in that same summer's examination papers examiners would have to deduct up to five per cent of marks for errors in spelling. It was an astonishing direct intervention and a cameo of what the Conservative style of managing education had become—dictatorial and non-consultative. Next in line were Her Majesty's Inspectors[16] who were replaced by the Office for Standards in Education, OFSTED. Privatized inspection teams now made bids for inspection contracts in schools. In *The Times*[17] Clarke condemned previous operation of schools as 'a closed shop that can only be entered by those already inside'.

In 1991 the services of the chairmen of the National Curriculum Council (NCC) and of the School Examinations and Assessment

Council (SEAC), Duncan Graham and Philip Halsey, were dispensed with. They were clearly offering unsuitable advice. Non-experts David Pascall and Brian Griffiths (Lord Griffiths of Fforestfach) replaced them. They had served in Thatcher's Policy Unit—Griffiths as its head—for years. Graham wrote in The Observer:[18]

> In the early days, Secretaries of State were careful not to meddle with syllabus content, or to tell teachers how to teach. Kenneth Baker . . . was well aware of the dangers of political interference . . . It was not Parliament or the National Curriculum Council which decreed that history should stop in 1962, but a Secretary of State who apparently feared that up-to-date stuff was dangerous for pupils and teachers alike . . . When Kenneth Clarke began to tell primary teachers how to teach, preferring his own gut prejudice to the evidence, the warning signs were clear.

There was evidence (Gipps, 1993) of the misinformation, whether deliberate or not, by government to make propaganda points. Gipps cites Clarke's revelation to The Mail on Sunday,[19] rapidly taken up by the wider media, that a quarter of seven-year-olds sitting the SATs for the first time had been unable to recognize three letters of the alphabet. In fact the figure for this group was less than 2.5 per cent and the figure of 28 per cent applied to those not having reached Level Two in reading. Clarke implied they had not even reached Level One. The Chairman of the BBC eventually apologized for broadcasting this untruth to the nation, but insisted it was too late to offer a televised correction. The public received a very clear impression that primary teachers were not doing their job properly. Clarke moved to the Home Office after Major's surprise victory in the 1992 general election. Major told the Conservative Party Conference (1992):

> When it comes to education, my critics say I'm 'old fashioned'. Old fashioned? Reading and writing? Spelling and sums? Great literature —and standard English grammar? . . . Tests and tables? British history? A proper grounding in science? Discipline and self-respect? . . . Well, if I'm old fashioned, so be it. So are the vast majority of Britain's parents. And I have this message for the progressives who are trying to change the exams. English examinations should be about literature, not soap opera . . . Yes, it will mean another colossal row with the educational establishment. I look forward to that. It's a row worth having . . .[20]

It was a remarkably combative statement, coming as it did from one who had slid into the grammar school C stream as a boy because of private reaction to financial stress and serious health problems in his family, and who might have wanted education to emphasize a more pastoral aspect. But the election showed a slight shift, in that only sixty per cent of Conservative MPs returned to Westminster had been to public school as children, a decline on the post-war average of seventy-five. Major's first appointment to the restyled DES (now Department for Education, DFE) was John Patten. Patten had been a don in geography, with a PhD and publications in the field. He tried to appease the Tory right wing, as his attack on examination boards at the Party Conference demonstrates. A summer of better results than ever was criticized as a lowering of standards, the same comment that would have no doubt been applied to a summer of worse results. The idea that better teaching might produce better results was not considered. Patten believed that he knew the simple answers to complex educational questions. Teachers did not agree. Their boycotts of government tests in key stage 3 English in the summer of 1993 spread to other tests. Fourteen attainment targets in mathematics and seventeen in science were viewed as unworkable, especially by GCSE examination boards. Teachers complained about the requirements of testing at key stage 1 and demanded the abolition of testing of seven-year-olds. They were given simplified tests instead.

Major continued to attack the control of teacher training by higher education institutions with the introduction of the Teacher Training Agency (TTA) in 1994. This controlled the number of places per institution, cash per student and course content to the detail of hours per subject (1996). Courses were open to scrutiny by inspectors. The TTA licensed institutions to run teacher training courses and could de-license them. A college dependent on its teacher training licence could close as a result. La Sainte Union College at Southampton was delicensed in 1997. There was a deep dislike by government for HE power in teacher training and a determination to break it. Schools themselves came under continuing review with the introduction of a four-year-cycle of inspection, using independent inspectors and contracts for tender. There was a published national framework for inspection and parents were to receive a summary of the report on their child's school. The Labour landslide victory and Liberal Democrat revival in the general election of 1997 were to remove some of the memories from the minds of education professionals of how deeply politicized education had become under the Conservatives—but in 1994 this could not be foreseen. At the time increasing political dictation of educational agendas and further 'reform' of the education system, like the proposal to open grammar schools in every town, seemed inevitable.

The Post-ERA World and RE

Religious educators continued to try to consolidate the situation after the Act. A survey of RE inspection reports in forty-four schools between 1989 and 1991 revealed what seemed to be the perennial problems besetting the subject: lack of curriculum time and resources. Orchard wrote 'It is the status of the subject which is at the heart of the problem.' In that single sentence he exposed the major failure of the 1988 Act in relation to RE. Slee[21] reflected on the 1988 Act and RE. She interpreted the debate as rooted in conflict between the confessional and phenomenological views of RE and asked: why had the parliamentary and public mind been so resistant to phenomenology? She concluded that although ignorance was a factor there were also weaknesses in the phenomenological approach: it was devised with adult students in universities in mind; it assumed, arrogantly, a consumerist view—that religions can be packaged and selected by the enquiring mind; that it is relativist in relation to truth claims; that it erases the questions about truth and commitment that pupils themselves want to raise. She proposed a rapprochement between the confessional and the phenomenological approaches to RE, citing as an example the title of the 1982 Berkshire agreed syllabus, Religious Heritage and Personal Quest.

Westhill, Birmingham

RE curriculum continued to advance. The Westhill Project for teaching RE in the five to sixteen age range produced a second edition of its teachers' handbook to take the Act into account. Their principles were:

1 Children need to develop their own beliefs and values and a consistent pattern of behaviour.
2 RE has a particularly important contribution to make to spiritual, moral and social development of children.
3 In RE, the role of the teacher is that of educator.
4 As in all other subject areas, the teaching of RE must be related to the ages and abilities of the children being taught.
5 RE will help children to explore a range of religious beliefs and practices and related human experiences.
6 RE has a major contribution to make in helping children to develop a positive and understanding attitude towards diversity in our pluralistic society.
7 RE does not make assumptions about, or preconditions for, the personal commitments of teachers or children.

The Westhill Project saw the main areas of RE content to be traditional belief systems, shared human experience and individual patterns of belief. Religions should be explored through their community life, family life, personal life and public life, leading to an understanding of underlying features—beliefs, spirituality, values and ultimate questions. The presentation of religions should aim to be objective, balanced and from several perspectives. It should consider the local and the global manifestation of the religion, the popular and the intellectual version of it, traditional and radical, and majority and minority views within it. Concept development would be an important teaching medium and suggested lists were provided for six religions. For Sikhism, for example, the key concepts suggested were Anand, Gurmukh, Guru, Hauma, Jivan Mukt, Khalsa, Sadhana, Sat Nam, Seva and Sikh. But Westhill urged that RE should emphasize attitudes as well: a sense of mystery and fascination about the world, willingness to acknowledge the controversial and ambiguous nature of many issues about beliefs and values and willingness to value diversity in religion and culture. There were also skills: using periods of stillness and silence for reflection, using technical religious language appropriately, using empathy to understand why other people believe and behave as they do. Significantly post- ERA, assessment, recording and reporting in RE were considered in some detail.

Infant and Nursery RE Advance

If Westhill College was making a clear statement of purpose for RE in the 1990s, the University of Birmingham was making a contribution potentially highly significant for primary RE at classroom level, for in 1990 *A Gift to the Child* appeared, a teaching pack with audio tapes, picture books and a 136-page book for the teacher, developed by a project team who had worked for more than two years with very young, i.e. nursery–infant children in West Midlands schools. After Goldman, in many primary schools an invisible dead hand had fallen across RE. Teachers had been made so wary of the dangers of bad teaching and so cautious about launching abstract ideas at too early a stage of child development that in many infant departments RE had all but disappeared. It was said by some infant teachers to be everywhere in the curriculum. Others confused it with either spiritual development or Personal and Social Education. It was specious to claim an omnipresence for RE within the total curriculum which would not have been accorded to other subjects, except perhaps English or, in Welsh-medium schools, Welsh. Infant teachers who claimed to do RE in topics such as Caring and Sharing, and People Who Help Us, were certainly confusing it with the Personal and Social Education. The thrust of the Birmingham work was to demonstrate that explicit RE on a multi-religious basis could be undertaken successfully with very small children by teachers who were not necessarily RE specialists. Their chosen seven topics were: Our Lady of Lourdes; Ganesha; Nanak's song; the Call to Prayer; Angels; Jonah and Hallelujah. The method was to take children through stages in relation to the topic: engagement; discovery; contextualisation and reflection. Children were encouraged to enter the topic for themselves to learn part of its meaning, but to stop at the point of respect for and empathy with the person or action, by means of distancing devices such as 'This is what Aideen does' rather than 'We ought to . . .'. Another means of distancing was for them to watch but not join in a religious ritual.

The prime teaching method was story. Thus for Our Lady of Lourdes the key vocabulary was defined as vision, devotion and pilgrimage. The engagement situation was children feeling and exploring a rosary in a mystery bag. The entering device was a lighted candle. Then the children are told the story of Bernadette and the Beautiful Lady. The distancing device is *Aideen's Book* (it is her story of devotion, not necessarily 'ours'). The children then learn about praying the rosary and Aideen's homecoming from Lourdes. The reflection situation is a discussion of who or what comforts you? What sort of person would you like to be with when you feel lonely or unhappy? The seven topics were intended to present a method and not to limit teaching to this specific content alone; indeed they lacked theological coherence as a group. But many first and infant schools that adopted the approach found it had transformed their RE.

'New Methods' in RE

Aware that some secondary RE was in danger of becoming too factual—an arid exercise appearing to emphasize vocabulary competence in different faiths (e.g. adhan, minbar, muezzin, minaret), caustically nicknamed by some commentators 'multi-faith, multi-fact', a new direction in RE was being explored by David Hay, John Hammond and others. Hay had conducted prior research on the religious experience of humans (1982, 1990). Like Alister Hardy, who had been interested in the idea of a 'biology of the spirit', Hay was a zoologist by academic background. He examined data which suggested that religious experience was more widespread than one might assume and much less destructible than a merely rational explanation could account for. He was influenced by the work of Unitarian Estlin Carpenter, who in Victorian times took the view that religious experience is a permanent element in the life of the human species. Hay saw religious experience as a natural, though not a universal, experience, avoided as a topic of conversation in modern society. Hardy referred to it as 'hidden religion'. Hay noted that biologically we are subjected to a nearly infinite number of stimuli from our environment and that psychologists must be right in predicating that there is some sort of filtering mechanism which selects the incoming messages that matter to us. Religious awareness might be a potential within this, which either is or is not attended to by the subject. Thus all might have a religious experience, but not all will.

> Yet even in a period when the tattered remains of an ancient interpretative system are all that is left to most people, it is clear that religious experience still appears with extraordinary frequency.[22]

'People who become religiously aware seem to *experience directly* [his Italics] their solidarity with their fellow human beings and their responsibility towards them . . . Life gains meaning. These would appear to be advantages of our biological heritage not to be lightly ignored.'[23] Hay examined religious experience against age, occupation, geographical distribution and experience of religious institutions. The British mainland area with the highest incidence of religious experience was found to be Wales (46 per cent). He linked this with Wales having the highest incidence of church-going. His research found the following percentages of people interpreting their experiences religiously:

> Awareness of the presence of God 80%
> Awareness of receiving help in answer to prayer 79%
> Awareness of a sacred presence in nature 61%
> Experiencing that all things are One 55%
> Awareness of an evil presence 38%
> Awareness of the presence of someone who has died 35%
> Patterning of events 32%[24]

The 'New Methods' team sought to compensate factual teaching by a move to what they viewed as a revival of the Platonic method,[25] to help children to explore what they already 'potentially know' about religion. They sought to re-establish common ground linking RE with spirituality. They held that people identified 'religion' too readily with external things like buildings, religious professionals and with public rituals such as weddings and funerals, that religion was often seen as cold and unattractive whilst spirituality is perceived more positively as personal, involving prayer, meditation and love. Hay thought that this attitude might stem from the post-Enlightenment Western ambivalence towards religion as a result of which, under rationalist influence, Europeans have been uncertain whether religion is the cure for disease of the spirit or is itself the disease. School RE was concentrating too much on the public phenomena of religion at the expense of the realm of personal experience, 'but it is the personal experience, *the inner intention* [their Italics], that matters to the religious believer, and *without some grasp of that intention, students will have no understanding of religion* [my Italics]. They will be rather like Victorian anthropologists, perhaps observing with real curiosity the habits, beliefs and artefacts of strange tribes, but separated by an experiential apartheid from genuine understanding.'[26] When RE is properly understood, they argued, it becomes clear that it is the reverse of indoctrination. It demonstrates that there is more than one perspective on reality. It enlarges, rather than diminishes, freedom. But the 'New Methods' team were aware that there were problems for RE: taking seriously any interpretation of reality which differs from the prevalent secularism; viewing as important different areas of experience from those often viewed as important; understanding religious language; and cultural distance from some of the religions studied. In the light of this their proposals for the RE agenda were:

> to help pupils to learn to be aware of and to take seriously their own inner experience and their potential to be aware, hence learning to respect the inner experience of other people; to take seriously the role of metaphor in focusing and interpreting our experience of life, thus (without being confessional) to become aware of the power of language and intention to structure human experience;[27]
>
> The implication of what we are saying is that if religious education is to do its job it cannot be conducted at arm's length.[28]

They found common ground with Personal and Social Education where, 'even though the model of the person . . . seems to be drawn implicitly from a secular perspective, it does respect the inward functions of the mind'[29] At the same time the team were emphatic that RE (and PSE) should not be used as a form of exerting social or political control. 'It was just such an attempt which corrupted and discredited religion for large sections of the population in nineteenth century Europe.'[30] They identified two approaches to RE which were in their view severely limited. The confessional approach had the merit that it took belief and commitment seriously, recognizing that belief can affect lifestyle and decision-making, but at the massive weakness of reducing reality to the faith perspective of the teacher and dismissing the experience of other faiths and their deeply held convictions. The other approach, the world religions school, is aware of many perspectives and tries not to distort what believers say and do, but pays a heavy price in that it neglects experience, offering no insight into the fascination of a faith that 'inspired the energy of its saints or the endurance of its martyrs'.[31] Netto, writing Chapter 18, noted the tendency in the UK to regard 'religion' as distinct from the 'secular', a distinction which did not apply globally. He felt that the model offered by Hay et al. broke through this imposed dichotomy.

The 'new methods' team provided practical examples of their approach. Changed classroom layout to facilitate group work, scene-setting by stilling exercises, leading pupils into an experience that is theirs rather than the teacher's and drawing out the learning by helping them to reflect on the event: these are at the core of the process. The teacher is essentially an enabler. Warm-up exercises are followed by awareness raising exercises, creative listening, breathing exercises and guided fantasy as a story-telling method. Guided imaging is related to the tradition of the Tibetan Book of the Dead and to Tony de Mello, who in turn relates to Ignatian techniques.[32] Detailed specific examples for classroom use are provided 'My Computer Mind', 'Waves', 'If I was a . . .', 'Life is like . . .', 'My Badge'. A grid offers links to a multifaith syllabus in a secondary school.[33] Application of these methods in implementing a concept-based agreed syllabus at Durham is described.[34]

Reaction to the 'New Methods' among RE teachers varied and it was hard not to take sides. For some these new methods were themselves a sort of conversion experience which transformed their whole teaching and their pupils' response, and from which there was no going back. It seemed to reunite RE with an educationally defensible spiritual base. At the other extreme came a more cynical reaction, hostile to such radical changes in teaching method and content as a rag-bag of New-Age-type trends applied to RE. More considered criticism came from Adrian Thatcher[35] who viewed it as oblivious to the work of Ryle, Wittgenstein, Heidegger, Rorty, Foucault and Derrida. It was 'the rise of the self', de-emphasizing the material, created order, making truth relative. Other commentators welcomed the experiment, and valued some of the skills as a vehicle for teaching RE content, but saw much of the recommended content-free or content-reduced approach as indistinguishable from Personal and Social Education. They raised a valid question: how far do the 'new methods' constitute *religious* education?

But the 'New Methods' team had captured a mood, which was also reflected in Webster (1989). He had been concerned that many of those trying to teach RE were finding that 'its meanings escape unfledged'.[36] He wanted pupils and teachers to be able to discover mystery without compromising integrity and suggested a study of religious poetry as one route in. 'It endlessly penetrates the experience of men and women to reveal to them their grounding in Mystery.'[37] Poetry always finds the hole in reason's ceiling and poets have the gift of making their readers poets too, nurturing creativity in a search for meaning, an openness to life, a union with the world, leading to self-actualization and self-transcendence. Webster concluded that 'a religious education which is sensitive to struggle, as old frameworks of meaning collapse, which allows an appreciation of believing thought, and which looks for ways of articulating what lies anterior to analytic thinking is a help in the journey to self- transcendence'.[38] The true realm of RE is emotional understanding and imaginative sensibility. This attempt at recovery of the imagination for education was developed in Starkings (1993). Brenda Wall[39] put it tersely, writing that she wanted children in RE to gaze rather than to gawp.

The Warwick RE Project

Changing paradigms about the nature of religion itself were reflected in the Warwick RE Project (1994). The Warwick group were concerned about the problems of locking young people into stereotypical religious and cultural identities. They argued that the current concepts of religions and religion were modern, post-Enlightenment constructions. They pointed to the role of the colonial power in defining 'other' in terms of the 'other' cultures and religions. They did not accept that religions are characterized by certain universal essences and held that the reference point should be the 'tradition', although it is conceived and delimited in different ways by different insiders and outsiders. Despite caution about use of the terms religion and religions they did not abandon them entirely. The project team included a theoretician (Jackson), ethnographers, curriculum developers and photographers. Children and adults who had been studied in the field were encouraged to comment on or contribute to draft curriculum materials. The disciplines drawn on included religious studies, cultural studies, anthropology and social psychology, and the intention was to present religions and culture as changing and evolving, trying to avoid imposing outside divisions on the traditions, such as dividing them into themes, and avoiding terms like the numinous or the spiritual, which might have different cultural connotations. They tried to present religious ways of life in the insiders' terms as far as possible. The first crop of classroom materials was aimed at infants and based on ethnographic studies of two Christian girls, a Jewish boy, a Muslim girl and a Buddhist boy.

Thus the nineties opened with a blossoming of new approaches and rethinking at the level of professional religious educators. Most of these advances were made as a result of funded project research in higher education institutions, working with classroom teachers to test and trial materials derived from new ways of looking at the nature of RE. It is striking that the stimulus for this did not come from the Education Reform Act and its provision for RE. Most of the new approaches either do not refer to the Act in detail, or refer only to applaud its sanctioning of teaching in schools the principal religions represented in the UK. It is possible to imagine that all these new developments could have arisen quite easily without the Act.

Agreed Syllabuses Post-1988

Early Day Motion No. 225 'RE in Maintained Schools'[40] called for the restriction of religions studied in school to two or at the most three, because of available timetable time. It was not debated in Parliament. The will for further political change was absent. Post-Education Reform Act consolidation and change in RE were more clearly evident in the crop of new syllabuses required to demonstrate conformity to the new legislation. Devon (1992) published a new syllabus in a format within an A4 ring-bound folder and logo resembling in size and appearance the folders produced in National Curriculum subjects. It was done deliberately and with NCC permission so that the RE syllabus could stand in the school staffroom beside the other subjects and be treated —it was hoped—with the same parity and status accorded to them. Not many new syllabuses seized the opportunity to be physically like other subjects. But change in new syllabuses was more than cosmetic. Devon identified RE targets:

1 Reflection on meaning
2 Knowledge and understanding of religion

Within these, six concept clusters were identified as key elements for teaching RE. These were awareness of mystery; questions of meaning; values and commitments (all related to Target 1); religious belief and teaching; religious practice and religious language and expression (related to Target 2). Each was further subdivided. Dorset (1992) asserted that RE should be concerned with religious belief, practice and expression, with students exploring, evaluating and reflecting on religious and life experiences. It identified key skills for RE: reflection, empathy, communication, analysis and evaluation. It identified key attitudes: respect, open-mindedness, self-esteem, sensitivity, critical awareness, appreciation and wonder. It introduced attainment targets:

AT1 Understanding and evaluating values, commitments and questions of meaning.
AT2 Knowledge, understanding and evaluation of religious belief and practice.

Bradford (1992) included in its targets: awareness and appreciation of life experiences and the questions they raise; appreciation of religious faith and the varieties of faith; knowledge and understanding of the practical and social consequences of religious faith; responding to life experiences and religion. They wished to emphasize 'the facts of religious and cultural diversity'. Buddhism (not one of Bradford's major religions) and Humanism could be included in RE, they argued. 'It is a question of balance.' To some outsiders these new syllabuses with their National Curriculum terminology might have looked jargon-packed. But unless they had used the language of the new National Curriculum, agreed-syllabus framers would have consigned RE to amateur status in the new post ERA world. Syllabus innovation was happening in the church (voluntary aided) school sector as well. Manchester Anglican diocese produced a new syllabus for its VA schools (1994) with aims from the [Church] Board of Education:

offering pupils a firm grounding in the principles and practices of Christianity and opportunity to explore the other faiths represented in Britain today.[41]

The recommended time allocation was that in most church schools 'about 66%' of the RE time should be spent on Christianity but that in schools with significant numbers of pupils from faith backgrounds other than Christianity it may be better to spend 'only 50%' of time on Christianity. More significantly 'it is not possible to pay proper attention to a World Faiths component in less than 25% of the time available to RE'.[42] 'RE is not a branch of sociology or cultural anthropology. This syllabus requires teaching of non-Christian faiths in a way that takes seriously both their basic religious premise and each faith's own understanding of itself.'[43] Units on five religions were offered for key stage 1 and 2 and a sixth religion, Buddhism, was added in key stage 3 and 4. The recommended method was separate religion teaching, with Christianity and two others at primary level, but thematic teaching was demonstrated as an option.

David Pascall, NCC Chairperson, attacked what he presumed were unquestioned assumptions in society:

> Who said that religion was dead—or that religious education has no part to play in a secular society? And where is this secular society anyway? We may not be a nation of churchgoers any more, but it would appear that our propensity to seek answers to profound theological questions is as alive as it ever was.[44]

While emphasizing that RE syllabuses could not be determined by the NCC he went on to indicate that RE was perhaps the only subject within the curriculum to dwell in depth on questions about the nature and origin of spiritual experiences and to ask what they might mean, with a role in moral development and helping children to understand the different religions present in British society. Pascall's view was echoed by one of his successors, Nicholas Tait (1995):

> A large part of what education is or ought to be is the transmission from one generation to another of what previous generations have thought and felt and believed. [Cp p. 1] This enables future generations to position themselves in relation to what has gone before, rejecting elements of the past if that is their wish but shaped nonetheless by a knowledge and understanding of the societies which preceded them. Anything less is supreme arrogance—as if each generation could create itself anew without reference to the past . . . It is therefore a disturbingly narrow secularist view of the world that leads some people in our educational system to regard the dispassionate study of religion . . . as something peripheral to the main purposes of schooling.

The 1988 Act had, however, left RE on the periphery.

Inspection Findings

OFSTED published a review of inspection findings for RE 1993/4. Its findings were that primary school RE was still very uneven, with standards unsatisfactory 'in many schools'.[45] In the majority of primary schools the work was only loosely related to the agreed syllabus. Standards in secondary school RE were found to be slightly lower than the average for all subjects, and patchiness of provision was cited as one contributory factor. Reviewing this evidence, Tait took the view that to persuade schools to provide religious education would depend on finding new ways of stating the case for its contribution to overall education. But Tait relegates RE again to voluntary and local effort again.

External examination group teaching by specialist teachers was commended and new syllabuses emphasizing continuity of learning and progression across the key stages were welcomed by OFSTED. But the insecurity of non-specialist teachers in the subject in primary and secondary schools was noted as having a serious adverse effect on quality along with lack of subject co-ordination in many primary schools, failure to meet agreed syllabus requirements, low resource provision resulting from 'the low priority given to religious education in recent years'[46] and lack of curriculum time, especially in many primary schools. The time pressure affected secondary schools in key stage 4, where a third of all schools failed to provide any non-examination RE provision for all pupils, and post-16, where 80 per cent of schools were failing to provide statutory non-examination provision for all pupils. In the vast majority of primary schools there was no policy for assessment, recording and reporting in RE and no evidence of its happening. In the majority of secondaries there was no 'well developed' policy in assessing and reporting RE—this in contrast to National Curriculum subjects. It was still necessary to reassure non-specialist teachers of RE that their own conscience need not be a stumbling block. Copley and Copley (1993) stated in a book for infant teachers:

> We as teachers have an absolute right to our own religious belief, whatever it is, or to our uncertainty or our disbelief. The children we teach have an absolute right to their beliefs and disbeliefs, but also, and equally important, the right to learn more about this whole area [religion] of human experience so their eventual stance in these matters is not founded on ignorance and prejudice. Trying to persuade children of the rightness of a particular religion is the province of the home and family, the church, the temple etc., rather than the teacher. The teacher's role when dealing with religion is to do with promoting tolerance, dispelling ignorance, raising questions, and introducing new ways to looking at life and the experiences of other people. In order to do this we have to be honest with ourselves and keep our own beliefs and disbeliefs under control . . .[47]

Copley and Copley (1993) saw the three crucial factors operating in developing RE programmes to be the needs, questions and experience of the primary school child; the wisdom and experience of the great world faiths and the experience of the teacher.[48] It was unusual to state the latter. But their view was that many non-specialist teachers in RE were being deeply influenced by their own experience of RE as pupils or by their own experiences (for better or worse) of religious institutions (synagogues, mosques, churches etc.) which were shaping their own teaching—or reluctance to teach—the subject.

Reports showed that if general RE provision was very variable, information technology in RE fared little better. A DfEE survey showed that only 8 per cent of schools used computers in RE, more than half reporting that IT was never used for the subject and only 2 per cent reporting 'substantial use' in RE. Of the 500 CD-ROM titles offered for review to the National Council for Educational Technology, only three were designed for RE and one of these was an electronic Bible, which could be viewed as a 'hi-tec' return to the forties.

OFSTED tried to identify specific areas of good and bad practice, e.g. weak RE in key stage 1 (infants) was characterized by patchy provision with no sustained consideration of religious practice or it was narrowly Christian or RE was subsumed under a consideration of moral values. In good work in the same age group, better pupils 'have a sound knowledge and understanding of relevant Bible stories and of the main features of Christian worship, and some knowledge of the major festivals of other faiths. They are given an opportunity to talk about their feelings and are developing an understanding of concepts and symbols.'[49] In primary schools in which the head-teacher was co-ordinator for RE the arrangement was often unsatisfactory, one suspects because of the busy-ness of heads after the 1988 Act, especially in small schools.

It was not all bad news. The report recorded that in 1994, Religious Studies GCSE examinations had been taken by 75,407 pupils (15.8 per cent of the 15+ age cohort). This represented 41 per cent of those entered for History and 36 per cent of those entered for Geography, both of which had guaranteed National Curriculum status and provision and a much higher proportion of lessons taught by specialists. Overall in Religious Studies 49.8 per cent of the pupils entered achieved passes in the range A to C, better than the average of 47.4 per cent in all subjects. AS examination entries in RS were higher (711 total) than some subjects which attracted more pupils in GCSE and Advanced Level. Advanced Level RE was entered by only 4.5 per cent of the 17+ age group cohort sitting examinations at this level, by four times more girls than boys and with 84.8 per cent achieving grades A to E.

Against this crop of problems, some of which had persisted since 1944, sprinkled with some encouraging signs, it was hard to see how any government since 1944 had effected good progress in RE. OFSTED implicitly highlighted the weakness of the 1988 settlement which had attempted to address curriculum and content without addressing staffing, in-service education and resourcing and without any real consultation with professionals in RE. Legislating for agreed-syllabus processes and general content and for the creation of a SACRE in every LEA was clearly having no bearing on RE in many primary schools. The lack of specialist teachers at primary and secondary levels and the refusal of government over many years to define RE as an official shortage subject like, for example, Physics (hence attracting cash bursaries for students in training) had created a climate of attrition which most other subjects did not have to operate in. Twenty-five per cent of secondary RE was being taught by teachers with no qualification in the subject whatsoever, compared with ten per cent of Mathematics and fourteen per cent of English. Moreover, since specialist RE teachers in secondary schools tended to be promoted more quickly to head of department posts than those in some other subjects, owing to the shortage, they also tended to be promoted on out of these posts and into pastoral or year head positions and beyond. This reduced their appearance time in the classroom to teach RE as a result of a diminished teaching timetable to compensate for increased pastoral or administrative duties. Paradoxically the success of so many RE specialists increased the dearth of specialist teaching. What was at issue in RE—what had always been at issue in the half century—was implementation (training, staffing, resourcing, curriculum position) and the percentage of time within the whole curriculum to be allocated to RE. However much percentage any religion received out of five per cent of total RE curriculum time was meagre.

Circular 1/94

On 31 January 1994 the document appeared that marks the end of our fifty-year cycle. This was DFE Circular 1/94, successor to Circular 3/89, to clarify and provide guidance about RE and collective worship. It only applied to England but a similar document, 10/94, was later issued by the Curriculum Council for Wales. The collective worship section proved to be extremely contentious but falls outside this study. But the Circular's presentation of the Act in relation to RE introduced subtle change. First (1/94) in the aim for RE, which was now:

> to develop pupils' knowledge, understanding and awareness of Christianity, as the predominant religion in Great Britain, and the other principal religions represented in the country; to encourage respect for those holding different beliefs; and to help promote pupils' spiritual, moral, cultural and mental development.[50]

It was the head-teacher's job to secure this provision, including time and resources, with the help of the governing body and (in maintained schools) the LEA.[51] It spoke blandly of the 'equal standing' RE shares with National Curriculum subjects; the real difference is described as RE not sharing national attainment targets, programmes of study and assessment procedures.[52] The circular reiterates the 1988 requirements for RE in different types of school, adding the 1993 Act permission for grant-maintained schools to select the agreed syllabus of their choice and its requirement on LEAs to review their agreed syllabuses every five years, spelling out clearly how they must meet the content requirements of the 1988 Act,[53] indicating at what ages or stages prescribed subject matter in relation to each nominated religion should be taught.[54] As a whole, and at each key stage, the content devoted to Christianity in the syllabus should predominate.[55] A 'range' of model syllabuses would be provided to help LEAs to draw up their own.[56] In fact the range that subsequently appeared consisted of two. Time allocated to RE was to reflect the Dearing Report: 36 hours per annum at key stage 1, 45 at key stages 2 and 3 and 'around' five per cent of curriculum time in key stage 4. In Circular 10/94 the recommendation for Wales was different: 36 hours per year for key stages 1 to 3 and five per cent of curriculum time at key stage 4. Parental rights of withdrawal were reaffirmed, though these were not to embrace spontaneous enquiries pupils might make about religion in other areas of the curriculum.

The shift in the RE provision in these Circulars was to tighten the definition of content and to make agreed syllabuses accountable on this. Renewed attempts to define status for RE were, as on previous occasions, fatuous; statements made about a subject excluded from the National Curriculum could not create status for RE alongside it. Most significantly of all, although firm steps were being taken to control the content of RE, no steps were being made to enforce a curriculum time allowance. It was merely recommended hours per annum. Yet again the importance of RE was being preached without the coercive backing that all other subjects were receiving.

There was detail on SACREs. Their advisory role is affirmed. They have to undertake agreed syllabus revision every five years and produce an annual report on their work. The 1993 Education Act emendation of 'denominations' for SACRE panels to read 'religions and religious denominations' is repeated. If LEA responsibility for securing school places in primary or secondary sector passes to the Funding Agency for Schools (as a result of 75 per cent of schools in either sector becoming GM schools) then the SACRE has to include a fifth committee (fourth in Wales, which has no Committee B, or Church of England panel), Committee E. This shall comprise the governing bodies of those GM schools equivalent to county or voluntary controlled schools. Decisions at SACREs are still to be taken by each committee having one collective vote. Section 104 specifically excludes from Committee A representatives of belief systems such as humanism 'who do not amount to a religion or religious denomination'. It might be said that the legal role of RE is to deal with religions rather than non-religions, that the secular alternatives are well represented in the whole of the rest of the curriculum, but granted that on many SACREs humanists were giving good service, helping to achieve co-operative results on the panels on which they served and generally supportive of teaching about religions, it seemed sectarian or simply mean to exclude them. Buddhism could be cited as a belief system which is not committed to a theistic view of life but it was allowed to remain. Of course humanists might be still be members of Committee C (teachers' associations) or D (the LEA) but in those cases they would not be appearing officially as humanists.

To critics 1/94 looked remarkably like some of the amendments that the 'Tribe' had been trying to write into the 1988 Act, reappearing now as 'advice' without further debate. It could be that Baroness Emily Blatch, by 1994 junior minister at the DFE and a member of the 'Tribe', was its main author. Her background lay in aviation, in the WRAF and air-traffic control, in work for Peterborough Development Corporation and as leader of Cambridgeshire County Council. Custom and practice allowed a junior minister such as her to see a Circular through. Although senior ministers could add their views, often they did not intervene or challenge but allowed their juniors to get on with it. It was accepted that if a strong-minded junior minister really wanted items to appear in a Circular, they often got their way. When Blatch was asked directly whether she wrote 1/94 her diary secretary replied that time constraints and diary pressures made it impossible for her to comment.[57]

Prescription in 1/94 for the processes of SACREs did not match prescription for time in the classroom. Despite this glaring anomaly by comparison to other subjects, official complaints about RE from 1988 tended to be about the amount of time devoted to Christianity within RE or more strictly not devoted to it, rather than about schools that were not delivering RE at all. Formal complaints were made to the Secretary of State against Ealing and Newham on the grounds that their syllabuses were not 'mainly Christian'. The DES followed with a letter passing on advice from legal counsel on what had to be done to ensure that new syllabuses complied with the law.[58] An analysis of agreed syllabuses carried out for the NCC in 1992–3 to prepare them to advise syllabus conferences was distorted in leaks to the media to suggest that all post-1988 syllabuses were illegal because they failed to spell out exactly what pupils should learn about God, Christ and the Bible. It suggested that twenty-seven LEAs might be held to be in breach because they were insufficiently precise about the position of Christianity within their syllabus. An orchestrated attempt was made to enforce allocation of 80 per cent of RE time to Christianity. Lady Olga Maitland, Conservative MP for Sutton and Cheam, campaigned for this in speeches and articles in the media, including the *Church of England Newspaper*[59] with headlines such as 'The Ultimate Betrayal' and 'RE at Sea'. Baroness Blatch caused a letter to be written to all LEAs whose syllabuses had been analysed to tell the Department within a month what action they intended to take to ensure that their syllabus 'clearly complies with the requirements of the law', but the National Curriculum Council was not told about the letter.

The Model Syllabuses

Secretary of State John Patten set two months for the production of model syllabuses to help agreed-syllabus conferences in drawing up local syllabuses. The models had no statutory weight. A SCAA monitoring group including members of different faith communities and professional bodies who were members of the RE Council resisted the attempt to apportion percentage time to religions. Members of religions framed the documents that interpreted their religion to outsiders; in that sense the model syllabuses continued the old tradition of the ecumenical approach to agreed syllabuses, this time on an interfaith basis. The consultation period on the draft models was very brief and the two syllabuses appeared in July 1994. Model 1, entitled *Living Faiths Today*, was phenomenological, 'structured around the knowledge and understanding of what it means to be a member of a faith community'.[60] Model 2, entitled *Questions and Teachings*, focused on religious practice, 'how these [the teachings of religions] relate to shared human experience'.[61] Both SCAA model syllabuses shared the same attainment targets:

AT1 Learning about Religions.
AT2 Learning from Religion [sic].

They also identified skills and processes in RE: investigation, interpretation, reflection, empathy, evaluation, analysis, synthesis, application and expression. Key attitudes for RE were also identified: commitment (to learning rather than to a particular religious position), fairness, respect, self- understanding and enquiry. They dealt with the 'big six' religions.

The Staff Inspector for RE later noted (Robson, 1995) that in the original drafts 'there was only really one model, namely the separate study of different religions' and that his own sponsoring of a model based on the categories used in the Faith Group Working Reports (including beliefs, religious practices, communities and ethics) was ruled out on grounds of lack of working-party time by chairperson Chris Woodhead, later Chief Inspector. As specimens for agreed-syllabus conferences the national models were never intended as schemes of work or local school syllabuses, and they were modified as a result of the Woodhead monitoring group. Some critics resented that they appeared content driven, though this hardly does full justice to the preamble and guidance notes. But two syllabuses presented little choice and hardly comprised the 'range' promised in Circular 1/94.

A group of four higher education tutors produced *A Third Perspective*, an alternative to supplement the existing two. It identified seven areas of common enquiry: the spiritual, cosmology, metaphysics, ethics, ritual, social organization and communication. The writers claimed that these were not themes but 'common areas of religious teaching and practice' in a syllabus intended for use in thematic and discrete ways.[62] They criticized the 'narrow view' of RE in the national models, the haphazard and uncritical rise of the 'big six' religions as dominating features of UK RE. They added humanism, justifying its inclusion on the basis that it addresses issues in which children are interested. They pleaded for child-related teaching again, against what was seen as too heavily religion-related alternatives and the ATs ('Learning about' and 'Learning from') which implied a passive role for the child. *The Third Perspective* writers wished children to 'engage with' religions and be more than passive agents in the RE process. They believed their syllabus was more child-related as it related to common human dimensions. But their own dimensions were selected by adults from a humanistic base to which not all religious educators subscribed. Their implicit view of childhood was as suspect as the passive child of the SCAA models. The *Third Perspective* child was a questioning child, aware of basic common human issues and trying to come to terms with them. But by 1994 society had produced a generation of largely secularized children, unaware of their own secularist outlook, who were not asking questions of meaning at all. Wintersgill defended the two SCAA national models.[63] Her defence was based partly on earlier work done by the National Curriculum Council whose efforts to produce thematic models sometimes fragmented, even distorted, religions they were addressing. She argued that what is distinctive in a religion is not easily placed in a framework which demands commonality and hence could be excluded from study altogether.

What RE offers *uniquely* [her Italics] is a study of religion. There has been a tendency to apologise for RE or to camouflage it as multicultural education, environmental education or some generalised path to self-understanding. Worst still many primary teachers, encouraged to teach RE for the first time, have been told that 'RE is in everything' with *Dogger* and *The Velveteen Rabbit* acquiring almost the status of sacred texts for key stage 1.[64]

This at least confronted a secular world-view.

SACRE Reports

A report from SCAA (1994) analysed and summarized SACRE annual reports for the previous year. Until SCAA was pressed to analyse these reports and publish the results the story, perhaps apocryphal, was that reports had languished in a cupboard in the NCC headquarters at York. What is certain is at first they were not used as significant evidence about national RE provision, not least because government did not wish to look at RE nationally at all. The summaries provide another window into RE at the end of our period. Ninety-eight out of 107 SACREs sent their reports to SCAA. Surveys of RE provision undertaken by reporting SACREs highlighted inadequate curriculum provision and a shortage of staff. Ignorance of the agreed syllabus in many primary schools was commented on.[65]. It was also noted that in one LEA 13 per cent of secondary schools had no designated head of RE department. But a fifth of SACREs noted stronger communication links between themselves and schools, mainly through visits. Initiatives at SACRE level were also taking place to strengthen links between the faith communities and schools and some SACREs were staging or hosting exhibitions, displaying good pupil work and providing local resource directories for teachers. Loss of advisory staff in RE as a result of cuts in education budgets was regretted in 'many' individual SACRE reports.[66] Only one reported a parental complaint about RE. Some SACREs expressed concern about the legality of their new or intended agreed syllabus and some had suspended work pending further advice. It is again a picture of dedicated professional work against the odds

In 1995 the Catholic Education Service published a report on quality in Roman Catholic secondary schools. They found that about a third of schools were not providing the 10 per cent of curriculum time for RE recommended by the Bishops' Conference of England and Wales. This confirmed the bishops' fears expressed before the 1988 Act was law that National Curriculum time pressures might squeeze RE harshly, but they would not be pleased to see this happening in their own schools. Seventy-five per cent of lessons observed in inspections of RC secondary RE were deemed satisfactory or better. In a third of schools lack of provision for less able pupils in RE and lack of differentiation, except through outcome, were criticized. However, excellent relations between teachers and pupils were keeping disciplinary problems to a minimum. RE in most of these schools was not surprisingly related to the wider spiritual life of the school, to their mutual benefit in the view of the Section 13 (diocesan school) inspectors.

Important as these various reports are as a form of evidence of the health of RE at school level, there was continuing commentary emerging on the nature of RE post-ERA. Watson (1993) identified eleven factors in the culture that should be 'RE friendly', yet each of which was in effect a double edged sword. These factors were:

1 the impact of science in increasing knowledge, yet at the risk of conveying the view that the scientific method is the only route to knowledge;
2 the achievements of technology in reducing drudgery, yet at the risk of promoting a utilitarian view of life;
3 more widespread opportunities for the enjoyment of life, yet at the expense of promoting distraction into unthinking materialism, consumerism, individualism and hedonism;
4 the revolution in communications, which might threaten particular traditions, including religious ones;
5 increased pluralism in society, with a consequent risk of relativism;
6 concern for human rights, which sometimes present religious cultures as oppressive;
7 stress on individual integrity and personal responsibility, which can present religion as authoritarian and dependence-inducing;
8 renewed interest in the spiritual dimension of life, yet with a tendency to see it as separate from religion;
9 the impact of the 'Green' movement, although some strands of the Green movement can be very critical of religion or hostile to its traditional institutional forms;
10 awareness and concern about global evil and suffering, which still raises the age-old question of God's role in it;
11 awareness of religion as a phenomenon and some resurgence of religious feeling, though often extremely critical of existing organized religion as hypocritical, smug, dogmatic, irrelevant, narrow-minded etc.[67]

To these she might have added

12 open recognition of sexuality as a natural, deeply satisfying, even mystical form of encounter, against which institutional religions have often seemed puritanically resistant or implicitly disapproving.

Watson saw the most fundamental problem facing religion and religious education as secularism. In schools this applied in two ways: the explicit curriculum which reduces RE to 5 per cent or less of pupil experience and in which, even within the RE curriculum itself, incipient secularism has led to the omission of the transcendent as a dimension to explore. She argued that the implicit curriculum transmits secular assumptions through particular styles of teaching but 'the null curriculum', by its omission of particular areas or points of view, conditions pupil thinking further. She cites as an example of this the national campaign against AIDS in the UK, which did not debate lifestyles or responsibility with regard to sexual activity but instead focused on mechanistic solutions (the use of condoms).

Watson went on to argue that in order to give religion a chance, the philosophically formidable case against secularism must be heard. RE should develop a rapprochement between the confessional model, the phenomenological model and what she named the Highest Common Factor model,[68], that is the desire to nurture in pupils those values, attitudes and interests associated with religion but yet which are also acceptable to the highest number of people, religious or not. The key to RE should be imagination, which is necessary to attune oneself to religious people, to gain knowledge in religion and for understanding religious concepts. Developing imagination should be done through the use of story, the study of symbolism and metaphor, and specific teaching on the concept of 'God'.

Clearly in Watson RE continued its well-established healthy professional tradition of vigorous self-examination and defence—even going on to attack secularism and provide a critique of other adverse factors acting on it. But this was within a legal provision which allowed its curriculum position to remain threatened. It was not a threat to its existence, but a threat to the time and resources, both human and material, required to produce quality RE.

Postscript

In Search of Serendipity

> The main thing at present for those who will teach [RE] is a conviction of the urgency and importance of right religious teaching, deep sincerity, a certain minimum of knowledge and the will to acquire more, the spirit and attitude that will lead to a right emphasis and aim, and a clear-minded resolution in carrying it out.

> Far too many syllabuses are not complying with . . . [the requirement to teach Christianity] which is why, according to a MORI poll, forty-four per cent of school-leavers leave school without a proper understanding of what happened even on Easter Day.

How far has RE really travelled in the fifty years of this study? The two quotations that appear above have been presented anonymously to raise the question: could one date them on the basis of their content? Could they both originate from anywhere between 1944 and 1994? In fact the first quotation is from Heawood, writing for teachers in 1939. The second is from Hansard for 3 March 1993. Conservative MP Lady Olga Maitland spoke in a debate initiated by Derek Enright, Labour MP for Hemsworth and a Roman Catholic. He was a one-time member of Wakefield SACRE and had taught RE for six months earlier in his career. He argued for the inclusion of Islam within RE 'not because we want to be tolerant of it—that is a demeaning attitude to take—but because we have a strong desire to understand it. Other religions can enrich us as we can enrich them.' It was as near as Labour had got to an explicit policy on RE other than to endorse the findings of the Swann Report on multiculturalism. Enright went on to criticize as unfair the provision that allowed for GM schools to be members of SACREs but then to opt out of the resulting agreed syllabus they produced. It was at this point that Olga Maitland raised the issue of 'so many' SACREs who do not comply with the 1988 Act provision that RE should, as she put it, 'in the main' be Christian. But she did not name defaulting LEAs. Nor did the Act use the words she used.

Politicians and RE

From a political point of view, the failure of the Labour and Liberal Democrat parties to develop a view of RE other than as an implicit adjunct to multicultural education or as something to be left to the individual conscience or initiative of MPs, allowed the more coherent Conservative picture of RE to dominate: that RE should make children aware of their Judaeo-Christian heritage, prevent them becoming blind travellers within a Christian culture whose signs they could not interpret, at the same time teaching religions separately in order to prevent 'mishmash', which seems to have meant confusion and triviali-zation. It would have been possible to combine the best in the explicit Conservative and implicit Labour and Liberal Democrat approaches to the subject and reshape it into a consensual manifesto for RE, based on understanding the cultural Judaeo-Christian heritage and under-standing the major living religions (including Christianity) represented in the UK, along with offering the child some opportunity for personal spiritual (though not necessarily theistic-based) development. But such compromise and consensus had ceased to be good politics long before the end of our period.

In 1944 such consensus as there was about RE reflected a wider political and social consensus about values. It also reflected a concern for the presence of religion in education as a whole, not confined to a classroom subject called RI. Whether even in 1944 this was a strong public concern or whether it was residual, despite its promotion by church leaders, is open to debate. As we saw in the Introduction, formative encounters between leading political figures and institutional religion may have influenced legislation but were untypical of the ordinary person, especially in the light of the spectacular post-war decline of the Sunday school movement. The issues that were to 'burst' on RE in the sixties—the ignorance of school-leavers about the Bible, the failure of Christian teaching, indifference towards RE itself, the need to address world religions—had all appeared in the thirties and early forties and lain dormant during the war and its immediate aftermath. In that sense the 1944 education provision was not only undermined by the need of British society to rebuild and to reorientate itself in a different direction in the post-war years, but it was also stillborn by virtue of ignoring the emerging evidence even before the war of the issues that eventually dominated the sixties debate on RE. Baker remarked that the 1944 Act 'left very few footprints'. That was perhaps unduly severe. However, the church and Sunday school presence in British society in the forties was still high-profile enough for the church lobby to have to be placated, as Butler realized. The 1944 settlement was a prescription by coalition politicians for what they saw to be the good of society; the 1988 education provision was the prescription by one party of what they believed to be the right solution to the multifarious problems besetting the education system. The 1988 legislation, as the very name of the Act records, was intended to be about the reform of malpractice, neglect or under-achievement in education. But it made no real attempt to reform the provision for RE.

The level of the failure of politicians of all parties in both Houses in their involvement in RE was that on the whole they were preoccupied during the half-century with its content rather than its provision. Some were aware of the continuing problem of teacher supply, but they did nothing effective to prevent its continuing throughout the whole fifty-year period. Few showed themselves willing to address the issue of time allocation within the timetable at school level. The 1988 settlement simply did not deal with this, despite repeated presentation of evidence by the RE Council and other bodies about the real and sometimes parlous state of RE at local school level. National Curriculum subjects squeezed out RE in many primary schools and in some secondaries in key stage 4, with the result that the status of RE looked more ephemeral than 'basic'. Those Conservative politicians who deplored that many children were not receiving their post-1944 entitlement to religious education were right to do so, but their subsequent legislation did nothing to solve this, apart from tightening the complaints procedure, in line with government philosophy of charters for consumer rights. It was assumed that school inspection would reveal the inadequacies. It was also naive to assume that control of the content of agreed syllabuses would of itself lead to better classroom provision. Had the legislators consulted the 'experts', who instead were maligned as special-interest groups opposed to change, they would have been spared such elementary mistakes. No other subject was left to these means of enforcement of provision. If parents were even aware of complaints procedures, SACRE reports suggest that relatively few were willing to invoke them and that when they did, they too were preoccupied with the content of RE. It was, after all, easier for religious or anti-religious groups or parents to take offence at syllabus or lesson content than over the time set aside for the subject. Even when school inspection revealed inadequacies, it did not always lead to remedial action. RE remained a Cinderella in many schools because it was never given the resources and staffing and status to compete on equal terms with other curriculum areas. The inspector's eye, seeing snapshot pictures of schools in action on particular days, did not always notice this. There was nothing to prevent schools claiming to be doing more RE than was the case. But standard testing as used in other subjects would have identified such failures easily on the basis of poor performance.

An Alternative Legal Settlement

In 1988 RE could easily have been made a 'special foundation subject' like the other foundation subjects, with a national syllabus and testing, but 'special' by virtue of retaining the withdrawal clause, if this was deemed politically necessary. The SCAA model syllabuses are de facto national syllabuses and the RE Council, with its representation across religions, could have helped to formulate a properly agreed national syllabus. Or it would have been possible to implement the preferred churches' option—RE as a foundation subject with a locally-determined syllabus. A third option in 1988 would have been to make RE a straightforward foundation subject removing the withdrawal clause but with options at key stages 3 and 4 into particular religions and non-religious stances for living, with a common core RE course including work on Christianity. Hull's variation on this (1996) was RE as a National Curriculum subject with a locally-determined element in the syllabus and with withdrawal extended to any subject over which parents might have a serious concern. In the Northern Ireland culture, with its stronger religious presence, RE had been given a core syllabus, 'not intended to represent the total provision for RE but [which] will provide the basis on which each individual school can build a programme to meet its particular needs'.[1] The three Northern Ireland attainment targets also relate to the cultural context:

> Target One: The Revelation of God
> Target Two: The Christian Church
> Target Three: Morality.

Leaving aside the semantic question of how these can constitute 'targets' and how one can 'attain' them, the point to note is that these would not have been culturally, politically or socially acceptable in more openly plural and secular England and Wales. But appropriate English and Welsh targets could and should have been defined.

In voluntary aided schools on the mainland, RE could have been made a core subject with English, Maths and Science in a variant national curriculum. National Curriculum exception and variation already existed: all independent (i.e. private, fee-paying) schools were exempted from the imposed National Curriculum, and Wales had a variation to deal with the position of the Welsh language which was altered in terms of its requirement for Welsh (Second Language) teaching in key stage 4 after the Dearing Report. This divergence from the English National Curriculum demonstrates that some variance was politically acceptable. The 'national curriculum' never was truly national across Britain or even England and Wales. It was merely a centralized curriculum with more commonality among participating schools than had hitherto been the case. Variation in provision could have been extended to RE, as in the other cases cited above. But the vision and the will to do this were lacking. Many politicians continued to see RE as a different type of subject from other curriculum subjects, somehow personal or voluntary and unsuited to intervention by government. The exception was that at times of major or horrific crime the public mind seemed ready to pounce, with concern that children should be taught 'the difference between right and wrong', with the implication that if the schools were discharging their duties in this regard effectively, there would be no unwanted pregnancies, no serial killers, child abuse etc.

English and Welsh Identity

The story of RE from 1944 to 1994 reveals perhaps a uniquely English and Welsh paradox: sincerely to affirm the importance of RE while simultaneously neglecting its position on the curriculum map. It might well have resulted from the ambivalence of the British, or in particular the English, about the place of religion in their national life and from the secular tendencies of the media to ignore the role of religion even when it was a potent force, as undoubtedly was the case in the collapse of communism in the former eastern bloc countries. The British media image of religion was one of inexorable decline peppered with occasional salacious scandal. But people still went to carol services in large numbers and the numbers attending churches on Sundays continued to exceed those attending football matches on Saturdays. Religious wedding and funeral ceremonies remained in great demand, even if not on the scale of pre-war years. Atheists did not refuse to sing Christmas carols.

A more disturbing aspect of this English–Welsh Christian-folk religious identity was that religions other than Christianity remained socially suspect among some people and liable to stereotyping. They were perceived as foreign, another time-honoured British method for disposal of them. It was to be the 1997 general election before the UK got its first Muslim MP. When the Prince of Wales asserted his wish as future king to receive the title of Defender of Faith rather than Defender of the Faith, i.e. the Christian faith, he was endorsing the view that Britain had become a plural country and that minority groups acting within the law had rights to existence and protection. Perhaps unconsciously he was also expressing a view that although religions are not the same, they do have some attitudes in common: provision of a critique of secularism and materialism; assertion of the importance of the quest for meaning; espousing an ethic that values other people rather than oneself; stressing spirituality etc.

RE Professionalism

If politicians failed to treat RE as a serious curriculum undertaking, equal to others, or to achieve a social vision of which it was a part, one must ask how far their failure was compounded by RE professionals. When political attacks on world religions teaching were launched, they came in part from people who accepted neither the failure of the 1944 settlement to fill the churches nor the questions that were being raised as early as the 1930s and 1940s about hostile or indifferent pupil response to Bible-centred religious instruction. But the attack on the way in which world religions were being taught still had some legitimate grounds. An intellectual critique from within the profession of the issues raised by thematic teaching of religions was by then overdue. If many parents and politicians presumed that the facile intention of teaching world religions was to give children a choice whether to be Jews or Sikhs or Muslims or Hindus, this impression could have arisen from the way in which the teaching was being given or the failure to explain to pupils, parents and RE student teachers in training what RE was really trying to do. The reality is that few adults and fewer children 'choose' a religion or cross religious boundaries, because such changes often involve an extremely difficult cultural reorientation as an inevitable consequence. Moreover by the eighties some school-leavers were just as confused about the 'facts' of world religions as an earlier generation had been about the Bible.

The RE profession had not always addressed sufficiently in its own debates the question of relativism and truth claims raised by the study of different religions to be able to provide a lead for educated outsiders to interpret its work clearly. They had not produced universally acceptable criteria for selecting religions to be studied. The 'big six'—Hinduism, Buddhism, Judaism, Christianity, Islam, Sikhism— had emerged. Omitted were Jehovah's Witnesses, Rastafarians, the 'old religion' or Wicca, as distinct from Satanism, and many other groups present in the UK. Some of these would not have been acceptable to many parents and politicians, but that alone is not a coherent policy for choice. What the chosen six have in common is a presence in the UK that dates back in most cases at least to 1900—albeit in small numbers—and that on occasions prominent members of the indigenous population have converted to them. Lord Headley's conversion to Islam in 1913 may not be much remembered now, but it led to the setting up of the British Muslim Organisation and a growing acceptability for the faith in Britain.

It was an unsurprising but not necessarily defensible, reversal that the Bible, which had dominated RI in 1944 had all but disappeared from RE by 1994. It survived as part of a unit on the theme Sacred Writings. A generation of children who were prepared to declare it boring had never read it, or part of it, to discover for themselves. It was to fall just outside our period for a research project, 'Biblos', at the University of Exeter (1995), to start to investigate whether and how the Bible might be taught in a society labelled variously 'plural' and 'secular' and to rediscover the Bible itself as a multi-religious text.

Classroom teachers in RE were faced daily by a different issue to the selection of religions or material for study, which was anyway done for them in the agreed syllabus. That was the tightrope to tread between sanitising religion on the one hand, thus rendering it tame and incomprehensible to their students, or so presenting the emotional and intellectual challenge of a religion that children might be overwhelmed by it in the classroom and inappropriately converted to the religion being taught. To tread the sanitising path would produce or increase pupil perceptions that religion and therefore religious education was a fruitless and wasted endeavour. To tread the other path was to renege on the whole theory of education and beliefs about the role of the teacher and the rights of the child that had been developed in the post-war years. In this situation it would not be surprising that some RE teachers could not sustain the balancing act.

If there were mistakes as well as triumphs in RE in the half-century there were also omissions. Religious educators were not always in dialogue with theologians. Theologians were not always sufficiently interested in religious education. The result perhaps impoverished both causes. In its efforts to be perceived as an essentially educational exercise, RE lost touch with the changes in and insights it might have gained from theology. Another serious omission was major research on the whole question of the use of agreed syllabuses. One can map developments in RE by a chronological study of how these syllabuses over fifty years. But there are serious methodological problems in this exercise. It is akin to trying to assess the quality of holidays over the same period by studying the brochures of tourist operators. It is still the case that in some primary schools agreed syllabuses are not being used. Some primary teachers resented an 'extra' subject added from a different base to their National Curriculum load and ignored RE despite the agreed syllabus.

The Achievements in RE

If all these were serious problems, however, the fifty years of RE was by no means a debit account. Perhaps the most astonishing achievement in RE is that in a half-century characterized by remorseless decline in organized religion in the UK and by continuing secularization within UK law and society, religious education transformed itself from a concern led by Christian educators, not necessarily specialists in the subject, into a professional activity containing members of all main religions in the UK and non-religious members, acting cohesively, consolidating their subject in school, initiating curriculum advance, raising the number of specialist teachers and external examination candidates, developing and in some measure communicating a philosophy that enabled RE as an activity to survive the apparent collapse of a Christian basis for education. That RE teaching could now be seen as a legitimate and fulfilling career (as opposed to a Christian vocation) was part of this achievement. Pupils and their teachers could express an enthusiasm for RE without automatically being presumed to be religious. Time proved that the ability of RE to shed its various skins like a snake—RI, RK, Divinity, Scripture, Bible Knowledge—demonstrated real resilience in the face of massive social change.

The professionalization of RE carried other benefits. Religious educators were able to address different religions not because they were relativists or were committed to a window-shopping approach to religion. Rather the transformation of Christian education into religious education took place mainly because of a simple realization that the leading 'world religions' are also UK religions, that children have a natural curiosity about them, and that it is therefore entirely appropriate to study them in RE. One commentator in the USA (Moran, 1989) described this aspect of UK RE as a microcosm of the world's future, urging educators in the USA not to neglect the UK debate and experience in RE. The espousal of world religions present in the UK as communities to be valued was perhaps also a largely unnoticed contribution made by RE to a society growing not always easily into pluralism. The Swann Report did note and applaud this. Even less noticed was that this endorsement of world religions in RE came originally from Christian religious educators whose vision was wide enough not to be threatened by diversity or dialogue with other faiths.

The Christian Education Movement and the Church of England remained significant forces in RE, neither pressing for Christian exclusivism or mission. If they were sometimes branded as liberals, it was often by opponents who could equally have been branded fundamentalist. By 1992 the ethnic minority population totalled about 2.58 million, some 4.7 per cent of the total population, of whom about 45 per cent were born in Britain. By 1994 there were more than 600 mosques (and 40 Muslim day schools), 160 gurdwaras, 150 mandirs, 50 Buddhist centres and 20 Buddhist monasteries in Britain. Outside the 'big six' there were at least 30,000 Jains, 5,000 Zoroastrians, 4,000 Baha'i, 15 Hare Krishna centres and many other groups. While the tendency to teach 'non-religions' such as communism in RE lessons disappeared, the commitment to world religions teaching was never challenged from a serious intellectual base. The politically contentious issues surrounding it remained the issue of theme teaching and deciding the balance between teaching the various religions. But the principle that the religions represented in the UK should be taught was accepted. If British society became more tolerant of its ethnic minority members and started to value diversity, RE could claim some credit for that.

Those Christians who feared that Christianity might disappear in a religious education context were simply wrong. Even before the 1988 Act a study of agreed syllabuses and of commercially produced classroom resources demonstrates that this was not happening. The 1988 Act legislated against it occurring subsequently. If the total teaching time allocated to Christianity was reduced from 100 per cent in the world religions framework, it underlined the need to present it selectively, sensitively and effectively. Teaching world religions added to the impetus to teach Christianity as a world religion and not merely an English or Welsh one. Orthodox Christianity—a third of the world's believers—began to appear in syllabuses and text-books along with Latin American or African or other cultural expressions of Christianity. Perhaps Roman Catholicism has still to be rehabilitated, outside its own school system, in RE schemes in a secular Protestant culture. Many religious educators continued to feel that Christianity was often the worst taught religion because teachers and children were often culturally tangled in it, or perhaps because children and teachers assumed that they knew it already.

Another aspect of RE to its credit was the steady output of books to explore and defend its rationale. For so small a subject, in terms of curriculum space in school, RE can claim one of the highest rates of production of literature dedicated to exploring its nature and developing the work. Perhaps religious educators felt called upon to defend their subject to pupils, colleagues and parents in the earlier decades of our study and to provide help for the many non-specialist teachers, but the result meant the production of a serious rationale for teaching which grew and changed with the times. One might wonder whether the teachers of Mathematics, for example, which occupied so large a portion of pupil time, put to defend their curriculum position, could have drawn on so extensive a body of documents and so many-sided a case to argue for their baronial status on the curriculum map.

The Church of England

The Church of England had both a visible and invisible role in RE throughout the period. It was visible as a stakeholder in education, with its own schools and its own syllabuses for voluntary aided schools, along with its network of diocesan advisers and inspectors for the subject. In this it had much in common with the Roman Catholic Church. But it had a real but less visible role by virtue of establishment and especially via the General Synod Board of Education, the work of the National Society for RE and the presence of senior bishops in the House of Lords, it had an entry into the political corridors and the influence to speak to the Secretary of State and be accepted as a legitimate and influential political lobby. Not all professional religious educators were aware of this, or if they were aware were happy to acknowledge it, but the reality was that the Church of England was very influential in both the 1944 and the 1988 settlements, even as they affected religious education in Wales where the Anglican Church was separate and disestablished. In the 1988 Act a government which set its face against the educational lobby, treating it dismissively as a vested interest, still had to listen to the Church. Towards the end of the period there was added a growing Muslim political lobby, but it had not yet shaped RE.

Educational Vision

The end of *Tom Brown's Schooldays* (1857) depicts Tom as a young adult alone in the chapel at Rugby School, mourning the sudden death of 'the Doctor', head-teacher Thomas Arnold. 'Here,' writes Thomas Hughes, 'let us leave him [Tom Brown]—where better could we leave him than at the altar, before which he had first caught a glimpse of the glory of his birthright, and felt the drawing of the bond which links all living souls together in one brotherhood . . .' For Hughes the Christian religion lay at the heart of education, as it had done for his schoolboy mentor Arnold, who added by choice to his duties as head-teacher the role of school chaplain. Hughes also acknowledges the link between religion and Englishness which survived into our period. He can talk[2] of the school's role in the 'training of Christian Englishmen.' In such a context all teaching expressed a moral and religious calling.

Today Hughes' values seem sentimental, inappropriate, even comic, although some of them survived in 1944. His male preserve of the public school with its muscular Christianity, character training through extra-curricular activities such as sport; the sometimes sycophantic hero worship; the romanticized power of 'the house', a climate in which bullies like Flashman are repulsed by peer-group pressure—these are distant from the 1990s comprehensive school with its day pupils not boarders, on whom the great extra-curricular influences are the media, the personal computer and fashion in music and clothing. But there are parallels: Arnold experienced the pressure faced by many modern teachers. In his case it was the work of running and reforming the school, advanced sixth-form teaching, preparing pupils for university scholarship examinations, writing and editing his own books in history and religion, working as chaplain both pastorally and in sermon planning and maintaining a heavy correspondence with former pupils. He died prematurely, partly of overwork, aged 47. His son Matthew, poet and school inspector, wrote of modern society (1855) 'wandering between two worlds, one dead, the other powerless to be born'.[3] Thomas Arnold's vision, like the vision of 1944, is no longer ours, but we may legitimately ask with Matthew whether any particular vision has replaced it. It is perhaps a commentary on our own times that the one character in Tom Brown to survive is the bully Flashman, brilliantly resurrected by George MacDonald Fraser.[4] Ironically, Fraser's Flashman Papers ran to more than ten volumes and nearly thirty years of writing. Tom Brown reached only one quickly forgotten sequel, Tom Brown at Oxford (1861). If Tom Brown evaporated, so did educational vision after 1944, to be replaced by utilitarianism, secularism and chronic overwork for teachers. One of the few post-1944 ideals, that of the comprehensive school, vanished under criticisms of social engineering, over-large schools, a culture of mediocrity, gross under-funding and a vociferous lobby resentful of the loss of grammar schools. The post-1960s world of education dispensed with visionaries and heroes, yet RE had traditionally been part of a Christian vision for education.

The Principal Achievement for RE

The greatest single achievement for RE within the half-century from

1944 to 1994 is that in a society which on the surface appeared to discard religion as a majority preoccupation and to have lost much of its educational sense of direction, religious education as a curriculum subject persisted at all. By its very name religious education makes a continuing claim, namely that religion or religions are important and are worthy of study and of serious attention by young people. It has never been difficult to demonstrate that religion is globally important. It has sometimes been difficult to raise the preoccupations of the British towards the world rather than the island nation. If religion seems less important in England and Wales than it was a half-century ago, English and Welsh sections of a small island can hardly be a reliable barometer for the world. The question is how far the English and Welsh are ready to recognize that and question their prevalent secular dogmatism.

With the proverbial cards stacked against RE in terms of resources, specialist staffing, curriculum position and status, even personal antagonism on the part of some non-RE teachers, RE has not only survived but in many cases thrived. That is both a reflection of the intrinsic interest of its subject matter and also of the work of those generations of teachers who have sought to engage children in the fascinating questions it poses, and those from outside the teaching profession in faith communities or political life who have sought to support it. RE still contains elements of both the Suffering Servant and Cinderella but it has also been true to a changing self-awareness in asserting that it is offering students a subject the study of which itself could claim to be life-enhancing, in terms of attitudes, skills and experiences it offers, whatever conclusions (if any) the student may reach about its content. That is no small achievement to carry forward as the credit account into the next century.

Appendix 1

Starting Out in Religious Education, 1935

From 1932 to 1935 I attended Furzedown College, Streatham, London, to train as an infant teacher. At college we had a whole afternoon per week, a two-hour session, of Divinity, run by visiting lecturers. We studied one topic per term and the emphasis was on theological understanding at our level. We were divided into Catholics and non-Catholics, each group having separate sessions. There was a third session for the small Jewish minority. Divinity was a popular session as, apart from music, it was the only session we had in each week with a male tutor, the college being for women only, and the full-time tutors were all female.

In September 1935 I took up appointment as assistant teacher at Brook Hill Infant School, Teignmouth, Devon. There were four classes in the school and roughly 200 children. The head-teacher taught the top class. My own class contained sixty children, what would now be called reception, although children started school then after the age of five and not before. The whole building was very Victorian, with high windows, well above pupil eye level. The infant school occupied the ground floor of the building and the junior school was upstairs. The classrooms were interconnected. There was no staffroom. Meetings were held in the head-teacher's office. School dinners did not exist, so most children went home for lunch. There was no school hall, but a screen separated the top two classes and it was pushed aside for assembly. We assembled for morning prayers after 9a.m. registration. The register was a precious document, which had to be protected in case of fire, had to be called aloud and was inspected by the school managers on their monthly visit. County grants to the school depended on the number of pupil attendances recorded. The children I taught were predominantly working class, from the Mill Lane district, which was at that time regarded as one of the least favoured in the town.

Some parents were agricultural or horticultural labourers. Some worked on the Great Western Railway or the docks. Few if any worked outside the town. A good many were unemployed.

Scripture took place every morning. It was the first thing we did after the register and prayers. How seriously it was taken in a school depended very much on the head-teacher. I called it 'story' to the children. A session lasted between fifteen and twenty minutes, but usually no longer, to allow for the limited attention span of the small children. Sometimes we had to practise hymns for assembly but I don't think that the children associated preparation for assemblies with scripture. It was a county school and we were following the Leicestershire agreed syllabus. I taught the syllabus for my age range on a two-yearly cycle. It was stories about children : the young Joseph, Moses, the childhood of Jesus, some parables, with an emphasis on story rather than on moralizing. We acted out some of the stories, which the children enjoyed, and we did murals using different coloured tissue-paper balls like a mosaic. We used to make individual models, Moses in a box in the rushes etc. But the expression work was mostly drawing and crayoning. Although it was a county school we related scripture to the church year. For example on Ascension Day the children were taken to church for a service and then had the rest of the day off.

Scripture was inspected annually by someone appointed by the county, sometimes a minister of religion. For many years it was Canon Hall, then Miss Savage was inspector of RI. Canon Hall was a marvellous man who would sit down among the five-year-olds and draw the story out of them. You didn't feel it was an inspection at all and the idea was to make the children think it was a sort of treat. The inspection lasted about half an hour per class. In all scripture you had to be careful not to teach doctrine in any way in a county school. It meant that teachers who didn't care about religion would tell the story, and that was that. The danger of this non-denominational approach, however, was that scripture could become very much a milk and water thing, of little import. That was where the church schools had an advantage, that their religious teaching could permeate the whole day . . . I used to enjoy teaching scripture. If you've got responsive children, it was interesting.

I left this school in 1939 to get married. The county did not employ married women teachers owing to the high unemployment rate. When I was called up (1941) I was drafted into teaching and I went to teach what were then called sub-normal children who had been evacuated to the Langdon Mental Hospital. We had simple prayers and taught our own simplified syllabus for scripture, very similar to what I had done with young infants, but now with older children. I taught there for two years, but then left to start a family. When I returned to full-time teaching in 1961 at Oaklands Special School, Dawlish, the world was very different. Scripture was still taught, again on a simplified syllabus, and I continued to do this daily, but by now it had become much more subject to the interest and inclination of the individual teacher.

Postscript by J. Brian Crispin

It was part of the 1902 Education Act that 25 per cent of grammar school places had to be free, scholarship places. Grammar school staff salaries were higher than those in other schools, I should think about 20 per cent higher. Not only that, but they also had longer holidays, because when I came here [Dawlish] in 1932 to teach in an elementary school, the grammar school had nearly double the holidays. There were grades of salaries for elementary school teachers. If you taught in London you were on the top grade, grade 4. If you taught in Devon, you were on the bottom grade, grade 1. Exeter was grade 2 and the big conurbations like Birmingham grade 3. My salary in 1932 (I was twenty-one years old) was £151.4s.0d. per annum [£151.20p] but I was better off than most men in Dawlish.

The boys' elementary school in Dawlish had a staff of three teachers plus the head, for about two hundred pupils. I taught the top class, 46 boys, in three groups 11+, 12+ and 13+, so it meant an enormous amount of marking. Every time I took a lesson I taught it verbally to a third of the class, while the other two thirds were doing written work based on their earlier lesson. Lamacraft [the head-teacher] was on the other side of a glass screen and could watch every move of mine. Sometimes he would open the door between his desk and my room and say 'Mr Crispin, those three boys in the back desk haven't done a stroke of work for five and a half minutes!'

The School Attendance Officer would visit every Monday morning and take down the names of boys who had been absent in the previous week. Missing boys meant less money. Once a boy who was marked present was sent into the village to buy a box of paper-clips. He had not returned when an inspector called in unannounced to check the register. Because the boy had not completed a full half-day session, but had been marked present for it, all the school's registers were sent to London for checking. On another occasion the whole staff had to stay until nine at night because of an unsolved error in register totals. It was found to be in the head's register!

When school milk was introduced it could be made as 'Horlicks milk', malted milk, with apparatus provided by the company. Two boys used to go out to make it and it took about half an hour, three-quarters if they were lucky. One morning in RI, a class had the story of the Prodigal Son and the teacher set them an essay about it. The milk monitor wrote: 'the Prodigal Son went away to a great city and wasted his living with Horlicks . . .'

Text based on an interview with Sallie Crispin on 23 September 1995. The reminiscence at the end by J. Brian Crispin is adapted from an address to the Dawlish Historical Society in December 1994.

Appendix 2

Starting Out in Religious Education, 1968

I went to a grammar school as a pupil and straight from the sixth form to Nottingham University to read Theology. I stayed on for my (in those days still optional) PGCE year. In the primary school where I spent four weeks in the autumn term of 1967, the RE topic was 'Stories Jesus was told'. Spring term 1968 was spent on teaching practice at a co-educational grammar school of 740 pupils, Swanwick Hall, in Derbyshire. My teaching practice notes for this survive and reveal that I had to cover from Jacob to Joshua (1st Year) the division of the Hebrew kingdom (922 BCE to the fall of Samaria in 722 BCE) in the 2nd Year, from Jeremiah to the Roman occupation of Palestine (3rd Year), recent developments in Bible study (4th Year non-examination groups), Buddhism and Christianity and social problems (5th Year non-examination groups) and the Passion narrative in the Synoptic gospels (4th Year GCE 'O' Level). I had to start the Hebrew prophets with the lower sixth 'A' Level group. No projector or tape-recorder were available and the main supplementary teaching methods had to be drama with younger children and discussion with older ones. A mock trial appears later in my notes.

In September 1968 I took up a post in a co-educational grammar school. It was already widely accepted that the days of grammar schools were numbered as most LEAs were planning for comprehensive schools. Secondary school teachers could see that their future would be in comprehensives. My teaching career therefore began in the last years of one era of secondary education and the first years of another. The school was Huntingdon Grammar School, descendant of the school attended by Oliver Cromwell and later by Samuel Pepys, but the town did not then have a future Prime Minister (John Major) as its MP. It was a three-form entry school of 550 pupils including sixth form, with a large rural catchment as well as Huntingdon old town, along with its London overspill estate. There was one RE specialist in the school (me) as Head of RE, assisted by other non-specialist teachers in their minority time. A couple of the older staff remained from the pre-war days of the grammar school. Their contracts had required male teachers to wear a suit and had specified which public houses they might use, most of which lay beyond the means of teachers. The school, in common with many then, had a Senior Master and Senior Mistress. The Senior Mistress had been on good terms with Lady Hemingford and Lord Hinchingbrooke. She had lived with her family for some years in a flat in the historic Hinchingbrooke House and later wrote a book about it.* Residual social status still accrued to grammar school teaching. There was an active association of former pupils, the Old Huntingdonians Association, which kept the school in living contact with the past. But the past did not dominate it; most heads of department were young and taught in what then were the most innovative ways available.

When I arrived the school had grown too big to fit its daily assembly into the hall, so the 1st Years had a separate assembly. The remaining years, ages twelve to nineteen, assembled in the hall. The staff sat on the platform behind the head-teacher. If the head was not conducting the entire assembly, he had to select a prayer suitable to the theme of the day from the book on his lap in time to deliver it when the speaker finished. The Senior Master, who was also head of music, played the grand piano for the hymns, which were sung reluctantly, in common with many secondary schools of that time. To compensate he seemed to play by elbow, with crashing chords designed to drown the apathy. Hymns were chosen by him without co-ordination with the theme or prayer of the day. His favourite was 'Book of books', words by Percy Dearmer (1867–1936). The first verse ran:

> Book of books, our people's strength,
> Statesman's, teacher's, hero's treasure,
> Bringing freedom, spreading truth,
> Shedding light that none can measure—
> Wisdom comes to those who know thee,
> All the best we have we owe thee.

This choice of hymn and pupil reluctance to sing it symbolized the end of an era not just in school worship but also RE; the 'Book of books' was no longer acceptable to a new generation. Although I had been appointed as 'Head of RE' according to the advertisement, I discovered

---

*W.M. Stuart, *Houseful at Hinchingbrooke*, (The Grasshopper Press, 1979).

on arrival at the school that on the timetable and in the classroom the subject was known as BK, Bible Knowledge, a title that was already archaic by a decade or more. The syllabus I inherited was entirely biblical, starting with the time-honoured trek through the history of the Jews from Abraham to Herod. 'O' Level consisted of the Gospel of Mark, with Matthew 5 to 7, and the Book of Acts. There were only biblical papers entered for 'A' Level. A few pupils sat 'AO' Level by attending half the 'A' level classes in their lower-sixth year. 'AO' was Alternative Ordinary Level, a precursor of 'AS', devised for more mature students than 'O' Level. It offered sixth-formers a chance to study RE for examinations who had not had the opportunity to do so lower in the school. This was useful, since when I arrived RE was set against French in the fourth-year examination option block, i.e. pupils had to choose between French and RE for 'O' Level study. This condemned RE to small teaching groups made up of inept modern linguists and religious fanatics ! I quickly learned that getting RE a fair placing in the options programme was one of the most important functions of the head of department. Without that the best teaching, the best resourcing and the best syllabus can be thwarted. Once moved on the timetable the group grew from nine or ten pupils to thirty-five in one year.

The RE room was, like many of its era, a mobile 'temporary' classroom on the periphery of the school campus. It had squatted there for a decade at least. In winter it was very cold and in summer it could be blistering. If a delinquent pupil kicked hard enough it was easy to put a hole through the door or the wall. I called it the Cardboard Classroom and recollect one day asking a class if they ever thought that God, if there were a God, intervened in everyday life. At this moment the oil heater blew up with a bang, expelling soot onto the front two rows of shocked, excited and screaming children, cascading the fullest covering onto me. My inherited text-books were either Bibles or child texts on biblical material, either by Youngman (see p. 49) or the *Story of the Scriptures*, an eight-volume series of which Volume 8 was daringly unbiblical. When I asked the caretaker to burn the worst of the Authorized Version Bible stock (1611 text) he went to the head-teacher and complained that although he was not a religious man, he drew the line at burning Bibles. The head-teacher, an agnostic, agreed with him.

As sole RE specialist I taught all the 'O' and 'A' Level work, which occupied just under half my very full timetable. Time allocated to 'A' Level teaching was less than other subjects on the grounds that the RE groups I inherited were smaller than most. I taught some classes in every other year group including statutory non-examination RE in the

4th and 5th Year and 'God's Putrid Rubbish', the sixth-form nickname for General Philosophy and Religion, GPR on the timetable, statutory RE at 16 plus. I took *Honest to God* as a text for these groups. It was still shocking and controversial, so the young adults were launched into the latest religious controversy. To most of them it was also an unintelligible text, but they forgave me that in my modernizing approach to 'BK' as a young teacher only four-years distant from them in age. Within a term the subject was re-named on all exercise-book covers and on the timetable as RE, with a new rationale that was made clear to all pupils. Gradually the biblical content of the syllabus was reduced, although many text-books in those days 'did' Islam and other religions in a couple of lessons per religion. Early additions to the RE syllabus were studies in the religious presence and history of the local area (St Ivo, St Neot etc.), work on beliefs and disbeliefs, on ethical problems and 'Me'. At 'A' Level a paper on Christianity in the twentieth century replaced the Old Testament. I retained the New Testament paper out of conviction that some biblical study at 'A' Level was worth undertaking for educational reasons. Visiting speakers were introduced as part of the core RE programme for all students from 1st year upwards. The biblical work that remained below the sixth form was revamped. So many of the insights of theologians like Bultmann, Jeremias, Dodd etc were not being applied at classroom level and I tried to relate them. Hence the life of Jesus began with Christians now, worked back to the resurrection faith of the first community and then into the person himself and the sources about him. Previously it had started with the birth narratives, treating the gospels as de facto biographies, even though the biography approach had been discredited in theology departments for many decades. I was soon asked to run an evening for parents on 'the New RE'.

After two years the school became comprehensive as planned. The three immediate consequences for RE were the arrival of a second, full-time specialist RE teacher, the arrival in the first-year pupil intake of eight, non- selective, mixed-ability forms (increasing the size of the school by about 40 per cent in one year alone) and the creation of a lower-school specialist RE room, no longer out in the cold in the huts, along with an upper-school specialist RE room in one of the newly built blocks. Comprehensive education led to a complete reappraisal of syllabus and teaching methods in all subjects, and the need to prepare staff and pupils for CSE examination work as well as 'O' Level. Mercifully there was no merger with another school, and so the non-selective entry gradually moved up the school until Huntingdon Grammar School was fully comprehensive as Hinchingbrooke School.

Terence Copley

Appendix 3

Starting Out in Religious Education, 1995

From 1991 to 1994 I studied Theology at the University of Birmingham. I stayed on to do a one-year PGCE course to train as a secondary school teacher. The course involved two weeks in a primary school to get a flavour of teaching, then 36 weeks of university and school-based training. I spent three weeks, then a further term, in a multi-cultural school in Handsworth, Birmingham. Here I taught a wide range of religious beliefs and practices, including GCSE Islam and Sikhism. At the end of the PGCE I spent a contrasting three-week period in a mainly middle-class, all girls, grammar school where the syllabus was more Christian based.

In September 1995 I took up my first post as teacher of Religious Education in an inner-London borough. The school has approximately 1,300 pupils aged 11 to 16, of diverse backgrounds. The majority are Muslims, although Sikhs, Hindus and Christians are well represented. There are a large number of Bengali speakers and most pupils have English as their second language. The ratio of boys to girls is 2:1, with most classes having eight to ten girls and 20 boys. The borough has an inclusive education policy which means there are a number of SEN (Special Educational Needs) teachers and ESL (English as a Second Language) teachers. The aim of these is to develop new methodology and resources accessible to all pupils. One challenge for me was adapting tasks for an autistic pupil in Year 7.

In late August 1995 I went into school to prepare my room. To my horror I found five-year-old faded display work hanging from the walls and glued to windows. They were removed with difficulty. The room had windows on two sides and in summer it was like working in a greenhouse. Pupils would moan incessantly that they could not see the video or that the sun was in their eyes. The room was repainted during 1996 and blinds added. The dilapidated blackboard was replaced by a bright new white board. Having developed handwriting skill on one, I had to improve my technique on the other. I still try to brighten up the room with mobiles, quotations from famous people and ample use of pupils' work.

There are two full-time RE specialists at the school. The head-teacher was an RE adviser and takes some lessons each week. Two other teachers take some RE alongside their other subjects. There are two main RE rooms. The department was not well-resourced when I arrived. There were a few text-books in the cupboard which were either 25 years old or unsuitable for bilingual children. Over the last year new texts have been bought. Hopefully in the not too distant future a computer and CD ROM will feature in our classrooms. With OFSTED and school league tables looming over all schools, there is a high emphasis on monitoring and observation of other teachers' lessons. This is beneficial to all concerned

I started with 18 (currently 19) different classes per week, each for a one-hour lesson. By the time pupils have arrived, taken off their coats, sat down and got their books out, about fifty minutes of quality teaching time is left. In key stage 3 we cover the following topics, one per term: The Inner Me; Celebration; Special Places; Community Rules; The Natural World; Expressing Meaning; Science and Religion; Beliefs and Values; Relationships. All the six main religions are covered and during a typical week pupils may be found studying Aborigines' views of the environment or Chinese New Year, devising their own wedding service, making an artefact, creating a pilgrimage round the local area or making a model of a holy place. Many of the classroom activities are group based; we produce a lot of display work projects, poetry, role play and discussion. A church, temple and gurdwara are all within easy walking distance and pupils love to visit these as part of their studies. Differentiation plays an important part in lesson planning. The pupils have wide-ranging abilities and tasks must be achievable by all and yet challenge the most able.

At key stage 4 RE is compulsory for all pupils. Last year pupils in Years 10 and 11 had no opportunity to sit an examination, so their study of RE was given no acknowledgment when they left school. This produced unmotivated and uninterested pupils who did not want to study religion, as they did not want to be a priest or RE teacher! Trying to convince the average 15-year-old that religious, moral and spiritual matters can and will affect their life was sometimes an impossible task. 'Going into battle' was sometimes how I described these lessons, and eventually some pupil interest was shown. I chose topics that I thought would motivate them, Life after Death, Relationships, The Miraculous. I made use of videos on numerous occasions.

But in 1996 it was decided that all pupils would study for a GCSE Short Course in Religious Education, the so-called 'Half GCSE'. As well as this great move, Religious Studies was to be offered as a full GCSE option for the first time for over five years. I asked if I could teach the option group and my head of department agreed. This option involves the phenomenological study of Christianity and Islam. It includes 20 per cent course work. The GCSE Short Course includes the study of five topics from the perspective of two religions. The topics include relationships, justice and moral questions.

As I have had a tutor group since I started teaching I have been able to observe some changes in collective worship. I remember my own school days with the hymn- talk routine on most mornings. As the school I teach in is so large, year-group collective worship occurs only once per week—even then there are only just enough chairs. Such assemblies are largely informative, with a short period of reflection. This allows pupils from all religious backgrounds (and none) to participate. As an RE teacher one cannot help but get involved in the major festivals. Divali, Easter and Christmas are now under my belt! The pupils love taking part in drama, dance and singing and this makes the hours of practice worthwhile.

The profile of RE has been raised, especially since some Year 7 pupils requested that I start an RE club. Many of them wished to do project work about a festival of their choice. I opened up my room every Friday for them to use books and equipment. The results were quite staggering; some 40-page-long theses were produced! Even better was their desire to continue the club when they went into Year 8. This group have now produced a high-quality display for Divali and a survey of beliefs in Year 8.

So far I have had little time for reflection on the start of my career. At times it felt like jumping into an ocean full of sharks. But there have been many occasions when I have seen the fruit of my efforts. The first year of teaching is certainly one huge learning curve, and although the PGCE provides some insight into the life of a teacher, there is nothing like the real thing!

Kathryn Wright

Appendix 4

The Withdrawal Clause in Religious Education

The British and Foreign Schools Society—a Victorian nonconformist body which established what became known as 'British schools'—had from its foundation accepted teachers and pupils of any denomination, whereas the National Society—the Anglican body which owned the majority of schools—taught the doctrines of the established church. But in 1863 when an Anglican school was funded in a village unable to support a school of each Society, a conscience clause was included in the school's foundation document. By 1867 even the Archbishop of Canterbury was said to approve of it (Braithwaite, 1995, p. 278f). The clause allowed nonconformist parents to withdraw their children from Anglican teaching or worship. W.E.Forster, introducing the 1870 Act, used the Conscience Clause (*Hansard* Vol 199 Cols 447–9) as a necessary condition to the receipt by any school of public funding. It applied to secular and denominational schools. Power of withdrawal lay with the parent not the pupil. The 1870 Act Section 7 provided:

> It shall not be required, as a condition of any child being admitted into, or continuing in the school, that he shall attend or abstain from attending, any Sunday School, or any place of religious worship, or that he shall attend religious observance or any instruction in religious subjects in the school or elsewhere, from which observance or instruction he may be withdrawn by his parent, or that he shall if withdrawn by his parent, attend the school on any day exclusively set apart for religious observance by the religious body to which his parent belongs.

The 1902 Act did not alter this principle and extended it into the new compulsory secondary schools:

> In a school or college receiving a grant from, or maintained by, a

council a scholar attending as a day or evening scholar shall not be required, as a condition of being admitted into or remaining in the school or college, to attend or abstain from attending any Sunday School, place of religious worship, religious observance or instruction in religious subjects in the school or college or elsewhere.

This was retained in the 1921 Education Act and substantially in 1944 and 1988 (see pp. 30 and 146).

Historically the provision has seen different waves of users, who gradually accommodated to RI and ceased to use the clause or found that RI itself was changing and becoming less objectionable. In the early days withdrawal was most often invoked by nonconformist parents whose children found themselves in Anglican schools which taught the catechism and the creeds. Later it was used by Roman Catholic parents with children in non-Catholic schools, to protect them against what was seen as non-denominational Protestant instruction. In time they integrated into RE. Next came Jehovah's Witnesses who objected to the 'doctrine' being taught in RI lessons and to the non-Witness credentials of the teachers. They too began to transition into integration. Finally groups of Islamic parents were orchestrated towards the end of the period of this book in attempts to create mass withdrawal, even from RE lessons which their children had previously been attending, as part of their campaign for government-funded separate schools. But in all these cases withdrawals by members of the particular groups were never universal. There were always members who were tolerant or apathetic enough to allow their children to remain in the lesson. Alongside all these were militant atheist or secularist parents, comparatively few in number, who did not want their children to encounter any curriculum attempt to portray religion in a favourable light. Some parents may have wished to withdraw their children, but perhaps felt that a certain social stigma or discrimination might accrue to such action. The 1967 Plowden Report recognized that as a problem, though it assumed that RE was intended to promote Christianity. A minority report 'Reservation on Religious Education' deplored that withdrawal often meant withdrawal to an empty room or corridor and that a secularist humanist programme could not be delivered to withdrawn children.

By 1988 no politician seemed willing to grasp the nettle of the withdrawal clause. Protection by withdrawal from religious *instruction* is a logical and defensible human right within a democracy. The option to withdraw from religious *education* is a complete anomaly. Logic suggests that in such a curriculum situation either no subject should be able to be dispensed with, or that the withdrawal clause should be extended to all subjects. Hull argued (*BJRE* Vol. 18. No. 3, Spring

1996) that if there were to be provision for withdrawal it should extend to any subject about which parents might express 'reasonable concern'. The interpretation of withdrawal rights became more absurd in 1995 when the Association of Metropolitan Authorities issued their Education Officer Circular 95/38 (18 May 1995) in response to the case of some parents in an East London primary school who wished to withdraw their children from non-Christian religions in RE but not from Christianity. 'The parents had filled in identical proformas, and an individual, known locally to be involved with an extremist political group, was . . . handing these out with a leaflet outside the school gates . . . It seemed evident that this multi-racial school was the target of an orchestrated campaign.' Yet despite this the school was required to supply parents with RE schemes of work based on the agreed syllabus so that the parents would have sufficient notice to withdraw their children from such parts of the RE as they chose, as long as it was not for less than a complete lesson. DFE legal advice that assisted this resolution of the issue reflected the political dogma of parental choice run amok. In no other subject were parents allowed to move their children in and out of lessons, often for the most specious of reasons, viewed from an educational perspective. The only educational benefit that might accrue from partial withdrawal arrangements of this sort are that some primary schools would have to produce a scheme of work for RE in accordance with the agreed syllabus when they might otherwise be neglecting to teach it.

By 1994 Religious Education was strangely vulnerable to parental whim or to withdrawal of children for racist motives on the part of their parents. If the emphasis on parents as consumers within the education system continues into the twenty-first century we may see the issue develop further, not necessarily to the advantage of RE. This lamentable situation has arisen because a piece of legislation produced for the most laudable of motives more than a century ago has survived unchallenged into a totally different educational and social context.

Notes

Preface

1. G. Moran, *Religious Education as a Second Language*, Religious Education Press, 1989, p100. As a US commentator Moran notes: 'In the UK teaching religion is sometimes used interchangeably with teaching religious education. Writers seem unaware of the logical problem with that and unaware of what a strange use of language it is to make religious education the object of the act of teaching ... In England, for all the talk about phenomenology and objectivity, the British public (and their politicians) think that religious education ought to have a personal and practical effect.'

Introduction

1. Broadsheet of Christian Thought and Action, SCM Press, No. 5, 25 January 1947, report by the editor, Robert C. Walton on a discussion group at Wath on Dearne Grammar School, Yorkshire.
2. R.A. Butler, *The Art of the Possible*, Hamish Hamilton, 1971, p. 7.
3. in A. Horne, *Macmillan 1957–1986*, Volume II of the official biography, Macmillan, 1988, p. 34.
4. K. Young, *Sir Alec Douglas Home*, J.M. Dent & Sons, 1970, pp. 43f, 72, 154f.
5. P. Ziegler, *Wilson: the Authorized life of Lord Wilson of Rievaulx*, Weidenfeld & Nicolson, 1993, p. 6ff.
6. ibid., p. 177.
7. R. Harries, 'Comrades in Christ', *The Times Higher Education Supplement*, 16 August 96.
8. J. Callaghan, *Time and Chance*, Collins, 1987, pp. 22–40.
9. J. Campbell, *Edward Heath*, Pimlico, 1993, pp. 9f and 62.
10. M. Thatcher, *The Path to Power*, HarperCollins, 1995, p. 5ff.
11. ibid., p.565.
12. After some debate about the name Ball, which ran in the family, the family decided to name the baby simply John Major, the name in which his birth was registered. At the christening, however, when asked to name the child, his godmother, a formidable Miss Pink (Anderson, 1991) or Fink (Junor,

1993), announced without warning that his name was John Roy Major. She felt John Major too plain. The family were very angry, but felt obliged to hold their peace and so the baby was baptized John Roy Major.

13. A.P. Stanley, *The Life and Correspondence of Thomas Arnold*, Volume I, Fellowes, 1858 edition, p. 125.

14. R.M. Jenkins, in M. Cadogan, *Frank Richards*, Viking, 1988, p. 162. Jenkins noted that the teachers in Richards' fictitious pieces were not 'cardboard constructions' but that part of their fascination was that the reader was allowed into their private thoughts and conversations, something that was denied in real life. 'Battles of the beaks' (Quelch v. Prout etc.) were especially popular with readers. Cadogan notes that over the years of the *Magnet*, Quelch's character sharpened rather than mellowed. By Magnet No. 1, 150 (1930), merely seeing a 'Greyfriars fellow' makes Quelch feel 'like the war horse snuffing the battle from afar', p. 163.

15. T. Copley, et al. *Forms of Assessment in Religious Education*: The Main Report of the FARE Project, University of Exeter School of Education, 1.4, p. 8.

16. R.A. Butler, op.cit., p. 91.

Chapter One—The Shadow of War: The 1940s

1. If you had passed certain examinations, you could be employed as an "uncertificated" teacher. Getting up at 6 a.m. I went by bus and bicycle from my home at West Mersea to a school at West Bergholt . . . I had a huge class of boys and girls from about nine to fourteen. Most of them did not have the slightest idea what I was talking about. Nor, for much of the time, did I.' R. Day, *Grand Inquisitor*, George Weidenfeld & Nicholson Ltd, 1989, p. 22.

2. N. Longmate, *How We Lived Then*, Arrow, 1971, p. 251.

3. H. Martin, in *Religion in Education Quarterly*, Vol. 6. No. 4, October 1939.

4. In W.O.L. Smith, *Education In Great Britain*, OUP, 1949, 3rd edition 1958, p. 7.

5. ibid., p. 8.

6. R. Acland, *What will it be like in the New Britain?*, Gollancz, 1942, p. 105.

7. A. Howard, *R.A. Butler*, Cape, 1987, p. 108.

8. ibid., p. 110.

9. in M. Gilbert, *Churchill, a Life*, Heinemann, p. 68.

10. ibid., p. 663.

11. ibid., p. 70.

12. 10 July 1942.

13. 12 February 1941.

14. 21 December 1940.

15. 16 January 1941.

16. CEM Foundation Document, p. 193.

17. A. Howard, op. cit, p. 113.

18. R.A. Butler, op. cit., p. 94.
19. A. Howard, op. cit., p. 115.
20. R.A. Butler, op cit, p. 94.
21. He was later to become a Labour Home Secretary and Leader of the House and remained an MP until 1964, when he was over 80.
22. Butler Papers, G13
23. Butler op. cit., p. 99.
24. London Borough of Brent, *Agreed Syllabus for RE*, self-published, 1995, pp. 5, 62, 68.
25. Butler op. cit., p. 106.
26. 24 April 1944.
27. F.A. Iremonger, *William Temple*, OUP, 1948, p. 569.
28. W. Temple, 14 May 1943, p. 8
29. E. Green, *Education For a New Society*.
30. *Hansard* for 29 July 1943 (Vol. 391).
31. *Hansard* for 10 March 1944 (Vol. 397).
32. Durham County Council, *Durham County Agreed Syllabus of Religious Instruction* (University of London, 1946) p. 1f.
33. Middlesex County Council, *The Middlesex County Agreed Syllabus of Religious Instruction*, (1948), p. 1f.
34. Cambridgeshire Education Committee, *The Cambridgeshire Syllabus of Religious Teaching for Schools*, CUP, 1951, p. 25ff.
35. ibid., p. 109ff.
36. Durham agreed syllabus, op. cit., pp. 6–13.
37. in N. Smart, and D. Horder, (eds) *New Movements in Religious Education*, (Temple Smith, 1975). p. 100.
38. B. G. Sandhurst, *How Heathen is Britain?*, Collins, 1948 edition, p. 43.
39. M. Avery, *Teaching Scripture*, REP, 1951, pp. 11 and 16.
40. A. Hastings, *A History of English Christianity, 1920–1990*, SCM Press, 3rd edition 1991, p. 421.
41. G. L. Heawood, *Religion in School*, SCM Press. 1939, p. 19.
42. Diary, 29 July 1943, paper 8/173.
43. K.O. Morgan, *The People's Peace*, OUP, 1990, p. 52.
44. July 1943.
45. 22 November 1941.
46. Vol. 21 January 1953.

Chapter Two—Post-War Reconstruction: The 1950s

1. A. Pierrepoint, *Executioner*, (Harrap, 1974), described the furore as 'the last great sentimental protest against capital punishment in Great Britain.' To end media speculation he revealed that Ruth Ellis spoke no last words, pp. 204 and 207.
2. A. Hastings, *A History of English Christianity, 1920–1990*, SCM Press, 3rd edition 1991, p. 437.

3. H.R.F. Keating, *Writing Crime Fiction*, A.&C. Black, 2nd edition, 1994, p. 14.
4. B. R. Youngman, *Teaching Religious Knowledge*, p. 17.
5. ibid., p. 18.
6. ibid., p. 20.
7. ibid., p. 21.
8. ibid., p. 23.
9. ibid., p. 27.
10. ibid., p. 39f.
11. It consisted of:
    1st Year: Life of Jesus
    2nd Year: History of the Hebrews
    3rd Year: Growth of the Church
    4th Year: Story of the Bible
    5th Year: Selected topics.
12. B.R. Youngman, op. cit., p. 44.
13. ibid., p. 117.
14. A.V. Murray, p. 194f.
15. Institute of Christian Education, *Religious Education in Schools*, SPCK, 1954, p. 30.
16. ibid., p. 36.
17. ibid., p. 83.
18. ibid., p. 74.
19. ibid., p. 75.
20. ibid., p. 112.
21. ibid., p. 64.
22. A.V. Murray, op. cit., p. 28.
23. Institute of Christian Education, op. cit., p. 76.
24. City and County of Bristol, *Agreed Syllabus of Christian Education*, self publ., 1960, p. xiii.
25. ibid., p. 2.
26. ibid., p. 177.
27. ibid., p. 183.
28. ibid., p. 187.

Chapter Three—Iconoclasm in RE: The 1960s

1. W.R. Niblett, *Christian Education in a Secular Society*, OUP, 1960
2. *The Times*, 21 April 1968.
3. *The Times*, 21 October 1974.
4. 1966. The score was 4–2.
5. F.H. Hilliard, *The Teacher and Religion*, James Clarke, 1963, p. 31.
6. 3 January 1957.
7. In 1956 29,070 pupils entered Ordinary Level, of whom 16,841 passed. By 1961, 46,536 entered with 26,276 passing. Between the same years Geography entries grew from 88,708 to 125,949 with 50,215 and 68,399

passes, respectively. For History the figures were 86,547 and 120,413 with passes 51,297 and 70,265, respectively. Rejoicing in the RE figures must be moderated by the comparison in number of entries with these two 'competitor' subjects. Hilliard ascribed it to the 'climate of opinion' being not very favourably disposed towards religion. This is an interesting comment for 1963. For Advanced Level the entries had risen from 1,193 (1956) to 2,645 (1961) compared with Geography 8,509 to 13,255 and History 11,997 to 17,831. Hilliard, F.H., op. cit., p. 60.

8. ibid., p. 68.
9. Surrey County Council, *Syllabus of Religious Instruction*, Surrey CC, 1963, p. 8.
10. *Religion in Education Quarterly*, Vol. 23, 2 and 3, 1956.
11. *Religion in Education Quarterly*. Vol. 28. 2
12. H. Loukes, *Teenage Religion*, SCM Press, 1961, p. 35f.
13. ibid., p. 41.
14. *Learning for Living*, Vol. 1 No. 1, 1961.
15. County Borough of Darlington, *Agreed Syllabus of Religious Instruction*, Darlington Education Committee, 1965, p. 3.
16. Cornwall County Council, *Agreed Syllabus of Religious Instruction*, Darton, Longman and Todd, 1964, p. 25.
17. Acland won Barnstaple for the Liberals in 1935. He left the Liberal Party in 1942, without resigning his seat, to found the Common Wealth Party. It was understood that when a general election came he would not stand in Barnstaple for Common Wealth.
18. R. Acland, *Unser Kampf*, Penguin Special, 1940, p. 33.
19. Diary, 11 July 1945.
20. R. Acland, *We Teach Them Wrong*, Gollancz, 1963, p. 33.
21. ibid., p. 69.
22. B.G. Sandhurst, *How Heathen is Britain?*, Collins, 1948 edition, p. 26f.
23. R. Acland, *We Teach Them Wrong*, op. cit., p. 166.
24. ibid., p. 191.
25. R. Acland, *Curriculum or Life?*, Gollancz, 1966, p. 64.
26. ibid., p. 115.
27. Cathy Mitchell, writing an obituary for Acland, BJRE Vol. 14 No. 1, 1990, p. 6f.
28. R. Goldman, *Religious Thinking from Childhood to Adolescence*, Routledge & Kegan Paul, 1964, p. 2.
29. ibid., p. 14.
30. ibid., p. 33.
31. ibid., p. 37.
32. ibid., p. 40.
33. ibid., p. 222.
34. ibid., p. 230.
35. West Riding County Council, *Suggestions for Religious Education*, WRCC, 1966, p. viii.
36. ibid., p. 3.
37. ibid., p. 3.

38. ibid., p. 82.
39. 22 May 1964.
40. Church of England Youth Council report, *The Church and Young People*, Church Information Board, 1955, p. 15.
41. E. Cox, *Changing Aims in Religious Education*, Routledge and Kegan Paul,1966, p. 83.
42. J.W.D. Smith, *Religious Education in a Secular Setting*, SCM Press, 1969, p. 105.
43. *Learning for Living*, September 1966.
44. P.R. May, and O.R. Johnston, *Religion in Our Schools*, Hodder and Stoughton, 1968, p. 80.
45. B. Wigley, *From Fear to Faith*, Longmans, Green and Co., 1969, p. 85.
46. CEM Executive Committee Minutes, 2 February 1968.
47. Stephen Orchard, General Secretary of CEM, interviewed by the writer in 1995.
48. *Learning for Living*, Vol. 14 No. 4, 1975.

Chapter Four—Controversies in RE: The 1970s

1. M. Thatcher, *The Downing Street Years*, p. 19
2. D. Lawton, *The Tory Mind on Education*, Falmer, 1994, p. 47.
3. A. Marwick, *British Society Since 1945*, Penguin, 1982, p. 265.
4. II Peter 3.8.
5. *The Fourth R*, 571, p. 274.
6. ibid., 573, p. 275.
7. ibid., 575, p. 276.
8. ibid., 248, p. 115.
9. ibid., 158 p. 80.
10. ibid., 15, p. 279.
11. ibid., 253, p. 117.
12. ibid., p. 345.
13. ibid., 10, p. 346.
14. ibid., p. 329.
15. ibid., 119, p. 61.
16. ibid., 264, p. 121.
17. ibid., 123, p. 63.
18. 17 October 70.
19. 4 November 70.
20. 10 November 70.
21. Letters from F. Gilbert and T.S.-B. Kelly, 17 November 70.
22. 19 November 70.
23. 20 November 70.
24. T.J. Cornish, 25 November 70.
25. *Schools Council Working Paper 36*, Religious Education in Secondary Schools, Evans Brothers and Methuen Educational, 1971, p. 73.
26. ibid., p. 21.

27. ibid., p. 21.
28. ibid., p. 21.
29. ibid., p. 22.
30. ibid., p. 24.
31. *REQ* Vol. 6 No. 4, p. 191.
32. *Schools Council Working Paper 36*, op. cit., p. 34.
33. ibid., p. 31.
34. ibid., p. 38.
35. *Learning for Living*, Vol. 15 no. 3, 1976.
36. *BJRE*, Vol. 11 No. 3, 1989.
37. Lancaster Education Committee, *Religion and Life*, publ. Lancashire County Council, 1973, p. 13.
38. D.A. Brown, 'A Christian Approach to Education', Methodist Church Division of Education and Youth Working Party Paper, 1991.
39. A. Dale, *The Bible in the Classroom*, OUP, 1972, p. 2.
40. ibid., p. 4.
41. *Learning for Living*, Vol. 15 No. 3, 1976.
42. *Learning for Living*, Vol. 15 No. 4, 1976.
43. *Learning for Living*, Vol. 15 No. 4, 1976.
44. W.O. Cole, (ed.), *World Faiths in Education*, George Allen and Unwin, 1978, p. 119.
45. ibid., p. 120.
46. ibid., p. 36.
47. ibid., p. 52f.
48. N. Smart, and D. Horder, (eds.), *New Movements in Religious Education*, Temple Smith, 1975, p. 243.
49. J. Holm, *Teaching Religion in School*, OUP, 1975, p. 102.
50. *REQ* Vol. 6 No. 4, p. 221ff.
51. M. Grimmitt, *What Can I Do in RE?*, Mayhew-McCrimmon, 2nd edition, 1978, p. 16.
52. *Learning for Living*, Vol. 14 No. 5, 1975.
53. *Learning for Living*, Vol. 17 No. 2, 1977.
54. M. Grimmitt, op. cit., p. 26.
55. *BJRE*, Vol. 18 No. 3, 1986.

Chapter Five—A New Deal for RE: The 1980s

1. M. Thatcher, *The Downing Street Years*, HarperCollins, 1993, p. 339.
2. ibid., p. 341.
3. S. Bruce, *Religion in Modern Britain*, OUP, 1995, p. 104.
4. 21 February 89.
5. N. Tebbit, *Upwardly Mobile*, George Weidenfeld and Nicholson, 1988, p. 267.
6. M. Thatcher, op. cit., p. 593.
7. M. Thatcher, *The Path to Power*, HarperCollins, 1995, p. 166.
8. ibid., p. 166.

9. J. Hull, (ed.), *New Directions in Religious Education*, Falmer Press, 1982, p. xiii.
10. *BJRE*, Vol. 11 No. 1.
11. *BJRE*, Vol. 15 No. 2, 1983.
12. J. Hull, (ed.), op. cit., p. xv.
13. ibid., Newbigin writing on p. 103.
14. The Shap Working Party on World Religions, World Religions in Education, publ. Commission for Racial Equality, 1987, p. 21.
15. ibid., p. 22.
16. *BJRE*, Vol. 18. No. 3, 1986.
17. *BJRE*, Vol. 15 No. 2 1983.
18. HMI, *Aspects of Secondary Education in England*, HMSO, 1979, 3.7.9. p. 29.
19. J. Hull, (ed.), *Studies in Education and Religion*, Falmer Press, 1984, p. 126.
20. *Resource*, Vol. 18 No. 1, 1995.
21. Swann Report, p. 518.
22. The Shap Working Party on World Religions, op. cit., p. 15.
23. ibid., p. 16.
24. M. Thatcher, *The Downing Street Years*, op. cit., p. 598.
25. ibid., p. 590.
26. ibid., p. 590.
27. K. Baker, *The Turbulent Years*, Faber and Faber, 1993, p. 61.
28. ibid., p. 167.
29. 3 May 1995.
30. Published in Royal Society of Arts Journal Vol. CXLIII No. 5464 November 1995, as an article: 'Alas! Sir Humphrey, I knew him well', G. Holland, pp. 39–51.
31. Speech given at University of Birmingham School of Education, quoted in C. Chitty, and B. Simon, (eds.), *Education Answers Back,* Lawrence and Wishart, 1993, p. 70ff.
32. M. Thatcher, *The Downing Street Years*, HarperCollins, 1993, p. 592.
33. ibid., p. 594.
34. ibid., p. 596.
35. ibid., p. 596.
36. A letter to me from Miranda Granger of Lady Thatcher's Private Office dated 2 August 1995. expressed Lady Thatcher's interest in RE but regretted that she had no time to go into detail.
37. K. Baker, op. cit., p. 207.
38. *BJRE*, Vol. 10 No. 3 1988.
39. ibid., p. 120.
40. 15 January 1988 Item 7.
41. K. Baker, op. cit., p. 207.
42. ibid., p. 208.
43. ibid., p. 209.
44. Letter to me dated 21 March 1996.
45. *BJRE*, p. 174.

46. Pamphlet: The Education Reform Bill: A Commentary for Catholics, published by the Catholic Bishops' Conference of England and Wales
47. E. Cox, and J.M. Cairns, *Reforming Religious Education*, Kogan Page, 1989, p. 69f.
48. *BJRE*, Vol. 11 No. 1.
49. *BJRE*, Vol. 12 No. 3.
50. ibid., p. 123.
51. ibid., p. 124.
52. *BJRE*, Vol. 11 No. 1, 1988.
53. *BJRE*, Vol. 18 No. 2, 1996.
54. Department of Education and Science, Circular 3/89, 1989, 20 p. 7.
55. ibid., 26(i), p. 9.
56. ibid., 29, p. 10.
57. ibid., 30, p. 10.
58. ibid., 52, 53, p. 17.

Chapter Six—RE after a New Act: 1990–1994

1. B. Castle, *Fighting All the Way*, Macmillan, 1993, p. 574.
2. M. Thatcher, *The Downing Street Years*, HarperCollins, 1993, p. 362. 835.
3. HMSO, 1992, p. 25.
4. 14 February 1996.
5. *The Church Times*, 6 October 1995.
6. P. Brierley, and V. Hiscock, (eds.) *The UK Christian Handbook*, Christian Research Association, Evangelical Alliance and British and Foreign Bible Society, 1994–95 edition, 1993, p. 729.
7. S. Bruce, *Religion in Modern Britain*, OUP, 1995, p. 46.
8. 'How religious are the British?' in T. Thomas, (ed.) *The British, Their Religious Beliefs and Practices 1800–1986*, Routledge, 1988, p. 236.
9. 1991, p. 670.
10. For a full analysis see D.J. Smith, *The Sleep of Reason*, Century, 1994.
11. 25 November 1993.
12. 3 March 1993.
13. The statement was prepared by Gillian Wood, the Education Secretary to the Free Church Federal Council.
14. D. Lawton, *The Tory Mind on Education, 1979–94*, Falmer, p. 89ff.
15. 21 May 1991.
16. Their numbers were reduced progressively from 450 to 180. Because they were structurally part of the DES/DFE they were suspect to the Conservative right wing.
17. 28 September 1991.
18. 6 September 1992.
19. Gipps in C. Chitty, and B. Simon, (eds.), *Education Answers Back*, Lawrence and Wishart, 1993, p. 31f.
20. ibid., p. 114.
21. *BJRE*, Vol. 16 No. 1.

22. *BJRE*, Vol. 11 No. 3.
23. D. Hay, *Exploring Inner Space*, Mowbray, 2nd edition 1987, p. 208.
24. ibid., p. 217.
25. J. Hammond, et al., *New Methods in RE Teaching*, Oliver and Boyd, 1990, p. 204.
26. ibid., p. 7.
27. ibid., p. 10.
28. ibid., adapted from p. 17.
29. ibid., p. 17.
30. ibid., p. 17.
31. ibid., p. 18.
32. ibid., p. 21.
33. ibid., pp. 179–182.
34. ibid., Ch. 14 passim.
35. *BJRE*, Vol. 14 No. 1 1991.
36. D. Webster, *Religious Education and the Creative Arts*, University of Hull, 1989, p. 3.
37. ibid., p. 6.
38. ibid., p. 15.
39. in D. Starkings, (ed.) *Religion and the Arts in Education*, Hodder and Stoughton, 1993, p. 180.
40. 12 December 1990.
41. Manchester Diocesan Board of Education, *Syllabus for Religious Education*, self-publ., 1993, p. 5.
42. ibid., p. 7.
43. ibid., p. 9.
44. Press release of the speech, dated 7 May 1992.
45. OFSTED 1993/4, p. 3.
46. ibid., p. 4.
47. T. Copley, and G. Copley, *Religious Education in Key Stage 1*, Southgate, 1993, p. 9.
48. ibid., p. 8.
49. OFSTED p. 6.
50. Section 16.
51. Section 20.
52. Section 33.
53. Section 34.
54. Section 35.
55. Section 38.
56. Section 48.
57. Letter, 26 March 1996.
58. 18 March 1991, from A.E.D. Charnier.
59. 12 March 1994.
60. SCAA Model 1, *Living Faiths Today*, self-publ., 1994, p. 3.
61. SCAA Model 2, *Questions and Teachings*, self-publ., 1994, p. 2.
62. *Resource*, Vol. 18 No. 1, p. 4.
63. ibid., p. 6ff.

64. ibid., p. 10.
65. SCAA, *Analysis of SACRE Reports*, self-publ., 1994, 2.1. p. 6.
66. ibid., 2.8., p. 9.
67. B. Watson, *The Effective Teaching of Religious Education*, Longman, 1993, p. 13ff.
68. ibid., p. 41.

Postscript: In Search of Serendipity

1. Department of Education for Northern Ireland, *The Core Syllabus for Religious Education*, HMSO, 1993, p. ii.
2. Thomas Hughes, *Tom Brown's Schooldays*, Penguin edition, 1995, p. 168.
3. 'Stanzas from the Grande Chartreuse', verse 15.
4. Series title, *The Flashman Papers*, by George MacDonald Fraser, appearing from 1969 onwards, Harvill.

Bibliography

Acland, R., *Unser Kampf*, Penguin Special, 1940

Acland, R., *What it will be like in the New Britain*, Gollancz, 1942

Acland, R., *Nothing Left to Believe?* Longmans, 1949

Acland, R., *We Teach them Wrong*, Gollancz, 1963

Acland, R., *Curriculum or Life?* Gollancz, 1966

Acland, R., *The Next Step* self-published, 1974

Alves, C., *Religion and the Secondary School*, SCM Press, 1968

Anderson, B., *John Major*, Fourth Estate, 1991

Arthur, C., *Biting the Bullet*, St.Andrew Press, 1990

Avery, M., *Teaching Scripture*, Religious Education Press, 1951

Baker, A.E., *William Temple and his Message*, Penguin, 1946

Baker, K., *The Turbulent Years*, Faber and Faber, 1993

Balen, M., *Kenneth Clarke*, Fourth Estate, 1994

Barratt, M., *The Seventh Day is Shabbat*, Heinemann, 1994

Barrett, D.B. ed. , *The World Christian Encyclopaedia*, Oxford University Press, 1982

Bath, City of, *Agreed Syllabus of Religious Education*, City of Bath, 1970

Baumfield, V., Bowness, C., Cush, D., Miller, J., *A Third Perspective*, self-published, 1994

Bedarida, F., *A Social History of England 1851–1990*, Librairie Arthaud, 1976, English trans. Methuen, 1979

Birmingham, City of, *Agreed Syllabus of Religious Instruction*, Birmingham City Education Committee, 1975

Birmingham, City of, *Together: a Teachers' Handbook of Suggestions for Religious Education,* Birmingham City Education Committee, 1975

Bloxham Project, The, *Heirs and Rebels*: Principles and Practicalities in Christian Education, self-published, 1982

Bradford Education, *Religious Education Syllabus and Guidelines for Attainment and Assessment*, City of Bradford Metropolitan Council, 1992

Braithwaite, C., *Conscientious Objections to Compulsions Under the Law*, Sessions, 1995

Brierley, P., and Hiscock, V., *UK Christian Handbook*, 1994/5 Edition,

Christian Research Association, British and Foreign Bible Society and the Evangelical Alliance, 1993

Bruce, S., *Religion in Modern Britain*, Oxford University Press, 1995

Bryant, C., *Possible Dreams: A Personal History of the British Christian Socialists* Hodder & Stoughton, 1995

Bulman, W., and Bulman, I., *The Power of Light*, Rupert Hart-Davis, 1966

Burridge, T., *Clement Atlee*, Jonathan Cape, 1988

Butler, R.A., *The Art of the Possible*, Hamish Hamilton, 1971

Butler, R.A., *The Art of Memory* Hodder & Stoughton, 1982

Cadogan, M., *Frank Richards*, Viking, 1988

Callaghan, J., *Time and Chance*, Collins, 1987

Calvocoressi, P., *The British Experience 1945–1975*, The Bodley Head, 1978

Campbell, D., *The Underworld*, BBC Books, 1994

Campbell, J., *Edward Heath*, Pimlico, 1993

Cambridgeshire Education Committee, *The Cambridgeshire Syllabus of Religious Teaching for Schools*, Cambridge University Press, 1951

Carpenter, H., *Robert Runcie*, Hodder & Stoughton, 1996

Castle, B., *Fighting All the Way*, Macmillan, 1993

Catholic Education Service, *Quality of Education in Catholic Secondary Schools*, self-published, 1995

Central Advisory Council for Education, *Children and their Primary Schools*, HMSO, 1967, commonly known as the Plowden Report

Chadwick, O., *Michael Ramsey: a Life*, Oxford University Press, 1990

Chadwick, P., *Shifting Alliances: Church and State in English Education*, Cassell, 1997

Charmley, J., *Churchill, the End of Glory*, Hodder, 1993

Chitty, C., and Simon, B., (eds), *Education Answers Back*, Lawrence and Wishart, 1993

Church of England Youth Council, the, *The Church and Young People*, Church Information Board, 1955

City and County of Bristol Education Committee, *Agreed Syllabus of Christian Education*, self-published 1960

Clark, D., *Between Pulpit and Pew: Folk Religion in a North Yorkshire Fishing Village*, Cambridge University Press, 1982

Cole, D., (ed.), *The New Wales*, University of Wales Press, 1990

Cole, W.O., (ed.), *World Faiths in Education*, George Allen and Unwin, 1978

Commission for Racial Equality, *Roots of the Future: Ethnic diversity in the Making of Britain*, self published, 1996

Cooling, T., *A Christian Vision for State Education*, SPCK, 1994

Copley, T., and Easton, D., *What They Never Told You About RE*, SCM Press, 1974

Copley, T., *RE Being Served? Successful Strategy and Tactics for the School RE Department*, Church Information Office Publishing, 1985

Copley, T., Priestley, J., Wadman, D., Coddington, V., *A FARE Deal for RE: the Interim Report of the FARE Project*, University of Exeter School of Education, 1990

Copley, T., Priestley, J., Wadman, D., Coddington, V., *Forms of Assessment in Religious Education: the Main Report of the FARE Project*, FARE, University of Exeter School of Education, 1991

Copley, T., *The RE Teacher's Christmas Carol*, National Society and Church House Publishing, 1991

Copley, T., and Copley G., *Religious Education in Key Stage 1: a Practical Guide*, Southgate, 1993

Copley, T., *Religious Education 7 to 11: Developing Primary Teaching Skills*, Routledge, 1994

Cornwall County Council, *Agreed Syllabus of Religious Education*, Darton, Longman & Todd, 1964

Cosgrave, P., *R.A. Butler* Quartet, 1981

Cox, C.B., and Dyson, A.E., *Black Paper Two*, Critical Quarterly Society, 1969

Cox, E., *Changing Aims in Religious Education*, Routledge & Kegan Paul, 1966

Cox, E., and Cairns, J.M., *Reforming Religious Education*, Kogan Page, 1989

Dale, A., *The Bible in the Classroom*, Oxford University Press, 1972

Dale, J., *The Spirit of the Age*, Swarthmore Lecture, Quaker Home Service, 1996

Darlington, County Borough of, *Agreed Syllabus of Religious Education*, Darlington Education Committee, 1965

Davie, G., *Religion in Britain since 1945: Believing without Belonging*, Blackwell, 1994

Davies, A.J., *We, the Nation: The Conservative Party and the Pursuit of Power*, Little, Brown and Co., 1995

Dean, J., *Religious Education for Children*, Ward Lock Educational, 1971

Dent, H.C., *Education in Transition*, Kegan Paul, 1944a

Dent, H.C., *The Education Act 1944* University of London Press, 1944b

Department of Education for Northern Ireland, *The Core Syllabus for Religious Education*, HMSO, 1993

Department of Education and Science, *Better Schools*, HMSO, 1985

Devon County Council, *Religious Education: Promoting Quality*, self published 1992

Dobinson, C.H. (ed.), *Education in a Changing World*, Clarendon, 1951

Dorset Education Authority, *REaction, REflection, REsponse*, Dorset County Council, 1992

Dudley Education Committee, *RE 1994: The Agreed Dudley Syllabus*, Dudley Education Committee, 1994

Durham County Council, *The Durham County Agreed Syllabus of Religious Instruction*, University of London, 1946

Ellacott, S.E., *A History of Everyday Things in England*, Volume V, 1914–1968 Batsford, 1968

Ellison, M., and Herbert, C., *Listening to Children, a Fresh Approach to RE in the Primary Years*, CIO, 1983

Evening, M., *Approaches to Religious Education*, Hodder & Stoughton, 1972

Farrell, M., Kerry, T., and Kerry, C., *The Blackwell Handbook of Education*, Blackwell, 1995

Felderhof, M.C. (ed.), *Religious Education in a Pluralistic Society*, Hodder & Stoughton, 1985

Fenwick, K., and McBride, P., *The Government of Education*, Martin Robertson, 1981

Flude, M., and Hammer, M., (eds), *The Education Reform Act, 1988* The Falmer Press, 1990

Garforth, F.W., 'Doubts about Secondary School Scripture,' in *Religion in Education Quarterly*, Vol. 28.2, 1961, SCM Press.

Gibberd, K., *Teaching Religion in Schools*, Longman, 1970

Gilbert, A.D., *The Making of Post-Christian Britain*, Longman, 1980

Gilbert, M, *Never Despair, Winston Churchill 1945–1965*, Heinemann, 1988

Gilbert, M., *Churchill, a Life*, Heinemann, 1991

Gill, S., D'Costa, G., King, U., (eds), *Religion in Europe*, Pharos, 1994

Gilley, S., and Sheils, W.J., *A History of Religion in Britain*, Blackwell, 1994

Glass, F., and Marsden-Smedley P. (eds), *Articles of War*, Grafton, 1989

Goldman, R., *Religious Thinking from Childhood to Adolescence*, Routledge & Kegan Paul, 1964

Goldman, R., *Readiness for Religion*, Routledge & Kegan Paul, 1965

Gordon, V.E.C., *What Happens in School*, Pergamon, 1965

Gosden, P.H.J.H., *Education in the Second World War*, Methuen and Co, 1976

Gosden, P., *The Education System since 1944*, Robertson, 1983

Gower, R., et al., *Religious Education in the Infant Years*, Lion, 1982

Green, J., (ed.), *Best Bible Bits*, Church Information Office, 1984

Griffith, J.A.G., and Ryle, M., *Parliament: Functions, Practice and Procedures*, Sweet and Maxwell, 1989

Griffiths, R. *Imagination in Early Childhood*, Routledge & Kegan Paul, 1935

Grimmitt, M., *What Can I do in RE?* Mayhew-McCrimmon, 1973, second edition 1978

Grimmitt, M., *Religious Education and Human Development*, McCrimmons, 1987

Grimmitt, M., Grove, J., Hull, J., and Spencer, L., *A Gift to the Child: Religious Education in the Primary School*, Simon and Schuster, 1991

Hammond, J., Hay, D., et al., *New Methods in RE Teaching: an Experiential Approach*, Oliver and Boyd, 1990

Harmer, J.W. (ed.), *The Scripture Lesson,* Inter Varsity Fellowship, 1945

Harms, E. 'The Development of Religious Experience in Children' in *American Journal of Sociology*, Vol. 50:2, 112–22.

Harris, A., *Teaching Morality and Religion*, George Allen & Unwin, 1976

Hastings, A., *A History of English Christianity 1920–1990*, SCM Press, third edition 1991

Hay, D., *Exploring Inner Space*, Mowbray, 1982, second edition 1987

Hay, D., *Religious Experience Today*, Mowbray, 1990

Heawood, G.L., *Religion in School*, SCM Press, 1939

Her Majesty's Inspectors of Schools, *Aspects of Secondary Education in England*, HMSO, 1979

Her Majesty's Stationery Office, *Aspects of Britain: Religion*, 1992

Herbert, T., and Jones, G.E. (eds), *Post-War Wales*, University of Wales Press, 1995

Hertfordshire County Council, *The Hertfordshire Syllabus of Religious Education*, self-published, 1995

Hilliard, F.H., *The Teacher and Religion*, James Clarke, 1963

Hilliard, F.H., Lee, D., Rupp, G., and Niblett, W.R., *Christianity in Education*, George Allen & Unwin, 1966

Holley, R., *Religious Education and Religious Understanding*, Routledge & Kegan Paul, 1978

Holm, J., *Teaching Religion in School*, OUP, 1975

Holmes, C., *A Tolerant Country? Immigrants, Refugees and Minorities in Britain* Faber and Faber, 1991

Horne, A., *Macmillan 1957–1986*, Vol II of the official biography, Macmillan, 1989

Howard, A., *RAB: The Life of R.A.Butler*, Jonathan Cape, 1987

Hubery, D.S., *Christian Education and the Bible*, Religious Education Press, 1967

Hubery, D.S., *Christian Education in State and Church*, Denholm House Press, 1972

Hughes, Thomas, *Tom Brown's Schooldays*, Oxford University Press, 1989 edition of 1857 original

Hull, J., (ed.), *New Directions in Religious Education*, Falmer Press, 1982

Hull, J., (ed.), *Studies in Religion and Education*, Falmer Press, 1984

Hull, J.M., *School Worship: An Obituary*, SCM Press, 1975

Hulmes, E., *Commitment and Neutrality in Religious Education*, Geoffrey Chapman, 1979

Hyde, K.E., *Religious Education and Slow Learners*, SCM Press, 1969

Iremonger, F.A., *William Temple, Archbishop of Canterbury*, Oxford University Press, 1948

Jackson, R., (ed.), *Approaching World Religions*, John Murray, 1982

Jackson, R., Barratt, M., Everington, J., *Bridges to Religions: the Warwick RE Project*, Heinemann, 1994

James, R.R. *Anthony Eden*, George, Weidenfeld & Nicholson, 1986

Jeffreys, M.V.C., *Truth is Not Neutral*, Religious Education Press, 1969

Jenkins, D., *The British: Their Identity and Their Religion*, SCM Press, 1975

Jenkins, S., *Accountable to None: the Tory Nationalisation of Britain*, Hamish Hamilton, 1995

Jones, C.M., *Teaching the Bible Today*, SCM Press, 1963

Jones, G.E., *Controls and Conflicts in Welsh Secondary Education 1889–1944*, University of Wales Press, 1982

Junor, P., *The Major Enigma*, Michael Joseph, 1993

Kavanagh, D., and Morris, P., *Consensus Politics from Atlee to Thatcher*, Blackwell, 1989

Kent County Council, *Guidance for Teaching the Kent Agreed Syllabus*, self-published, 1995

Kincaid, M., *How to Improve Learning in RE*, Hodder & Stoughton, 1991

Kushner, T., *The Holocaust and the Liberal Imagination*, Blackwell, 1994

Lancashire Education Committee, *Religion and Life*, Lancashire County Council, 1968, revised edition 1973

Lancashire Education Committee, *Agreed Syllabus of Religious Education*, Lancashire County Council, 1994

Lawton, D., *Education and Politics in the 1990s*, Falmer, 1992

Lawton, D., *The Tory Mind on Education, 1979–94*, Falmer, 1994

Leonard, G.L., *Firmly I Believe and Truly*, Mowbray, 1985

Leonard, G.L., *Priorities in Pastoral Theology*, Churchman Publishing, 1988

Lester Smith, W.O., *Education in Great Britain*, Oxford University Press, 1949, 3rd edition 1958

Lewis, P, *The Fifties*, Heinemann, 1978

London Borough of Barking and Dagenham, *Learning for Life Together*, self-published, 1995

London Borough of Brent, *Agreed Syllabus for Religious Education*, self-published, 1995

London County Council, *London Syllabus of Religious Education*, London County Council, 1947

Longmate, N., *How We Lived Then*, Arrow, 1971

Loukes, H., *Teenage Religion*, SCM Press, 1961

Loukes, H., *Teenage Morality*, SCM Press, 1973

Macy, C., (ed.), *Let's Teach Them Right*, Pemberton, 1969

Madge, V., *Children in Search of Meaning*, SCM Press, 1965

Manchester, Diocesan Board of Education, *Syllabus for Religious Education*, self-published, 1993

Mantle, J., *Archbishop*, Sinclair Stevenson, 1991

Marwick, A., *British Society Since 1945*, Penguin, 1982

May, P.R., and Johnston, O.R., *Religion in Our Schools*, Hodder and Stoughton, 1968

Mathews, H.F., *Revolution in Religious Education*, Religious Education Press, 1966

Mathews, H.F., *The New Religious Education*, Religious Education Press, 1971

Mathias, D. 'Ideas of God and Conduct', unpublished PhD, Teachers' College, University of Columbia, 1943

McCloughry, R. (ed.), *Belief in Politics*, Hodder & Stoughton, 1996

Melrod, G. (ed.), *Israel*, APA Publications, 1992

Methodist Conference, *The Methodist Hymn Book*, Methodist Conference Office, 1933 edition

Middlesex County Council, *The Middlesex County Agreed Syllabus of Religious Instruction*, self-published, 1948

Moran, G., *Religious Education as a Second Language*, Religious Education Press, USA, 1989

Modood, T., *Not Easy Being British*, Ruunymede Trust and Trentham Books, 1992

Morgan, K.O., *The People's Peace*, Oxford University Press, 1990

Murray, A.V., *Education into Religion*, Nisbet and Co., 1953

Murray, A.V., *Teaching the Bible*, Cambridge University Press, 1955

Murray, P., *Margaret Thatcher*, W.H.Allen, 1980

National Curriculum Council, *Starting out with the National Curriculum*, NCC, 1992

Newbigin, L. 'Teaching Religion in a Secular, Plural Society', in Hull, J.M. (ed.) *New Directions in Religious Education*, Falmer, 1982

Niblett, W.R., *Christian Education in a Secular Society*, Oxford University Press, 1960

Northamptonshire County Council, *Religious Education in Northamptonshire*, self-published, 1994

Office for Standards in Education, *Religious Education, A Review of Inspection Findings 1993/4*, HMSO, 1995

Otto, R. *The Idea of the Holy*, OUP, 1923

Parker, C., *Readiness for Religion I: What I am like*, Hart-Davis, 1967

Parsons, G., (ed.), *The Growth of Religious Diversity: Britain from 1945*, Volume I: Traditions, Volume II: Issues, Routledge, 1993

Peart-Binns, J.S., *Graham Leonard, Bishop of London*, Darton, Longman and Todd, 1988

Piaget, J., *The Child's Conception of the World*, Routledge & Kegan Paul, 1929

Piaget, J., *The Child's Conception of Physical Causality*, Routledge & Kegan Paul, 1930

Piaget, J., *The Moral Judgment of the Child*, Harcourt, Brace & World, 1932

Pierrepoint, A., *Executioner Pierrepoint*, Harrap, 1974

Revised Syllabus of Religious Instruction for the Schools of Wales, University of Wales Press, 1963

Read, G., et al., *How Do I Teach RE?*, Stanley Thornes, 2nd edition, 1992

Read, S, *Hello, Campers*, Bantam, 1986

Rentoul, J., *Tony Blair* Warner Books, revised edition, 1996

Robinson, J.A.T., *But That I Can't Believe!*, Fontana, 1967

Robson, G. 'Religious Education, Government Policy and Professional Practice, 1985–1995', in BJRE Vol. 19:1, 1996.

Routledge, P., *Scargill*, HarperCollins, 1993

Ruthven, M., *A Satanic Affair*, Chatto and Windus, 1990

Sandhurst, B.G., *How Heathen Is Britain?* Collins, 1938, revised edition 1948

Sayers, D.L., *The Mind of the Maker*, Methuen, 1941, re-issued by Mowbray, 1994

School Curriculum and Assessment Authority, *Analysis of SACRE Reports, 1994*, SCAA, 1994

School Curriculum and Assessment Authority, *Model 1, Living Faiths Today*, SCAA, 1994.

School Curriculum and Assessment Authority, *Model 2, Questions and Teachings*, SCAA, 1994.

Schools Council Working Paper 36, *Religious Education in Secondary Schools*, Evans Brothers and Methuen Educational, 1971

Schools Council Working Paper 55, *The Curriculum in the Middle Years*, Methuen, 1975

Shap, The Shap Working Party on World Religions, *World Religions in Education*, The Commission for Racial Equality, 1987

Smart, N., *Secular Language and the Logic of Religion*, Faber & Faber, 1968

Smart, N., *The Phenomenon of Religion*, Macmillan, 1973

Smart, N., and Horder, D., (eds), *New Movements in Religious Education*, Temple Smith, 1975

Smith, D.J., *The Sleep of Reason*, Century, 1994

Smith, J.W.D., *Religious Education in a Secular Setting*, SCM Press, 1969

Somerset County Council, *Religious Education and Collective Worship*, self-published, 1981

Somerset County Council, *Agreed Syllabus for Religious Education*, self-published, 1992

Stanley, A.P., The Life and Correspondence of Thomas Arnold, Vol I, Fellowes, 8th edition 1858

Starkings, D. (ed.), *Religion and the Arts in Education*, Hodder & Stoughton, 1993

Steel, D., *Against Goliath*, Weidenfeld & Nicolson, 1989

Stevens, R., *Education and the Death of Love*, Epworth Press, 1978

Surrey County Council, *Syllabus of Religious Education*, self-published, 1963

Tate, N. published conference address in symposium 'Religious Education at key stage 4', Christian Education Movement, 1995

Tebbit, N., *Upwardly Mobile*, George Weidenfeld and Nicholson, 1988

Temple, W., *Christianity and Social Order*, Penguin Special, 1940

Thatcher, M., *The Downing Street Years*, HarperCollins 1993

Thatcher, M., *The Path to Power*, HarperCollins, 1995

Thomas, T., (ed.), *The British, Their Religious Beliefs and Practices 1800–1986*, Routledge, 1988

Tickner, M.F., and Webster, D.H., (eds), *Religious Education and the Imagination*, University of Hull, 1982

Tindal Hart, A., *The Country Priest in English History*, self-published 1959 and by the Country Book Club, 1960

Watson, B., *The Effective Teaching of Religious Education*, Longman, 1993

Webster, D., (ed.), *Religious Education and the Creative Arts*, University of Hull, 1989

Wedderspoon, A.G., *Religious Education 1944 to 1984*, George, Allen & Unwin, 1966

Welsh Society of the Institute of Christian Education, *A Syllabus of Religious Instruction in the Schools of Wales*, University of Wales Press Board, 1945

West Riding County Council, *Suggestions for Religious Education*, self-published, 1966

Who's Who 1995, A. & C. Black, 1995

Wigley, B., *From Fear to Faith*, Longmans Green and Co., 1969

Wilson, H., *The Labour Government 1964 to 1970*, Weidenfeld & Nicolson and Joseph, 1971

Wintersgill, B., 'The Case of the Missing Models: Exploding the Myths,' in *Resource* Vol. 18:1, 1995, Professional Council for RE

Wolffe, J., (ed.), *The Growth of Religious Diversity*, The Open University, 1993

Yeaxlee, B., *Handbook to the Cambridgeshire Syllabus of Religious Teaching for Schools*, SCM Press, 1940

Young, K., *Sir Alec Douglas-Home*, Dent, 1970

Youngman, B.R., *Teaching Religious Knowledge*, University of London Press, 1953

Ziegler, P, *Wilson: The Authorized Biography of Lord Wilson of Rievaulx*, George Weidenfeld & Nicholson, 1993

Index